THE CHALLENGE
OF LEGISLATION

THE CHALLENGE OF LEGISLATION

BIPARTISANSHIP IN A PARTISAN WORLD

John L. Hilley

BROOKINGS INSTITUTION PRESS
Washington, D.C.

Copyright © 2008
THE BROOKINGS INSTITUTION
1775 Massachusetts Avenue, N.W., Washington, D.C. 20036
www.brookings.edu

Library of Congress Cataloging-in-Publication data

Hilley, John L.
  The challenge of legislation : bipartisanship in a partisan world / John L. Hilley.
       p.   cm.
  Summary: "Insider's account of the bipartisan passage of the Balanced Budget Act of 1997. Weaves together detailed narrative and portraits of key players and offers unique insight into the relationship between party leaders and their rank-and-file, the interplay between elected officials and their staff, and the delicate art of partisan negotiations"— Provided by publisher.
  Includes bibliographical references and index.
  ISBN-13: 978-0-8157-3654-7 (cloth : alk. paper)
  ISBN-13: 978-0-8157-3653-0 (pbk. : alk. paper)
  1. United States. Congress. 2. United States. Balanced Budget Act of 1997.
  3. Legislation—United States. I. Title.
  JK1021.H52 2007
  352.4'97302—dc22   2007043782

2 4 6 8 9 7 5 3 1

Printed on acid-free paper

Typeset in Minion

Composition by OSP, Inc.
Arlington, Virginia

Printed by R. R. Donnelley
Harrisonburg, Virginia

To Rosemary Mulholland Hilley,
the love of my life

Contents

Acknowledgments   ix

Introduction   xi

1   We're Fixing a Hole   1

2   Launch   23

3   Circle 'Round the Consumer Price Index   41

4   The Handoff   57

5   Staking Out Territory   71

6   Offer and Counteroffer   85

7   An Agreement   98

8   What Was That We Agreed To?   116

9   The Center Must Hold   129

10 The Challenge of Reconciliation   137

11 House on Fire   157

12 Tax Tribulations   168

13 Into the Hands of the Leaders   188

14 Taxes and Death   202

15 The Triumph of Responsibility   215

Postscript: The Limits and Potential of Bipartisanship   226

APPENDIXES
A. Primer on the Budget Process   235

B. Key Budget Terms   240

C. Chronology of Important Dates   249

D. List of Participants   251

Notes   255

Index   269

Acknowledgments

In writing this book, I have conveyed the story of the 1997 balanced budget agreement as I lived it as senior advisor to President Bill Clinton. I have drawn on extensive notes and narratives written in 1997, as well as numerous source materials that figured prominently in the effort. Those include detailed budget tables, position papers, memos to the president and others, updates and summaries written by White House staff involved in the negotiations, and public documents released as part of the budget agreement. To the best of my ability, I have tried to accurately convey the true story of how the 1997 budget agreement was created and enacted.

I have a number of people to thank for help on the book. First and foremost is my wife, Rosemary, to whom the book is dedicated. She edited and commented on every draft, serving as the principal sounding board for the book. Her help and encouragement were indispensable. My sons Brendan and Ryan also offered helpful advice at several stages, as did Melanie Lynn Hilley, Betty Mulholland, and Peggy Brennan.

I am grateful to Mary Kwak and Bob Faherty of the Brookings Institution Press for being open to a different kind of book about Washington. Mary's help was critical. She asked the right questions, insisted on clarity, and made the book much more readable. I am also indebted to Martha Gottron for her expert and insightful editing. She simplified, cleared up, corrected, and significantly improved the book.

Several former White House and congressional colleagues were kind enough to read drafts and offer suggestions. Bill Hoagland, Ken Kies, and Barbara Chow read the entire manuscript, provided their insight and recollections, and made the story much better. Chris Jennings provided significant help on health care issues, and Larry Stein provided important assistance in formulating several key topics. Janet Holtzblatt provided expertise in the complex area of the Earned Income Tax Credit. The Congressional Budget Office was generous in making documents available, and I thank Melissa Merson and Linda Schimmel for that. I am also grateful to Paul Cullinan for his insights on baseline issues.

I also owe thanks to two outside-the-Beltway friends for their assistance. Jon Noll read major portions of the manuscript and raised important issues of balance and clarity. Eric Redman, author of the classic *The Dance of Legislation,* offered valuable guidance at several points.

I intentionally waited a decade to tell the story. I wanted the dust to settle and give time a chance to lend its perspective. Being in the trenches every day and working to see the agreement to success was an immersion experience. I wanted the distance that would allow the effort to be put in a broader context. The 1997 agreement was the culmination of a sixteen-year effort, the capstone, but not the foundation. I have tried to credit previous efforts without which the 1997 agreement would have been impossible. I also hope that I have been fair to the participants. In fact, there was a great deal to admire in each one. Although I worked on behalf of the Clinton White House, we were ultimately successful because people on both sides dealt in good faith, seeking and achieving an outcome in the national interest.

Introduction

Unlike most books about Washington, this book deals in good news. It tells the true story of how responsible leaders in both parties overcame their differences to enact the most significant bipartisan achievement of the last two decades. This bright shining moment occurred in 1997, when Republicans and Democrats reached across the aisle to balance the federal budget while enacting major tax policies and initiatives in education, health, welfare, the environment, and many other areas. The Balanced Budget Act of 1997 not only brought an end to a period of massive federal budget deficits, but it also provided health insurance for five million children, created the HOPE scholarship for postsecondary education, enacted a child tax credit, increased funding for environmental programs, strengthened incentives to move people from welfare to work, and provided new incentives for saving and investing.

The story of 1997 forms the backbone of this book, but only the backbone. What I hope this book also reveals is how Washington works when it works. In writing this account, I have tried to capture the reality of governing in modern America—the competing political forces, the complexity and challenges, and the exhilaration of accomplishment. I hope this story is not only interesting and instructive, but also inspirational.

The partisanship that dominates our politics today has made the already difficult dance of legislation truly daunting. In our time, the challenge facing responsible leaders is to harness that partisan power to the public interest. Bipartisanship is not an absence of partisanship; it is partisans coming together to reconcile their competing political and policy objectives—as they did in 1997. Once committed to constructive engagement, leaders in both parties learned to trust one another and work as teammates. On several occasions, the budget agreement would have been lost without acts of good faith and courage on both sides of the aisle. While both sides fought hard for what they wanted, they came to understand that winning did not mean imposing losses on the other side—it meant finding common ground. Ultimately, the people's representatives rose to the challenge of legislation.

A careful reading of the story also reveals less encouraging facts. Both sides operated within tight political constraints. More could have been done in the national interest than Congress and the president accomplished. Both sides were limited in their flexibility by fear of political attack, by beneficiaries entrenched in the status quo, and by the special and financial interests to which they had become beholden. Despite all this, the participants were ultimately successful in crafting a bipartisan agreement that served their own and the country's interests.

In writing this book, I have conveyed the story of the 1997 balanced budget agreement from my perspective as senior advisor to President Bill Clinton and head of the White House legislative affairs office. Of the hundreds of issues in play, I have focused on the central ones that propelled the agreement, using those to reveal an inside story of politics and policy in the hands of the nation's top leaders. Here is the story of how one group of partisans embraced bipartisanship to act together for the good of the country. Perhaps this account will help others do the same.

CHAPTER ONE

We're Fixing
a Hole

In November 1996 the American people voted to retain Democrat Bill Clinton as president and to keep Republicans as the majority party in Congress. These partisans were no strangers to each other. In 1995 they had fought an epic battle of the budget, waging a political war that shut the federal government not once, but twice. Partisanship reigned supreme as the two sides held the federal government and the American people hostage. When the dust finally settled, the only sure results were negative: bitterness, distrust, and, despite all the sound and fury, an enormous deficit hole that still needed fixing.

Now it was January 1997, and the American people had bestowed a fresh start on their elected leaders. At this critical juncture, America's leaders would either reignite the partisan wars or perhaps, just perhaps, overcome their wounds and launch a bipartisan effort to balance the budget. To succeed, they would have to reach out to each other and find a way to accommodate their competing political and policy objectives—while hopefully pointing all that partisan power toward the national interest.

Immediately after the 1996 election, President Clinton instructed the administration staff to prepare a balanced budget plan that could serve as a starting point for the bipartisan route, touting Democratic priorities but also leaving room for the necessary compromises with the Republican Congress. Given the hard feelings and mistrust that lingered palpably after the 1995 debacle, it would be a major accomplishment simply to forestall the partisan warfare that usually accompanies the president's budget submission to Congress. With that in mind, Erskine Bowles, the White House chief of staff, agreed that I should launch a secret foray into the Republican camp—not to weaken the opposition but to build a modicum of trust before the president presented his budget proposal to Congress. As head of the White House office of legislative affairs and a former congressional staffer, I would make the first contact.[1] These talks had to remain hidden, not just from rank-and-file Republicans but also from many Democrats, both in Congress and in the White House. Erskine and I knew our outreach to the other side would never get off the ground if we first ran our intentions past congressional Democrats bent on partisan warfare. The same was true for many of the White House staff with all their Capitol Hill connections.

Friday, January 24, 1997

There was a natural place to start—in the Senate with Pete Domenici, the Republican chairman of the Budget Committee. For institutional and cultural reasons, the Senate is more bipartisan than the House. The filibuster and other procedural roadblocks available only in the Senate grant a great deal of stopping power to the minority party. As a result, the legislative path in the Senate often runs down the middle, and senators are more accustomed than House members to working with the other side.

The son of a grocer and one of five children, Domenici was a self-made man. He had served ably as one of Republican leader Bob Dole's principal lieutenants but had been rebuffed for leadership posts.[2] He had suffered the disappointment of being passed over for the vice presidential nomination in 1988 in favor of Dan Quayle. But he had borne it all with good grace and fortitude, and he had mastered the feat of being a hard-nose budgeteer while generously helping his home state of New Mexico from his seats on the Appropriations and Energy Committees.

Domenici was an accomplished legislator and a tough negotiator who could work with the other side. He had been a central part of every budget negotiation since the early 1980s, and he had proven his willingness to take unpopular stands.[3] Equally important, based on years of experience, I knew that I could trust Domenici to be open to our overtures while keeping our talks confidential.

On budget matters, Domenici was inseparable from his extraordinarily capable Budget Committee staff director, Bill Hoagland. So it was the three of us who met in the quiet of Domenici's office in the Hart Building late on a Friday afternoon—thirteen days before the president's budget would become public. It quickly became apparent that Domenici's main concern was the role he would play in the Senate over the coming year. For nearly two decades he had been Senator Dole's confidant and strength. But Domenici was not certain where he stood with Trent Lott, the new and more conservative Republican leader from Mississippi who had succeeded Dole in mid-1996. Hoagland put Domenici's concerns bluntly: was the White House negotiating privately with Lott? Of course not, was my honest reply. We were not negotiating with anybody yet; Domenici and Hoagland were the first contacts the White House had made on the Republican side.

Domenici was also worried about the challenge facing the budget committees in both the Senate and House. They were charged with drafting the initial budget blueprint setting overall tax and spending levels for the federal government. Only when that resolution had been passed could the congressional appropriations committees begin to allocate spending to specific government programs.[4] An important part of the budget committees' effort was to compel the other congressional committees to legislate program changes to back up the numbers in the budget resolution. Domenici knew it would be a tough job in the Senate. His first instinct was to try to put together a bipartisan budget in committee in partnership with Senator Frank Lautenberg of New Jersey, the new ranking Democratic member. But he had no illusions about the prospects for success. The membership of the Senate Budget Committee was badly skewed. The Democrats were more liberal than the majority of their caucus, and the Republicans more conservative than their Senate brethren.[5] It was not a recipe for compromise.

Domenici wanted to know the prospects of working out something in advance with the White House. If an agreement could be reached, his committee would craft a bipartisan budget resolution reflecting the compromise. And if his committee would not cooperate, he had a backup plan. He would bypass the Budget Committee and take the agreement with the White House directly to the Senate floor.[6] It was a startling offer from a veteran chairman: he was willing to circumvent his own committee if that's what it took.

In response, I explained that the White House believed that a major deficit reduction package could achieve a balanced budget by 2002. Moreover, the White House believed that a balanced budget could be achieved through spending reductions alone, avoiding the need for tax increases and even leaving room for a tax cut as part of the bargain. But in the midst of all those spending reductions, there would have to be room for the president's initiatives in health care, education, the environment, welfare reform, crime and drug prevention, and science and technology. Domenici did not miss a beat. He said he understood the need to accommodate many of the president's priorities, but he would do so only if the budget agreement restrained the growth of entitlement spending in programs like Medicare and Social Security. He followed with a bold suggestion to adjust the consumer price index (CPI), the economic measure used to determine cost-of-living adjustments (COLAs) in government benefit programs. Economists generally agreed that the CPI overstated the true rate of inflation.[7] Domenici was asking the obvious question: why not make the CPI adjustment part of an agreement and take credit for it in the budget? The effect would be enormous. Lowering the CPI by half a percentage point would reduce COLA payments to beneficiaries—and thus reduce the budget deficit—by $25 billion in 2002 alone. But forcing an adjustment in the CPI would bring into play the third rail of American politics, Social Security. It would also send the labor unions into a frenzy since wage adjustments are negotiated in light of the measured rate of inflation.

Domenici knew the fallout that any proposal to reduce the CPI would create, so he was quickly, but very privately, putting the idea on the table. Republicans had been badly burned in the past by advocating COLA reductions. This time the party would venture forth only in partnership with a Democratic president.

Returning to the White House, I reported back to Erskine Bowles, who had recently succeeded Leon Panetta as White House chief of staff; Erskine had been deputy chief of staff in 1994 and 1995 in the first Clinton administration before returning to the private sector. He was a moderate who would work hard to see all sides and find the middle. Perhaps particularly important, he had not been a party to the divisive budget battles of 1995.

I had good news: Domenici wanted to engage. Erskine and I quickly decided to expand our quiet diplomacy on both sides of the aisle. On the Democratic side we would do our normal briefings on the president's budget proposal to leaders and committees before the State of the Union address on February 4 and the president's budget submission on February 6. Given our quiet initiatives with the Republicans, it was essential to show the flag of party unity by very publicly briefing key Democratic members and staff. On the Republican side, our goal would be to make enough contacts to ensure that the president's budget submission would "arrive alive." This would be no easy feat. In the 1980s and 1990s, members of the opposing party had adopted the vocabulary of forensic examiners to rate the survival chances of the president's submission. When the two sides were far apart, the president's budget would quickly be declared "dead on arrival," or, if the president were lucky, on life support, barely breathing, or on its last leg. Congressional Democrats had done it to Presidents Reagan and Bush, and during his first administration, the

Republicans had returned the favor to President Clinton. We were determined to avoid this fate.

THAT MEANT ANTICIPATING all sorts of wild cards. On the House side, perhaps the wildest was Budget Committee chairman John Kasich of Ohio. In 1995 he had played a key role in moving the Republican Contract with America budget bills through Congress and onto the president's desk, setting the stage for the veto showdowns that closed the federal government. The Contract with America, the cornerstone of the successful 1994 Republican campaign to gain control of the House, laid out a sweeping agenda whose lead items were balancing the budget and cutting taxes.

Kasich was a man of strong convictions who wanted to cut taxes, cut spending, and balance the budget under the deficit projections produced by the Congressional Budget Office (CBO), which were more austere than those generated by the White House Office of Management and Budget (OMB). He was a true believer in small government and fiscal responsibility. We would need to talk with Kasich before the president's budget saw the light of day.

WHAT ERSKINE AND I had not counted on, however, was our own wild card, President William Jefferson Clinton. He was doing his own outreach to Senate Republican leader Trent Lott. Domenici's suspicions were more accurate than our inside information.

Lott had succeeded Dole as Senate majority leader the previous spring after Dole decided to leave the Senate in order to devote all his efforts to his presidential campaign. Wanting to establish a record of legislative accomplishment, Lott had quickly proven his ability to work with the Clinton White House in passing welfare, health, and environmental legislation in the closing days of the 104th Congress.[8] Sensing electoral peril in the wake of the government shutdowns, the House Republican leadership had done its part to move those pieces of legislation, giving up on the kinds of controversial legislative riders and poison pills that voters might see as extreme.[9]

The president's desire to reach out to Lott was natural and recognized the new reality in the Republican leadership. The 1995 budget collapse and the loss of several House seats to Democrats in the 1996 elections had weakened House Speaker Newt Gingrich inside his caucus and in the public eye. The Speaker was also weakened by an ethics investigation into allegations that he had improperly mixed political and other funds.[10] In contrast, Senator Lott had risen in profile and power, particularly since the 1996 election, which had strengthened his party's majority in the Senate by two seats. As he had done on several key pieces of legislation in 1996, Lott was the man who could muster his troops to deal with the president. Perhaps most important, he had not been a party to the confrontations and failed negotiations of 1995–96. He had been granted a fresh start as Republican leader at the most propitious time.

TUESDAY, JANUARY 28, 1997

Reaching Senator Lott by phone, I pressed him on the budget. He was happy to report that he and the president had indeed been talking a balanced budget and wanted to push ahead. That was Lott's legislative strategy: push, push, push. Don't sweat the little stuff, just get it done. He was taking the same approach to the president. He even suggested that the two of them should agree to the outlines of a deal and then push it through Congress.

But that would not work. In 1996 the Republicans had cooperated with the administration because they feared political obliteration—payback for government shutdowns and a lack of accomplishment. Now they were back, stronger and more conservative in the Senate. Moderates like Senators Nancy Kassebaum of Kansas, Mark Hatfield of Oregon, and Bill Cohen of Maine had retired, and Lott's more conservative caucus would want to assert itself. No budget deal could be cooked over the phone or in the back room. For an agreement to carry, all four party caucuses in Congress would have to be fully engaged.

THAT EVENING, THE president's senior advisers gathered for the weekly White House political meeting in the Yellow Oval Room, a large comfortable room on the second floor of the White House residence looking directly out to the Washington and Jefferson memorials. It was here that the president, the vice president, and twenty or so of the president's top advisors had met over the past year to put their collective efforts into one overriding objective— victory in the November elections. With that goal achieved, it was time to govern.

Walking to the meeting from the Oval Office, I told the president of my conversation with Lott. His first reaction was to talk about anything but the budget—a mini-filibuster. He had been found out and he knew it. Finally, I was able to convey a few simple points: After 1995–96 we were dealing from strength; a secret budget deal with Lott would undermine us with congressional Democrats, who would be outraged at their exclusion from the process; and our early outreach to Democrats and Republicans had to include the guys who understood the budget—Domenici and Kasich and their Democratic counterparts, Lautenberg and Representative John Spratt of South Carolina. Otherwise any deals that were reached might soon crumble.

During the meeting, the political team focused on second-term initiatives and the State of the Union address.[11] In these early days of 1997, it was all good news. White House polls showed that 57 percent of those surveyed thought the nation was on the right track, compared with 35 percent who thought it was on the wrong track. The president's favorability rating was 67 percent, while Speaker Gingrich's was a dismal 33 percent. Now was the time to capitalize on the public's support by adopting policies that were close to Democrats' hearts. More than fifty possible initiatives were on the table, ranging across the spectrum—a balanced budget, the HOPE scholarship for postsecondary education, expanded health care for children, tax cuts, welfare-to-work proposals, technology investments, environmental clean-up, consumer protection, more cops on the street, drug abuse prevention and enforcement, shored-up pensions, improved race relations, foreign affairs. It was an expansive agenda, destined to be delivered in rapid-fire, laundry-list fashion in the State of the Union.

But most important, the president was intent on setting a constructive tone. He would be forward looking and magnanimous and offer the hand of bipartisanship, perhaps opening the way to a constructive engagement with the Republican Congress. Both parties had strong incentives to finish the job of balancing the budget. For Democrats, a balanced budget would free them of the big spender bogey, shifting the public's focus to the party's strengths in education, health care, environment, and public investments. The macroeconomic arguments for balancing the budget were also compelling. The baby boomers with their impending claims on Social Security, Medicare, and other social programs would soon place the country—and the federal budget—under extraordinary financial stress. The federal budget needed to increase, not reduce, national savings if future generations were to be prosperous enough to honor those collective promises.

Republicans had their own reasons for wanting a balanced budget. It would fulfill one of the central pledges of the Contract with America and prove that the Republicans could be fiscally conservative while achieving several policy objectives, including tax cuts and reductions in government spending. And if the budget turned to surplus, the stage would be set for further rounds of tax cuts in the following years.

AFTER THE MEETING, I alerted Erskine to the president's intramurals with Lott. The president came clean, and Erskine raised the same warning flags. A backdoor agreement with Lott would cause a firestorm among Democrats who favored partisanship over a bipartisan budget agreement. To top it off, a quick deal with Lott likely could not carry the Republican House. When it came to budget matters, House Republicans were not used to playing second fiddle.

One thing was clear: it was time to ramp up and catch up with the president. We would have to help keep the boss pointed toward a bipartisan agreement. That would require us to accelerate and deepen our conversations with Republicans. OMB director Frank Raines and I would reengage Domenici immediately with the hope that our discussions with him would keep Lott from jumping too far ahead. If Domenici became the point man, the White House would be dealing with the expert on the budget who understood the nitty-gritty of policies and programs and where the compromises might lie. We agreed that I would also meet with John Kasich privately even though we knew our quiet shuttle diplomacy could not last for long. Secret talks would need to yield to a more inclusive process; the two sides would have to engage in the open. But that coming into the open—the handoff—would be very tricky. The participants were leery of each other and had different agendas. Our quiet outreach was intended to point the key players in the same direction—hoping they would take ownership of the process once they were convinced that their efforts could bear fruit.

THURSDAY, JANUARY 30, 1997

John Spratt was the newly elected ranking Democrat on the House Budget Committee.[12] He was an immensely popular member, and with good reason. Sincere and kind, he lacked pretension and was very smart in a nonthreatening way. He had a facility with numbers and budget concepts and was a quick study. In budgetary matters, he was allied with the House Blue Dogs, a group of conservative Democrats who believed in tough budgets, opposed tax cuts, and were much less afraid to cut spending than were their caucus colleagues. But now he had a broader mandate—to represent the House Democratic caucus. Although a moderate, he had earned the trust of those who were more liberal. And he was a friend of Erskine. From the White House perspective, he was the right person in the right place.

Spratt was frustrated with Kasich, his Republican counterpart, and more broadly with the difficulty of communicating with House Republicans. He was picking up signs that unlike the Republicans in the Senate, the House Republicans did not yet have a game plan. Spratt also worried that with the president and Republicans on record favoring tax cuts, there could be a bidding war leading to a replay of the fiscal hemorrhage begun in 1981. And he feared that neither Congress nor the White House would muster the courage to make the necessary spending cuts. He told me that Republicans might grab a few Democrats and enact a Republican budget that was anathema to the majority of House Democrats. But it was clear he was really talking about something different. No significant number of Democrats would abandon their party for a simple reason: the conservative Democrats who liked the Republican spending cuts hated the Republican tax cuts. No, what John Spratt was really saying was that he and other Democrats were worried about the White House—worried that the president might reach an agreement with the Republicans and leave congressional Democrats in the lurch.

Friday, January 31, 1997

Meanwhile Senator Lott had given us the green light to engage Domenici as his deputized budgeteer. Frank Raines and I came to the Hill separately and convened with Domenici and Hoagland in his office in the Hart Building, away from the Capitol and the press.

I arrived first, late in the afternoon. Domenici was dressed casually, sipping red wine from a paper cup. In the first minute he laid out his personal stakes, declaring openly, "My reputation is on the line." He had proven himself numerous times, but he could not rest on his reputation; it was a new day, a new caucus, and a new leader.

At the opening of budget season, Domenici was worried about all the moving parts. Numerous political and budget factions would be competing to leave their imprint on any budget agreement. In the Senate there was the bipartisan Breaux-Chafee group whose budget plan had garnered forty-six votes the year before.[13] In the House, there were the austere Blue Dog Coalition, the liberal Democratic Study Group, the moderate Republican Lunch Bunch, the in-the-middle New Democrats, the Black Caucus, the Hispanic Caucus, and more. All would have to be engaged.

This task would be all the more difficult because we all understood that a bipartisan agreement could not be a normal budget resolution setting only the overall levels of revenues and spending. Given the political differences between the parties, the administration could not simply announce an overall agreement and then leave it to the Republican Congress to enact the specific policies. In critical areas such as Medicare, taxes, welfare, and immigration, negotiators in the White House and Congress would have to agree on both the policies and the numbers. And everyone would need to pull together to make sure the committees followed behind and actually enacted the agreements.

This sounded fine, if optimistic, in the Senate. But what about the House, I asked? Domenici's answer was detached from the reality he knew so well. His response: once the White House and key senators had an agreement, Lott would take the deal to House Speaker Gingrich who would deputize Kasich to mobilize the House to follow. This was what Lott had been telling the president; work with us, and the House will follow. But there was no way this scenario was going to happen. The Constitution empowers the House of Representatives to initiate spending and tax bills, and it had been in the driver's seat on the last major budget round. Did anyone think Gingrich and Kasich would swallow a Senate–White House deal? Given the apparent lack of communication between Senate and House Republicans, it was clear that the White House would need to expand its quiet outreach to all sides.

MONDAY, FEBRUARY 3, 1997

On "Meet the Press" over the weekend, Senator Lott had invited the president to come to the Hill the day after Tuesday's State of the Union address to discuss ways the Democratic president and the Republican-controlled Congress could work together. The invitation was constructive, a first public reaching across the aisle. But conflicting schedules meant that the meeting would have to be delayed a week. And what was Lott hoping to accomplish, what was his agenda?

At his Capitol office, Lott told me that his call for a leadership meeting was just what it seemed—an effort to get the sides engaged, for the participants to talk about their legislative priorities, and perhaps start a process leading . . . somewhere. This was the Senate leader we liked: move quickly, get the balls in the air.

Senator Lott said he was not tied to the regular order—the normal deliberative process in which legislation is introduced, referred to committees, and considered and reported for consideration by the whole House or Senate. He was a risk taker and believed in "finding a seam and driving through it." I knew he must have uttered those same words to the president. He was a deal maker at heart, strong on the close, but not overly interested in the details. He did not like sitting through the long back-and-forth and nitty-gritty of negotiations. He would sometimes leave the room, return in a few hours, and upon reentering demand to know in a good-natured way what the hell was taking so long.

Republican Senators were lined up behind his bipartisan overtures. But what about the House? His answer: "Newt knows I'm up to something and can be brought along." But that sentence contained two contradictory notions. One had Gingrich on the inside; the other had Gingrich in the dark. Well, how about Kasich, I asked? He groped for words, finally saying that with Gingrich on board, they could get Kasich to come along. I held my counsel but knew that would not work. In House budget matters, the path ran the other way, from Kasich to Gingrich. It was Kasich who exercised an almost compelling influence on the budget. He was chairman of the House Budget Committee, but more important, he was the true believer and the real expert. Kasich was the central figure who would have to validate an agreement and provide the foundation on which Gingrich would build his political support.

WHEN I RETURNED to the White House, Erskine asked how long it would be before anyone discovered our quiet shuttle diplomacy. That would depend on the number of people we approached and who they were, I said. Domenici and Hoagland were used to working quietly and there was little chance that they would slip up. But the president or Senator Lott could be too open; they enjoyed talking to each other, to friends, and to colleagues.

Moreover, we were accelerating our activities and needed to expand the outreach and negotiating team. That process would start with Bob Rubin. A former Wall Street financier who had served as head of the president's National Economic Council, Bob had become the most influential member of the cabinet since succeeding Lloyd Bentsen as Treasury secretary in 1994. More than any other cabinet secretary, he was a part of the White House team, a central figure in the inner circle. Erskine would bring him into this one.

TUESDAY, FEBRUARY 4, 1997

It was time to roll up the sleeves with Domenici and Hoagland, taking the view from a very long perspective. These men had been a part of the now-sixteen-year effort to repair the fiscal damage caused when an enormous breach was opened in the nation's finances in 1981. At that time, the Reagan administration, the Republican-controlled Senate, and the Democratic-controlled House of Representatives jumped outside the normal budget bounds, enacting massive tax cuts that proponents claimed would be largely self-financing. Citing the principles of supply-side economics, they argued that tax cuts would boost economic activity and ultimately generate more tax revenue. Any remaining budgetary shortfall, they promised, would be covered by cutting government spending—even though President Ronald Reagan was firmly committed to major increases in defense spending. As it turned out, both the self-financing of the tax cuts and the spending reductions proved to be illusory, and despite a decade of congressional efforts to turn the tide of red ink, $1.4 trillion was added to the national debt between 1982 and 1989.

By the end of the 1980s deficits were rising and projected to increase further. Into the breach stepped President George H. W. Bush. He provided the political leadership that made it possible for Congress to enact a massive, $500 billion, five-year deficit reduction package in November 1990.[14] To achieve this goal, he was forced to repudiate what had been perhaps the central message of his successful 1988 campaign—his pledge not to increase taxes.[15] In a tumultuous political year, President Bush shepherded the passage of the bill, despite the defection of House Republicans over tax increases that accounted for 30 percent of the deficit reduction. But the president was not rewarded for his fiscal virtue. A weakening economy drove the deficit higher and undermined his bid for reelection. His loss to William Jefferson Clinton in 1992 strengthened the antitax resolve of the emerging Republican congressional majority. From their viewpoint, Bush had committed the unforgivable political error of following the Democrats into the tax briar patch.

When President Clinton took office in January 1993, the fiscal outlook was bleak. The new president inherited a stunning amount of red ink, with the federal budget deficit projected at $1.8 trillion over six years, according to CBO.[16] Repairing the fiscal damage became the administration's number one priority—in line with the message of "It's the economy, stupid," that had been the centerpiece of the president's campaign. But the prospects for a bipartisan approach were doomed by the inclusion of significant tax increases in President Clinton's first budget proposal.

The administration's first budget reduction effort was manna from heaven for the Republicans, who were intent on capturing Congress. Not a single Republican voted for President Clinton's 1993 budget package. Enactment was secured with Democratic votes only, including the tie-breaking vote of Vice President Al Gore acting in his capacity as Senate president. Partisanship ran rampant as Republicans accused Democrats of raising taxes rather than cutting spending to reduce the deficit—although the $500 billion, five-year deficit reduction package was equally split between spending cuts and tax increases.[17] These attacks paid off in the 1994 midterm elections, which gave Republicans control of both chambers when the 104th Congress convened in January 1995.

Once in power, House Republicans moved swiftly to implement their campaign platform, which had been astutely packaged as the Contract with America.[18] The contract laid out a sweeping agenda to balance the budget, cut taxes, reform welfare, strengthen national security, grant regulatory relief, and implement congressional reform and terms limits, among other priorities. At the center of the Republican program was the commitment to balance the budget while cutting taxes. With Social Security, which amounted to 22 percent of the budget, off the table, that meant that the rest of government would have to absorb nearly $900 billion in spending cuts over seven years.[19]

In a legislative tour de force, the Republican-controlled House rode roughshod over the opposition to pass the major components of the Contract with America—including the tax and spending bills—in the first hundred days of the 104th Congress. In quick succession, the House passed legislation that cut spending on major entitlement programs, including Medicare and Medicaid, as well as funding for many of the government's core services. The Republican-controlled Senate then tweaked the program, setting the stage for a confrontation with the White House and congressional Democrats.

In the ensuing test of wills, neither side blinked. President Clinton vetoed the Republican budget package, arguing that it cut too deeply into the government's core functions and distributed the benefits of tax cuts largely to the well-to-do. The Republicans held their ground, maintaining that their budget rightly reduced the scope of government and let taxpayers keep more of their hard-won earnings. In the face of the two sides' refusal to compromise, the federal government was forced to shut down, not once, but twice—in November and again in December 1995. President Clinton refused to sign legislation that so altered the nature and responsibilities of government, and the Republicans refused to fund a bill that didn't. Finally, the public rebelled, assigning blame for the standoff to the Republican Congress and demanding that the government be reopened. On January 6, 1996, the Republicans presented, and the president signed, a funding bill without the deep cuts the Republicans had advocated.

But now in 1997, thanks to the brave but politically perilous efforts of George H. W. Bush in 1990 and Bill Clinton in 1993—and to a booming economy that was filling the Treasury with revenue—the long-sought goal of a balanced budget was in sight. The remaining gap could be eliminated by spending cuts alone, which meant that tax increases could be taken off the table.

Frank Raines and I outlined the president's budget proposal to Domenici and Hoagland (table 1-1).[20] It was a budget that had been worked to death for months inside the White House, in cabinet agencies, and with key Democratic leaders and committees on the Hill. It was a masterpiece of politically informed

Table 1-1. *President Clinton's Proposed Savings for FY1998 to FY2002 Using the OMB Baseline*

Item	Proposed savings
Net reductions in discretionary spending	$137 billion
Defense	*$79 billion*
Nondefense	*$58 billion*
Reductions in Medicare spending	$100 billion
Reductions in Medicaid spending	$9 billion
Receipts from spectrum auction	$36 billion
Net mandatory spending increases	($24 billion)
Net interest savings	$16 billion
Net spending cuts	**$274 billion**
Net tax cut	($22 billion)
Net deficit reduction	**$252 billion**

Source: OMB, *Budget of the United States Government: Fiscal Year 1998* (GPO, 1997), table S-4.

policy that reinforced the support of our core Democratic constituencies even as it left room for the necessary compromises with Republicans.

Under OMB's deficit projections, enactment of the president's program would turn a projected deficit of $100 billion in 2002 into a $17 billion surplus. Over the five-year budget window, the president proposed a total of $274 billion in net spending cuts. Of that amount, $252 billion would go toward deficit reduction and $22 billion would pay for a net reduction in taxes.

The bulk of the $274 billion in net spending cuts would come from four big categories: reductions of $100 billion from the Medicare program, $79 billion from defense spending, and $58 billion from nondefense (domestic and international) programs funded annually through the appropriations process; and receipts of $36 billion from the government's auction of portions of the electromagnetic spectrum to private users. Those big pieces, along with other savings, allowed the budget to pay for a small tax cut and numerous presidential spending initiatives while still coming into balance.

The administration had labored for months to achieve a net reduction of $58 billion in nondefense discretionary spending while allowing targeted programs in that category to grow in such areas as education and training, the environment, crime and enforcement, and science and technology (box 1-1). The administration also proposed new spending initiatives in entitlement accounts that would provide health coverage for children and for families between jobs, encourage employers to hire those on welfare, restore benefits denied legal immigrants under the 1996 welfare reform legislation, and fund

Box 1-1. *Selected Domestic Spending Initiatives in President Clinton's FY1998 Budget Proposal*

HEALTH. Expand health insurance for children and the temporarily unemployed; increase funding to the National Institutes of Health for research on AIDS, breast cancer, and genetic medicine; expand funding for substance abuse and mental health programs; increase support for the Centers for Disease Control and Prevention.

EDUCATION. Modernize schools; upgrade teaching and learning standards; increase the number of tutors for child reading; link every school to the Internet; support remedial and special education; expand grants and loans for low-income college students; raise funding for the Job Corps, youth summer employment, and Head Start.

ENVIRONMENT. Fund Superfund hazardous waste cleanups and brownfields cleanups, to enable redevelopment of industrial sites.

IMMIGRANTS. Restore Medicaid and Supplemental Security Income payments to qualifying legal immigrants who were in the United States before enactment of the 1996 welfare reform bill.

TECHNOLOGY. Fund the advanced technology program, the manufacturing extension project, and national infrastructure grants to link to the Internet.

DEVELOPMENT. Increase funding for community development block grants for urban renewal and housing, empowerment zones and enterprise communities, and urban cleanup.

CRIME. Increase funding to the FBI, Drug Enforcement Administration, and Border Patrol; initiate grants to the states to put an additional 100,000 police officers on the nation's streets.

Source: OMB, *Budget of the United States Government: Fiscal Year 1998.*

school construction. Finally, the president's proposals used the tax code to achieve several policy objectives, aimed at expanding college education, extending health care to low-income children, giving homeowners a tax break on their principal residence, encouraging workers to save more, and encouraging businesses to hire former welfare recipients (box 1-2).

Box 1-2. *Selected Tax Cuts in President Clinton's FY1998 Budget Proposal*

HOPE SCHOLARSHIP. Allow a $1,500 per year tax credit for the first two years of postsecondary education for families earning less than $100,000 a year.

LIFETIME LEARNING DEDUCTION. Allow an income-tested $10,000 tax deduction for postsecondary education expenses, including job training.

CHILD TAX CREDIT. Allow a $500 per year tax credit for children under thirteen for families with income under $75,000.

CAPITAL GAINS. Waive taxes on capital gains up to $500,000 on the sale of a homeowner's principal residence.

INDIVIDUAL RETIREMENT ACCOUNTS. Increase the limits on the amount of income that can be set aside for traditional pretax IRAs; establish an income-tested tax-deferred IRA.

TAX INCENTIVES. Allow targeted tax incentives to businesses for pollution cleanup, investment in inner cities and the District of Columbia, and the hiring of long-term welfare recipients.

Source: OMB, *Budget of the United States Government: Fiscal Year 1998.*

In response, Bill Hoagland gave us a one-pager with nine lines and seven columns of numbers. (For the basics of the Republican plan, see table 1-2.) Their initial proposal contained not a word of description. But the gulf between their position and ours was apparent. At the start of this good-faith effort, the two sides were once again miles apart. The Republicans would cut Medicare and Medicaid and domestic discretionary funding far deeper than the administration would. They had to. They were using tougher CBO deficit projections while also making room for tax cuts that went well beyond those proposed by the Clinton administration. Even with all this politically imprudent cutting, they were still $22 billion short of balance in 2002. No wonder Domenici wanted to reach outside the normal budget box and adjust the consumer price index downward, knocking billions of dollars off the deficit—and out of the pockets of millions of Americans.

Table 1-2. *Senator Domenici's Initial Proposed Budget Plan for FY1998 to FY2002 Using the CBO Baseline*

Item	Proposed savings
Freeze defense and nondefense discretionary spending	$217 billion
Reductions in Medicare spending	$158 billion
Reductions in Medicaid spending	$22 billion
Other mandatory savings	$49 billion
Net interest savings	$48 billion
Net spending reductions	**$446 billion**
Net tax cut	($108 billion)
Net deficit reduction	**$386 billion**

Source: Republican offer sheet prepared by Senate Budget Committee majority staff.

The four of us—Domenici, Hoagland, Raines, and I—started looking for areas of agreement. We were close on defense spending. Some Democrats would feel the number was too rich, but with U.S. troops in Bosnia and the nation's worldwide commitments, defense would not be a battleground in this year's budget. After the fall of the Iron Curtain in 1989, the nation was eager for a peace dividend, and America's leaders had given it to them. Defense spending peaked at $320 billion in 1991 and then fell steadily over the next five years, to $266 billion in 1996.[21]

Then Domenici launched a trial balloon, saying that the difference between the OMB and CBO deficit projections was not as great as it might seem. Fully half the difference was the result of a judgment call on an arcane economic assumption affecting corporate tax payments. Forget whose judgment call would turn out to be more accurate, Domenici was opening a door—indicating a willingness to move toward the administration's less pessimistic deficit projections.

If that was to happen, Frank and I knew Domenici would want something in exchange. He was not a supply-sider; it would not be "self-financing" tax cuts. Domenici had worked too long and hard cleaning up messes to believe in free lunches. What he wanted was "entitlement reform," code words for reducing spending on Medicare, Medicaid, welfare, and other programs whose spending flows from formulas set in law. Unlike government programs that are funded yearly, entitlement spending is automatic. If you meet the eligibility requirements, you are entitled to get the money.

Entitlement programs make up most of the federal government's social safety net, with Social Security, Medicare, and Medicaid being the largest.[22] Social Security, a cornerstone of Franklin Roosevelt's New Deal, was enacted in 1935 during the Great Depression; it provides income for retirees with a sufficient work history, as well as income for the disabled. Both Medicare and Medicaid were part of President Lyndon Johnson's Great Society. Medicare funds health care for seniors, and Medicaid provides grants to states to support health care for the poor. Other major entitlements include unemployment insurance, farm price supports, and means-tested programs such as food stamps and Supplemental Security Income (SSI)—cash that is given to the very needy. Entitlements were a growing share of federal expenditures, with the fastest growth in the area of health care—caused by more enrollees, more generous benefits, and sharply rising health care costs.[23]

Entitlement spending had become a flashpoint for competing philosophies of government. The differences tended to follow party lines, but not always. To many Republicans and some Democrats, entitlements were a blank check on the Treasury. They increased spending automatically, and once under way with their vested beneficiaries, the programs were difficult to rein in. The programs were viewed by some as an inevitable path to an expanding government, one that would make ever greater claims on the Treasury and the economy.

The other side of the argument was that entitlement spending was the proper means to fulfill society's commitments. If the collective judgment of the nation's citizens was that government should provide pensions in the form of Social Security, health care through Medicare or Medicaid, or other forms of support, then entitlement spending was an appropriate way to fulfill those promises. A retiree's Social Security check or health care should not be held captive to the whims of the economy, a fickle Congress, or the latest budget impasse. Entitlements are thoroughly democratic because no privileged position or special favor is required to qualify. If you meet the standard, you are in.

On the question of entitlements, Domenici's position was not in doubt. His sheet of numbers could not have been clearer. Over the five-year window, he would reduce Medicare by $158 billion, Medicaid by $22 billion, and other entitlements by $49 billion. If he had his way, over half the deficit hole would be filled from these programs. And if a CPI adjustment were included, these entitlement cuts would skyrocket.

He had kept his counsel on the president's budget proposal until the end of the meeting, but he could no longer resist. What was the White House doing suggesting $62 billion of new entitlement spending?[24] Weren't we supposed to be reducing existing programs, not starting new ones? We let it pass. It was getting late and the president's State of the Union Address was that evening. We would convene again on Saturday, off-campus at Frank's house.

WEDNESDAY, FEBRUARY 5, 1997

The president's State of the Union address hit the right chords. "The people of the nation elected us all. They want us to be partners, not partisans. They put us all here in the same boat, they gave us all oars and they told us to row."[25] As was his custom, he went through his extensive set of initiatives: education, health care for kids, a welfare-to-work program, anticrime initiatives, environment, national service, and on and on. A very full agenda, but all of it paid for within his balanced budget.

The launch of the budget would follow the State of the Union address by two days. So Wednesday was a critical day to make the rounds. Erskine and I would meet with Senate Democratic leader Tom Daschle of South Dakota, and I would visit with John Kasich by myself. And on the day of the launch, the president would host one of his semi-regular meetings with the two Democratic leaders, Daschle and Representative Richard Gephardt of Missouri.

Senator Daschle was entering his third year as leader. After Democratic leader George Mitchell of Maine retired in 1994, Daschle had won the leadership race by a single vote, with most of the senior members of the Senate Democratic caucus supporting his opponent, Senator Chris Dodd of Connecticut. From that tenuous beginning, Daschle had solidified his position in the caucus. He had had a remarkably successful first two years, proving to be not only a consensus builder within the caucus, but a tough and able adversary. He was nominated for his second term by Senator Robert C. Byrd of West Virginia, the most senior and, at one time, the most powerful Senate Democrat.

Daschle was a trusted ally of the White House, and we quickly brought him along on Republican leader Lott's intentions on the budget. In public Lott had been talking regular order—receive the president's budget, let the Senate Budget Committee do its work, and then take the long march through the rest of the committees. But in private, as we told Daschle, Lott was promoting a quick agreement with the White House.

Daschle reported that Democrats in Congress saw no advantage to an early sit-down with Republicans. They were hell-bent on making the Republicans come up with their own budget—in public. The most recent slight riling Democrats was the introduction of the Republican tax bills, posted as S1 and S2 on the Senate calendar, proposing unrealistically large tax cuts of $193 billion over five years.[26] The Democrats' reaction was swift and predictable. If the Republicans were serious about their tax cuts, then let them produce a budget that paid for it all. They would have to cut spending deeply, including the programs they had been skewered on just a year earlier. And if, as everyone knew, they could not possibly produce a budget with those large tax cuts, Democrats would make them eat their words.

But forcing Republicans into the open would not be so easy—nor necessarily advisable. There was no legal requirement to reduce the deficit, no deficit targets that had to be hit. If partisanship really took hold, Congress would simply take a pass on the tough decisions to balance the budget. The appropriations committees could be turned loose to draft their annual funding bills, and that would be it. Congress could get out of town without a meltdown and with no deficit reduction. The Democrats could not make the Republicans walk off a budget cliff. Only they could do that, and our White House budget team was sure they had absorbed the lessons of their failure in 1995.

KASICH WAS FINALLY back in town, and just in time. "So, John," he said, "tell me what we ought to do." White House staff had been engaged with Domenici for two weeks but was running late with Kasich. The president's budget plan would be out tomorrow, and we needed Kasich to be part of a bipartisan solution. There was no time to lose.

I told him that in his position, I wouldn't have a clue what to do. The president's budget only got to balance because it used OMB rather than CBO deficit projections. The difference between the two projections came to more than $65 billion in the last year alone. So the Republicans, using the CBO numbers, were starting with a bigger deficit to fill, and they wanted a bigger tax cut, costing probably $20 billion to $30 billion in the last year. Some of the savings in the president's budget had little chance of enactment, so that was another $10 billion that had to be found somewhere. To balance the budget, the Republicans would need up to $100 billion more savings in 2002 alone, and about $300 billion over the five-year budget window. And they had no easy way to fill the deficit hole. They could not politically afford to run the Medicare gauntlet again, could not make the CPI adjustment without holding hands with the White House, and would not dare cut defense spending.

Kasich paused, smiled, and then let out a big laugh, "So you're telling me we're screwed!" As he and I started back over the numbers, I was amazed that he had not yet fully focused on the challenge of putting all the pieces together. Kasich started to push back, criticizing previous Democratic budgets, questioning the president's dedication to deficit reduction. Why not stretch to hard numbers and give ourselves the best chance of success, he asked. He wanted to use CBO numbers and to err on the side of caution—and on the side of the deeper spending cuts he favored.

We all had been down this road before. In the budget standoff of 1995, Republicans had insisted that the president produce a balanced budget plan under tougher CBO numbers. When President Clinton did just that in January 1996, Kasich and others dismissed it as too little, too late. I told Kasich that if the Republicans had claimed victory then and passed that balanced budget, they would have validated their budget crusade and could have justified, if not erased, the memories of the government shutdowns that had so tarnished their party.

"You know, one of the reasons that 1995 didn't work is that Pete Domenici and I were left out of it," Kasich commented. He was acknowledging opportunities lost, but he was also laying down the rules for this year's hoped-for agreement. When the budget negotiations moved to the White House in late 1995, Domenici and Kasich had been relegated to the back room, while the president, Senate majority leader Dole, and House Speaker Gingrich tried their hand at deficit reduction. As the negotiations began to rush toward collapse, the two budget committee chairmen became accomplices to the failure, upping the ante on what was being demanded of their leaders. In the end, no one's deal would have been good enough.

But now was a new day, and all of us were hoping to avoid repeating the many mistakes of the past. Kasich agreed to meet on a confidential basis— neither of us would share information without the permission of the other. One of the key players in the House was joining a team on which he had not been given the full roster of teammates nor all the avenues those teammates were pursuing. This is the result the White House team had been hoping for. For the time being, the lack of communication and coherence on the Hill suited us just fine, as long as those paths ultimately led to an agreement.

THAT AFTERNOON, THE White House budget and economics team gathered in the residence to brief the president for the following day's release of the budget. Erskine asked me to begin. I said that we were in a good political position. We had a sound budget and could deal from strength. The Republicans were traumatized by the 1995 budget meltdown and would have great difficulty moving a serious balanced budget by themselves, especially one that used CBO deficit projections and contained tax cuts. But the Republicans were open to a compromise, and we had already engaged some of their key people. Domenici and Kasich wanted to be inside the tent.

I warned that we had to be extremely mindful of congressional Democrats. The agreement had to win a strong majority of Democrats in both houses. For them, the tax cuts would be hard to swallow unless they had clear victories on education, health, and other high-priority issues. In addition, congressional Democrats were not ready for a sit-down with the Republicans. It would be unwise for the president and Lott to run too far ahead.

Frank Raines followed with the numbers. If we were forced to use CBO numbers, if we split on taxes, if we got our priorities, the budget would remain billions out of balance. The president absorbed it all; he understood the federal budget as well as anyone. In preparing his first budget submission in 1993, he had gone line by line through the whole thing. In areas he had dealt with as governor of Arkansas such as welfare, education, and other social services, his knowledge surpassed that of the policy experts. He also had a remarkable facility with numbers. He said passing this budget agreement would be tough but easier than the failed attempt of 1995. If we had to split the differences to get a balanced budget, we would. As the meeting came to an end, President Clinton gave his blessing to continue our multiple channels, both in the open and underground.

CHAPTER TWO

Launch

February 6, 1997—the official launch of the fiscal 1998 budget. The president did the formal unveiling in the morning; OMB and the economics team followed with detailed briefings.

The president's budget was alive on arrival for the first time in many years. The Republicans were taking some shots, but the tone was very different from the normal partisan assaults. The Republicans knew they could not be negotiating with the White House in one room and kicking the hell out of the Democrats in another. Some Democrats misread the signals, misattributing the muted Republican response to the clever political construction of the president's budget. But that was not the explanation. In Washington almost nothing is beyond being questioned, spun, and criticized. Without the administration's early and quiet outreach, the natural tendency toward partisanship would have taken hold.

THE LAUNCH OF the budget was a good opportunity to invite the two Democratic leaders, Tom Daschle and Richard Gephardt, to the White House. It is essential for the White House to maintain close and open relations with its party's leaders on the Hill. Their judgment and help are indispensable to the president; they are in a position to rally their caucuses for or against presidential initiatives. And on this day our team knew Gephardt would be firmly opposed to our desire to reach a budget agreement with the Republicans

First elected in 1976, Richard Gephardt was a moderate-to-liberal Democrat, a careful listener, and a consensus builder who had the support and trust of his caucus. Not only was he bright and committed, but he was also a dedicated campaigner, working tirelessly on behalf of Democrats. He became majority leader in 1989 when Representative Tom Foley of Washington moved up to become Speaker of the House. Along with Senator George Mitchell and Speaker Foley, he had been instrumental in persuading President George H. W. Bush to repudiate his "no new taxes" pledge, paving the way for the massive deficit reduction package that was enacted in 1990. And he had helped Speaker Foley rally House Democrats to support President Clinton's 1993 deficit reduction package, which passed in the House by a single vote and with no Republican support. Without those two budget agreements, the federal government would not even be close to a balanced budget.

Now Gephardt was in the minority, and he was focused on one objective—retaking control of the House of Representatives. A loss of control in the House is catastrophic. Everything changes. The majority runs the place, and the minority watches, remonstrates, objects, holds press conferences, rallies the troops, questions, and delays. But that is all done from the outside, with no access to the true instruments of power—the ability to set rules, pass legislation, control committees, and conduct investigations. That is why the political fights in the House are so intense, the tone so severe, the campaigns so tough and bitter. It is "winner-take-all" politics.

For Democrats, it had been two rough years under Republican control. The Republicans had marginalized them, responding tit for tat to past Democratic treatment. Key decisions on policy, schedule, bill consideration, amendments, committees, and investigations were all made by the Republicans. In 1995 the congressional Democrats had been spectators, powerless to stop the Contract with America juggernaut. Its derailment was not caused by congressional Democrats, but by Republican mistakes and a president who would not fold.

To make things worse, the administration had parted company with its congressional allies in the buildup to the 1996 election. President Clinton and congressional Republicans had a mutual interest in demonstrating an ability to govern. As a result, in the eyes of many House Democrats, the administration had conspired with the enemy to get things done—welfare reform, the expansion of health care coverage, safe drinking water regulations, an increase in the minimum wage, and business tax cuts. Many House Democrats would have preferred continued gridlock and an impoverished record of accomplishment on the part of Republicans, believing that a plague on both houses would fall hardest on the Republican majority. And now the Clinton administration wanted to balance the budget. Given the political facts, that would require the White House to work once again with the Republican leaders across the aisle.

Given all this, Gephardt had a suggestion: rather than negotiate with the Republicans, Democrats should rally around a slightly modified version of the president's budget—one that would unite Democrats. His suggestion was to peel off twenty to forty moderate Republicans in the House to pass a Democratic budget. He said Democrats could carry the day over whatever alternative the Republican leadership came up with.

Hmmm, peel their moderates off. I thought to myself: not only unlikely, but impossible. The Republican leadership had subdued its moderates in 1995. The whole caucus had jumped as one, moderates and all, with only one defection. Peeling off members of the other party's caucus was always a rare event, and it was an even more difficult task in a Republican caucus over which Speaker Gingrich had consolidated his power by gaining control over committee appointments and chairmanships, overriding the normal seniority system. Breaking ranks with the party leadership carries many costs: a loss of legislative power, a drying up of party resources and fundraising, and the psychological burden of being on the outside of both sides.

Furthermore, the House Republican leadership had learned many valuable lessons; their next budget would not have all the sharp edges of its predecessor. Moderate Republicans were not about to jump ship to join Democrats; too much bitterness and water had already flowed over the dam and too many real disagreements remained on policy. What dueling budgets would produce would be no agreement at all. And all of us in the Oval Office that day knew whose agenda that was—-Mr. Gephardt's.

Gephardt also emphasized the difficulty of uniting House Democrats behind a bipartisan compromise. He ran quickly through the factions in his caucus. The only ones in favor of even modest tax cuts were the moderate New Democrats. The mostly conservative Blue Dogs hated tax cuts because they made balancing the budget that much harder. They wanted to balance the budget first and foremost, using the toughest numbers possible. That included a willingness to cut everything: entitlements, defense spending, and domestic spending. The liberals in the caucus hated tax cuts for a very simple reason: they deprived the government of the resources to address national problems, such as health care, education, environment, and the inner cities. Without the tax revenue, liberal Democrats would not have the wherewithal to pursue an activist agenda.

Partially in response to Gephardt, but mainly because of the sentiments of his own caucus, Senator Daschle returned to the discussion he, Erskine, and I had had the day before in his office. He told the president that his was a strong budget, and now it was the Republicans' turn. Make them create their own budget in the light of day. Doing that would expose the ridiculousness of the five-year, $193 billion tax cut proposal they had posted on the Senate calendar. If Republicans were serious, they would have to go back to their old ways, cutting Medicare and other popular programs. That approach could soften them up and weaken them, driving them to an agreement on our terms. Daschle was sounding a call to arms to beat up the other side just as Gephardt had, but to give us a better bipartisan agreement rather to kill one altogether. Partisan warfare could serve its purposes if it drove the other side to the middle, not over the edge.

It was the president's turn. He sometimes used indirection, talking about one thing to address a second, closely related topic. He did not question the premise or logic of Gephardt's suggestion. But he wondered aloud if we could peel off Republican votes in the Senate. Many of their moderates had retired and been replaced by more conservative members. Trent Lott was in command of his caucus and could surely keep his team in check. It was very hard to see how the Democrats could split the Senate Republicans. It was a skillful turning of the issue, and it gave an unambiguous signal of where the president was headed.

There was one area where the White House and the Democratic leadership in Congress could come out united, and that was beating up the Republican tax bills. Never mind for now that the White House had a fundamental disagreement with the House Democratic leadership about budget strategy. The president, Gephardt, and Daschle agreed to a first step they could all support—to step forcefully on the Republican tax proposals. There would be time enough to deal with all the problems on the horizon. For now, it was enough—and all the White House could do—to point the daily steps in the right direction.

FRIDAY, FEBRUARY 7, 1997

Friday morning, and the president was calling. He had just spoken to Senator Lott who had given him a heads-up. He was going to blast away at the president's budget, in particular the $62 billion of new entitlement spending. Lott was reading right off Domenici's play sheet. The president seemed genuinely surprised. But I said Lott was doing to us on entitlements what we were doing to the Republicans on taxes. The good news was that Lott had called beforehand, an adversary giving notice before he struck. And he had told the president he thought they could work together.

SATURDAY, FEBRUARY 8, 1997

It was a wet, snowy Saturday morning. Domenici and Hoagland were a little late to arrive at Frank Raines's big old place right off Connecticut Avenue— the fruits of his days in investment banking and at Fannie Mae. Frank had big little shoes to fill at the Office of Management and Budget, those of Alice Rivlin. The OMB position had come open in 1996, when the president appointed Rivlin as vice chair of the board of the governors of the Federal Reserve System. She was the consummate budgeteer, having served as the first director of the Congressional Budget Office from 1975 to 1983. She was not only expert, but credible. Her honesty made her words count.

Frank was a quick study. He had taken advantage of the expert staff at OMB to cram a lot of the federal budget into his head. He could explain it and argue it. But the politics and players were new to him. It takes years to grasp the complexity of Capitol Hill, that wonderfully democratic branch of government where 535 elected entrepreneurs struggle to survive and prosper. Power is distributed and overlapping among numerous centers: leadership, committees and subcommittees, party caucuses and subcaucuses, and personal fiefdoms. There are a constant churn of issues being addressed and processed, an ongoing jockeying for position and power, and the ever-present need to keep money and press releases flowing to home districts and states, all with a mind to the interests of constituents and campaign contributors. Add to that the members' leeway to make many of their own rules, and you have the United States Congress: a dynamic but sometimes derailed institution—one that can produce great successes as well as failures. To get anything done in Congress, one has to understand the players and what motivates them, as well as who can deliver and who can be trusted. No expert can teach those things; they have to be learned and practiced on the job.

DOMENICI AND HOAGLAND were anxious to start with Medicare, the government's health program for the elderly. Their priority was throttling back entitlement spending, and next to the sacrosanct Social Security program, Medicare was the biggest spender. Medicare was also where the Republicans had made their biggest political mistakes in 1995. The Contract with America budget would have cut Medicare by $270 billion over seven years. The Republicans argued that these reductions would extend the life of the soon-to-be-bankrupt Medicare trust fund.[1] True enough. But somehow they failed to notice, or did not fully appreciate, that their Medicare savings were equal to the size of their tax cut. The Democrats could not believe their luck. A lot of senior citizens got very wound up thinking they were going to lose health benefits to pay for a tax cut going largely to the wealthy.

Frank and I were happy to start with Medicare. Having won the issue so decisively in 1995, the White House would dictate the terms of the Medicare settlement. We would just have to be careful not to settle too early or let Medicare get detached from the rest of the package. It was a big engine, both to generate savings and as a political lever. If Republicans wanted the White House to go along with large Medicare savings, they would have to give us what we wanted in return.

If corrective action were not taken, the Medicare trust fund was expected to go belly-up by 2001.[2] Extending the life of the trust for another decade would take some $400 billion of Medicare cutbacks over the next five years—far beyond the political tolerances. An increase in the payroll tax or any other tax to make up the shortfall was not even on the table, so that left three options: cut back the amount hospitals and other providers are paid for their services, make beneficiaries pay a greater share of the costs, or rejigger the services that the trust fund covered. Given the size of the problem, all three were likely to be needed.

The trust fund sleight of hand was simple. Part A of Medicare provides hospital and related medical services to seniors. Increasing numbers of seniors and rising health care costs were driving the Part A trust fund into the red, and quickly. The solution was to move some of Medicare's rather large expenses out of Part A and therefore off the trust fund ledger.[3] Presto! Problem solved. Of course, those hefty expenses had to go somewhere. The solution was to move them into Part B of the Medicare program—the part that was not financed through a trust fund. Part B provides physician, nursing, and related health services to seniors. Twenty-five percent of the financing comes from premiums paid by seniors, and the rest from the government's general revenues. Moving program costs from Part A to Part B would "save" the Part A trust fund by effectively piling the expenses onto the general budget.

The trust fund ploy solved a political problem, but it did not change the bottom line. The unified federal budget lumps everything together, and it was the unified federal budget that had to be balanced by 2002. Congress and the White House could make up new boxes and categories, move them around, change the labels, and juggle the parts. Those manipulations would help navigate the tough political territory of deficit reduction. But as long as the budget to be balanced included all the revenues and spending of the federal government, it all had to add up. It was that big bottom line the president was intent on bringing into balance.

None of this was lost on Domenici and Hoagland. They understood the need to rejigger the Medicare trust fund. But Medicare was politically charged. Some Republicans wanted to hold firm on the current definition of the trust fund, forcing the president to make tough cuts in Part A of Medicare or admit that it was going bankrupt. They had subliminally suppressed the memory that the Contract with America budget had relied on the same sleight of hand. Now it was the president's budget that advocated the shift, and they wanted the administration to take the heat. But Domenici and Hoagland were too smart to hoist themselves on an issue that could bite them just as hard. They would go along with "our" trust fund transfer; they just wanted to make sure that the final compromise contained plenty of real Medicare savings.

Toward the end of the meeting, Domenici turned to a crucial topic. He said that many people in his caucus—like Senator Phil Gramm of Texas—would want some sort of budget enforcement backstop to make sure the budget actually got to balance. After all, the White House was proposing to balance the budget based on projections of an uncertain future. What if that future did not turn out to be as rosy as originally forecast? How would the president guarantee that the budget would actually balance in 2002?

Domenici was talking budget process, a topic on which nearly as much time, effort, and angst had been spent as on the job of balancing the budget itself.[4] And with good reason. The budget process sets the rules that the players must follow. A near-universal truth is that the one who sets the rules usually wins. And as the nation had grappled with massive federal budget deficits, those budgetary rules had been changed several times in an effort to build a box that would force elected leaders to bring the budget into balance.[5] These rules were not invented and enacted in a vacuum. They were the result of political initiative and strength, one more crucial battleground in a struggle to determine the nature and control of the government's activities.

It was hard to tell what Domenici might have in mind. President Clinton's budget proposal already contained an enforcement mechanism that ensured the budget would be balanced by 2002.[6] That enforcement would kick in quite late in the five-year budget window and would cure any shortfall by both increasing taxes and cutting spending. The administration's plan was deemed to be legitimate by the Congressional Budget Office, providing a way to deflect calls for enforcement mechanisms that were counterproductive, unrealistic, or politically slanted. But clearly, Domenici was laying the groundwork for demanding some other enforcement process.

TUESDAY, FEBRUARY 11, 1997

The president, vice president, and a full retinue of aides were headed to Capitol Hill in response to Senator Lott's invitation to meet with the bipartisan congressional leadership. These meetings were important for the human element. By coming together, the two sides might find it easier to find common ground. A legislative process might be initiated, but the real purpose was for the nation's elected leaders to be in the same room, talk to each other, and observe that human beings have a capacity to work together.

Elections are important, and not just for the obvious reasons. The mood on the Hill is much better after an election. The brutal partisanship of the election has passed, and only the winners are present. The policy struggles have yet to be engaged or reengaged, and optimism and civility are evident. A window of opportunity opens, bestowed by the people on those they elected to serve them.

For this meeting, a pecking order was in place, with each participant expected to comment on his or her priorities for the year. The president went right into his welfare-to-work proposal—a very smart place to start. In 1996 Clinton had signed a Republican-passed welfare reform bill to the consternation, if not chagrin, of many Democrats. It was the most right-leaning of all the major bills enacted in 1996. The Republicans had the president between a rock and a hard place during an election year on an issue he had championed since his days as governor. The bill had many good provisions and was a significant improvement over the welfare bill Clinton had vetoed in 1995.[7] But it contained some bitter pills, such as ending Medicaid and SSI benefits to many legal immigrants. The merits of the bill were argued strongly inside the White House, even though there was never any doubt that the president would sign it. Although Clinton said nothing at this meeting, he was determined to fix the offending immigrant provisions as part of this year's hoped-for budget agreement.[8]

The president talked about how the welfare rolls had dropped by 2.5 million people, while jobs had increased by 11.5 million. He anticipated that as many as 4 million people could be coming off the welfare rolls in the next few years. He wanted to make sure there were jobs, training, and transitional assistance so that the move to the workforce was permanent and productive. He was asking the Republicans to implement his welfare-to-work proposal, thereby making a success of the welfare legislation they had so strongly advocated in 1996.

Next in the pecking order was House Speaker Newt Gingrich. The Speaker was interesting from many perspectives. To most, he was the hard-nosed revolutionary who broke the forty-year Democratic grip on the House of Representatives in the 1994 elections, smartly pulling all the political, press, and procedural levers to win. In taking control, the Republicans were good, but also lucky. Democrats in the House and Senate had been hit by a nearly perfect political storm that was largely of their own making. Three factors loomed large—the Democrats-alone tax increases in 1993, the inept handling and ultimate failure of Democrats' efforts at health care reform in 1994, and the House banking scandal, in which members' personal overdrafts seemed to reflect and magnify their lack of care to the nation's business.[9]

The Speaker was more than a revolutionary. A skilled negotiator and legislator, Gingrich was not only quick on substance but very smart about where to make his stands. At times, he could be unyielding and obdurate, wanting to fight rather than compromise. That was the Gingrich who drove the Contract with America legislation through Congress and into confrontation with the president. At other times, if it suited his political agenda, he could be amazingly accommodating, ready to concede on a variety of issues.[10] In a negotiation, the White House was happy to deal with Gingrich for an important reason—he was good on his word and could almost always deliver. His power may have weakened since the 1996 elections, but if he said he could do it, it almost always got done. If an agreement was reached inside his office, he would do the lifting on his side.

There was another side to Gingrich, and it was on display as he followed the president's remarks. This was the expansive Gingrich who was able to see the big picture, the Gingrich who liked to throw out ideas and see what stuck. He thought this year's budget efforts should focus not on existing programs but on goals for the nation. If both sides could agree to a handful of goals, then they could try to come together around the policies that might achieve them. He suggested there was a ready-made test bed in the nation's capital. Why not try out some of these initiatives in the District of Columbia, a challenging microcosm of what might work in the rest of the country?

As for the year's legislative prospects, he suggested that each side rack up its goals, see which ones could win agreement, and then enact the legislation. If both sides agreed to something, it would be enacted as stand-alone legislation rather than wrapped into a big budget bill. Take the wins where we could get them, he said, and then suggested that the parties might even reach an early agreement on Medicare and pass that as a stand-alone bill.

In one sentence, the Speaker had made the world's quickest transition from the novel and expansive to the old and contested. The proposal to deal with Medicare separately was manifestly against the interests of the White House.

It was a nonstarter. Medicare was one of the budgetary and political engines that would be needed to carry the entire agreement. It would not be done separately. But, in fact, Gingrich was not trying to put one over. The larger truth was that unlike Lott, he was not even thinking in terms of an agreement to balance the budget; he had not yet embraced the possibility that had been driving White House efforts for months.

Senator Lott went next, going through a list of issues headed by tax cuts. But he was open about how these could be enacted; he did not rule out revenue raisers, particularly those that broadened the tax base and got away from special carve-outs benefiting narrow interest groups. But he wanted to reduce the capital gains tax rate, particularly for small businesses and farmers. He was smart to appeal to Democrats, who also favored capital gains tax cuts for these constituents. Then he began to reel off his priorities in other areas: education, crime, trade, and then Superfund, the government's program to clean up hazardous waste sites, arguing that the government should ease the burdens on business for these massive clean-ups.

In these early mood-setting political meetings, there is an implicit understanding that some topics are out of bounds, not to be discussed in polite company. Everyone knew not to raise abortion, flag burning, gay rights, unions, a constitutional amendment mandating a balanced budget, a hike in the minimum wage, and a few other hot topics on which the sides were dug in and would be forced to speechify if the topic were raised. Superfund was close to being on this list for most politicians and already was for some. Inadvertently or not, Senator Lott had pushed one of the vice president's hot buttons.

"Mr. President, let me respond to that," Al Gore gathered himself upright. Throughout his many years in the House and Senate, the vice president had been a tireless advocate of the environment, and he was now the Democrats' lead spokesman on the issue. He had initiated environmental programs to crack down on polluters, clean up messes, monitor environmental conditions, and expand environmental education. And on many of these issues, he was often at odds with Republicans. There was no love lost between the vice president and congressional Republicans. He was an aggressive spokesman for the administration, adept at hitting the other side. When congressional Democrats needed to sharpen and amplify their message, they called on Vice President Gore to lend his strong voice.

Responding to Senator Lott, the vice president stated forcefully that the administration would insist on having financially solvent polluters pay the major share of cleaning up hazardous waste sites. This position was anathema to most Republicans, who preferred to have the public pick up the rather substantial costs of cleanups.

Silence descended as the vice president finished. For an instant, there was an opening for the rhetorical battle to be joined, but the participants let it pass, and the momentarily threatened decorum was once again reestablished. Representative Gephardt was next, sounding very positive, stating the need for both parties to work together. He suggested the leaders focus on a single issue at a time and pass it in a bipartisan manner. But he did not want these leadership-driven initiatives to end-run Congress. The regular order, including committee consideration, should be followed. His message was pointed both at Republicans and the White House. He knew both were interested in reaching a bipartisan budget agreement. Gephardt's regular order would put the Republicans in the position of passing a budget that would reveal its numerous politically incompatible objectives. Regular order also did not include the White House reaching a quick bipartisan agreement.

Senator Daschle spoke last. He closely echoed Gephardt. Let's work together in a bipartisan manner but respect the regular order, he urged. It was the same message Daschle had given the president the previous week. And the two men's position was understandable. The Democrats wanted the Republicans to be called to task for the large tax cuts they continued to advocate, even as they were pledging allegiance to a balanced budget. If they were serious, Democrats believed, Republicans should walk the very perilous political gauntlet such conflicted desires would create.

Then began the process of deciding what to do next. After a lot of round and round, all agreed that five topics should be the focus of bipartisan efforts: education, juvenile justice, welfare-to-work, taxes, and the District of Columbia. In fine political fashion, the list had something for both sides and ensured that both the president's and the Speaker's suggestions were adopted. Everyone was for education, taxes were a Republican priority, and juvenile justice sort of popped out. Nonetheless, it must have been evident to all these veteran politicians that the "working groups" delegated to handle these topics would not get far at all. They would be too far from the institutional centers of power where decisions were actually made.

As the meeting was breaking up, the issue of budgetary constraints came up. Senator Strom Thurmond, the ninety-four-year-old senator from South Carolina and the Senate's most senior member, roused himself from a drowsy silence as if on cue: "All inside a balanced budget." Everyone smiled.

After the meeting, the White House group walked back to the vice president's Capitol office, right off the Senate floor.[11] Inside the room, the president asked me how I thought it had gone. All fine, I said, except for Gingrich's invitation to settle quickly on Medicare. Medicare would need to be part of the overall agreement. The president smiled: "I figured that too, so I just played dumb." And Medicare had not ended up on the chosen list of five topics.

WEDNESDAY, FEBRUARY 12, 1997

The president's budget had been above ground for six days. It was time for White House chief of staff Erskine Bowles to meet House Budget Committee chairman John Kasich. Kasich was late. After the pleasantries, he launched into a soliloquy that revealed the yawning gulf between his position and the president's. His vision of a budget was not even in the same political ballpark as Clinton's. Kasich wanted to cut spending more than even most conservative Republicans had proposed in the past. He wanted to use the most conservative possible deficit projections: from his viewpoint, the deficit projections in the president's budget were not even in play. He said he would actively work to blow up any agreement that failed to use the CBO deficit projections. And he said he and Domenici would force the necessary spending cuts by hauling in the committee folks and bludgeoning them into submission!

That was a cold blast, and there was only one way to counter his rhetorical unwinding—by seeing how serious he was. Would he be offering such a budget and, more important, would he be passing it out of his committee, Erskine and I asked. Democrats certainly were not going to help move a budget like that. Would he have the needed Republican votes?

Kasich was taken aback at our response. Sure he would produce his own budget as a starting point, but he was not sure he would move it through his committee. There it was: rhetoric meeting reality. The trial balloon of budget purity had been pricked by the prospect of the sharp objects in his committee. To emphasize the point, Erskine and I urged him to produce his own budget, and to do it in public. Let the world see how he would fill the $80 billion to $100 billion hole in 2002. There would be no Democratic support for such a plan. Would there even be Republican support?

Kasich backed off, growing reflective. "You know, guys, I know how to get it done, how to get off the dime." He was coming back, absorbing once again the fact that he could not square the circle by himself. He had tried that in 1995 and come up empty.

Erskine was amazed at Kasich's performance. As we walked down the hallway, he started to laugh, reverting to one of his pet phrases, "He done drunk the Kool-Aid." The meeting with Kasich had been disorienting, and we would need to circle back—to him, but more important to his leader, Newt Gingrich.

THURSDAY, FEBRUARY 13, 1997

Meeting with Gingrich the next day, Erskine and I found an upbeat leader. The Speaker had just concluded a near-death experience on ethics charges. In effect, he had admitted misusing organizations he directed to promote his political causes and himself and had agreed to pay a $300,000 fine. He dwelt for a few moments on the personal ordeal of the daily assaults and attempts to deprive him of his position as Speaker. He said that some days it was all he could do to get through the next hour, hoping that at some point it would be over, but not focusing on when, fearful that the thought of its continuation would overwhelm him. He told us he had forced himself to segment his life; to put his fight for political survival in one corner, apart from the day-to-day issues confronting the Speaker. He had been putting one foot in front of the other for many days now, he had been hunkered down for a long time. But now the burden was lifting, and he was beginning to look ahead.

Gingrich complimented the president on the 1996 election campaign. He admired the use of "values" issues, issues directed at the various constituencies whose support was critical to the victory in November. Targeted initiatives had supported the president's standing on education, health care, crime, and the environment.

Erskine mentioned an article he had recently read in the *New York Times*. The article was about Clinton, but Bowles said he could have substituted Gingrich's name for the president's and the article still would have rung true. Newt sure liked that. And there was much truth to it. Clinton and Gingrich both were skilled politicians and survivors and were enamored of big ideas. In meetings the president and the Speaker were clearly comfortable with each other. They shared the same sense of humor, the same southern roots, and the same ambition to be productive in service to their country. But, of course, they came at the world differently: one seeing the tumult and reforms of the 1960s as a positive step forward, and the other as a dangerous interlude in the ongoing march of conservative values. These two were truly cut from the same cloth, but on one the shears had cut left of center, and the other to the right.

Erskine and I needed to get Gingrich focused on the budgetary challenge and on the fact that a bipartisan agreement was within reach. We walked him through the arithmetic: if the president got his spending initiatives and the Republicans got their tax cuts, the remaining deficit could be $80 billion to

$100 billion in 2002 alone. We asked what he thought we should do to fill it. He was temporarily at a loss. Then he said that maybe everyone had to look at balancing the budget as a long-term proposition. Perhaps there would be too much "political grinding" to try to do it all in a single year. He suggested triage. Put aside the issues that were too tough and focus on the pieces that were possible as part of an agreement.

The Speaker's response was understandable. He had just begun to focus on the budget, and we had just thrown a polite but cold $80 billion bucket of water in his face. Gingrich was responding in a wholly rational way: the White House and Congress should do whatever they could, even if they could not get all the way there this year.

We told Gingrich we were receiving more than mixed signals from John Kasich and were fearful he would be too dug in and doctrinaire to help find the middle. I reminded Gingrich of January 1996 when the president laid down a seven-year budget that balanced under CBO deficit projections—exactly as the Republicans had been demanding. But that budget had not met with Kasich's exalted standards. We told the speaker that Kasich might be more demanding than the system could bear.

The Speaker said that Kasich had a moral commitment to balancing the budget, a commitment that was anchored in the memory of his parents' premature and tragic deaths resulting from an automobile accident. He said that Kasich was seeking to meet a self-constructed ideal rooted in his personal circumstances. It wasn't gamesmanship, it was real.

Moving from the personal to the procedural, Gingrich started expounding a diffuse and complicated process, the kind of structure the president and the bipartisan leadership had launched two days before. It would lead to the same dead ends. He wanted to decentralize the job and let numerous informed members go about the business of putting together the smaller pieces. He would build a small group of "those who really matter" to coordinate the overall effect.

We did not respond directly. Gingrich's plan was bubble-up decisionmaking, a model we at the White House believed suffered from critical defects: it was too complicated, too slow, and without the institutional structures needed to reach, protect, and enact a budget agreement. In contrast, we believed that an agreement would have to be driven from the top. The broad outlines had to fit the political objectives of both parties, and the leaders were the ones best positioned to make those judgments. If the outlines of an agreement could be reached, a congressional budget resolution would provide the procedural protections to ward off unwanted amendments and hold the deal together. It would also compel the committees to hit their deficit reduction targets as part of an expedited and protected reconciliation process.

Nonetheless, it was a good, if inconclusive, meeting. The speaker was reengaging, but he was not yet fully organized or up to speed. We and the Senate Republicans were ready to move ahead, but the Speaker was just regaining focus. It was time to see the man who was always on the move. We would ask Senator Trent Lott to help get his House compatriots on track.

Friday, February 14, 1997

Our inner circle—Erskine Bowles, Bob Rubin, Frank Raines, and I—had grown to a group of five with the addition of Gene Sperling, head of the National Economic Council. The council had evolved into one of the two main domestic policy shops in the White House, splitting duties with the Domestic Policy Council under Bruce Reed.[12] Gene had been with President Clinton since the 1992 campaign, having worked for New York governor Mario Cuomo before that. There was no one in the White House who worked harder or put more into the job—he rightly demanded a lot from his people as well as himself. The economic council was invaluable to the president's efforts, both in fashioning policies and in presenting them in politically smart ways.

Over the coming months, our group would meet daily in the chief of staff's office. Under Bowles's steady hand, information would be exchanged and parsed, issues analyzed and debated, and next steps agreed upon. Treasury and OMB were the only two cabinet agencies directly involved in the day-to-day deliberations. Agency input was mainly gathered and consolidated through White House policy advisers, although agency staff often played significant roles with their congressional counterparts.

Today the group was meeting with the president. Clinton was a night owl. The mental engine would still be warming up in the morning, but purring very well by afternoon, up to full speed by evening, and into overdrive as the small hours neared. This meeting was at 10:00 a.m. in the Oval Office. But the subject matter was right in his wheelhouse—politics and all the moving parts. This budget agreement would be like no other attempted by this White House. Instead of going it alone, as the Democrats did in 1993, or engaging in outright partisan warfare as happened in 1995, this time we wanted to walk the bipartisan path.

I told the president we had made progress on three fronts. First, we had pushed along the Lott-Domenici process, and although it was still early, we felt that an agreement could be made with Senate Republicans. Second, we had consulted widely on both sides of the aisle, meeting with leadership, committee chairmen, and other influential members – the president breaking in to insist that we must "get caught talking" to everybody, particularly Democrats. Third, we had successfully sounded the wake-up call on the size of the challenge—all the leaders and key budget people now knew about the $80 billion hole in 2002.

I said that House Republicans were just now discovering the nature of the challenge and did not yet have a coherent game plan on the budget. Gingrich had just put his ethics problems behind him and was still coming into focus. Kasich was somewhere we could not quite locate: trying to set conditions that a bipartisan agreement could not meet but still wanting to be part of the solution.

On the Democratic side, the president already had the lay of the land, having met with Democratic leaders Daschle and Gephardt a week before. Fortunately, both Democratic budget leaders, John Spratt and Frank Lautenberg, wanted to be part of the solution, as did others Erskine and I had reached out to, such as moderate senator John Breaux of Louisiana and Representative Vic Fazio of California, the chairman of the House Democratic caucus.

The president started ticking off his list of particulars. He wanted to get a lot of Democrats down to the White House to talk with them about the politics of this year and next. He had a fundamental disagreement with the popular Democratic view that confrontation was the path to political success. He believed that was a misreading of the 1996 election. He would be the essential validator to convince Democrats that a balanced budget agreement was in their own interest as well as the nation's. Despite their differences over political strategy, he wanted to reassure Democrats that he would pursue an agreement that a majority of them could support. And the president also wanted to reach out to more Republicans, particularly in the House.

RIGHT AFTER THE meeting, I reached Senator Lott, who was traveling in Mississippi. Starting in about our House problems, I told him that he and Gingrich were on very different tracks. The speaker was talking decentralization, bubble-up, and a slow walk that might not even have a balanced budget as its goal. Kasich was a big problem, far off the path the White House was following with Domenici. Kasich was talking massive spending cuts that neither party would support in the light of day. Lott needed to help get his House brethren on track.

Lott was upbeat, even confident. He had to be or he could not persevere as leader. Being leader means being the backstop for a lot of nasty problems. The common term for a legislative hot potato was "a leadership issue." It meant the problem was being kicked upstairs. And, almost by definition, finding a solution was not easy.

Lott had been active. He had met with some House Republicans and claimed they would be supportive. He asserted that Gingrich knew that Lott was "up to something." He felt that Kasich could be brought along. Lott would check with one of his friends on the House Budget Committee. I asked about the working groups and Gingrich's plan for bubble-up consensus? Lott chuckled. Those working groups "were to keep everybody busy." He did not expect much to come from them other than to divert attention from the real work. Lott and I seemed to be on the same wave length, but we were still wondering where the Speaker stood.

LATER, IN THE afternoon, Raines and I met with Domenici and Hoagland. We had covered all the options on Medicare on Saturday. Now they wanted to talk about the president's $62 billion in proposed new entitlements. These were smart guys, so they started with our weakness—an entitlement for Alzheimer's respite care. The proposal was worthy on the merits, they said, but could create a major budgetary problem. The president's budget assumed thirty-two hours of respite care a year, a woefully inadequate amount to deal with consequences of this devastating disease. Domenici was right to press us. Wouldn't our good intentions lead to a rapid expansion of the program to cover the true need, he asked, and wouldn't that cost a fortune? How would the government pay for what all of us knew would be the true cost of the program? Frank and I did not have an answer.

We were on stronger ground on the president's initiative to provide health insurance for an additional five million children. The entitlement was not open-ended, that is, one in which the dollar costs could soar to any level.[13] The total dollars that could be spent were capped. The White House had done its estimate of the program's cost, and we were willing to stand by that.

The other big item was the restoration of Supplemental Security Income and Medicaid benefits to legal immigrants. Those cash and health benefits had been eliminated in the 1996 welfare bill. From our viewpoint, this measure did not represent a new entitlement; it restored benefits that had been unwisely and unfairly taken from deserving individuals. These immigrants had waited in line, followed the rules, and entered the country legally, but had fallen on hard times. On this issue, it was good to be dealing with Pete Domenici. He was from New Mexico and had both a natural sympathy and constituent interest. This issue would not be so easy in the House.

Then to Medicaid. The 1995 Republican budget bills mandated that federal funding for Medicaid be turned into a fixed block grant to the states. Give the states the money, along with some guidelines, and let them handle the program. Democrats had vehemently opposed this provision, fearing that austere or uncaring state governments would curtail the reach and quality of health services for the poor. In 1995 the White House had vowed to veto a block grant for Medicaid, and when the budget collapsed, the Republicans had been forced to retreat. This year there would be no serious attempt to resurrect a block grant for Medicaid spending.

But we had a shared interest in curbing Medicaid spending. Initially a well-intentioned inducement for states to address the health needs of the poor, Medicaid's payments to states had become a cash cow to some. These states had learned to game the system, sucking dollars out of the federal Treasury, even if they did not spend the money on health care. To stop the outflow, the Clinton administration wanted to cap payments to states and tie payments to the number of poor served by the program—a per capita cap. Lott, Domenici, and Hoagland all agreed with that approach. But getting the proposal adopted would be tough. The stumbling block was not ideological or particularly partisan; it was about the money. The states' governors would lobby hard, spinning the loss of money and their political clout in many directions.

CHAPTER THREE

Circle 'Round
the Consumer
Price Index

Erskine Bowles and I felt confident we were pushing in the right direction—those daily steps. We felt even more confident after the Speaker called Erskine on Saturday to say that our meeting with the leaders on Thursday had been "providential." Before that meeting, Gingrich had believed the budget could not be balanced before 2005; now he thought 2002 was in reach. He was ready to roll up his sleeves and work.

Before that happened, however, the White House team was working on solving the problem of the handoff—that all-important moment when the two sides would engage in the open for the first time. We were dealing with a Republican Senate in a hurry, an unfocused Republican House, and a bunch of congressional Democrats mostly interested in beating up the other side. To get agreement on a balanced budget, we had to get Republican leaders in both houses on board. But most important, we had to get Democrats inside the tent. Even if the Republicans were to agree to every penny and policy in the president's budget, congressional Democrats would not be party to an agreement they were not party to.

The natural venue for the handoff was the Senate Budget Committee. It is the first Senate committee to move after receipt of the president's budget. Its mission is to examine the president's budget, consider alternatives, and craft a congressional budget resolution setting overall levels of taxes and spending for the federal government. Once Domenici convened his committee, both sides would be forced into the open. To help the proceedings, we would ask Senate Democrats to offer their own budget or some variation of the president's budget proposal. Once the process was under way, members would vote on plans and amendments, revealing where they stood and perhaps moving toward a compromise. A failure of the committee to get off the ground would strengthen the case for the White House and congressional leaders to step in. The problem with convening the committee was that in solving our problem, it was creating one for Domenici. He was happy with our quiet discussions, preferring to reach agreement with the White House before showing his hand. Why should he invite a partisan fight in his committee if he didn't have to?

WEDNESDAY, FEBRUARY 19, 1997

Returning from the Hill, I stopped to see Erskine, who was on the phone with Gingrich. The Speaker and Trent Lott were in Palm Beach with some of their large contributors. They had found some quiet time and were talking budget strategy. More important, Gingrich had been talking with the president. The Republicans were proposing a two-bill strategy. The spending bill that balanced the budget would be passed in advance of the bill that cut taxes. Their political motivations were clear. They had been drubbed in the last budget round because Democrats had successfully tarred them with cutting Medicare to finance their tax cuts. This time, by separating the two bills, it would be more difficult to draw the link. This strategy would also make life easier for congressional Democrats. They would want to vote for a balanced budget before endorsing tax cuts.

Packaging alone would not solve the numbers issues. Budget savings had to be high enough both to balance the budget and to pay for tax cuts. But Gingrich had a solution for that too. To keep down the costs of the tax cuts, he would make several automatically expire, or "sunset," in a few years. The Republicans believed this was smart politics for them and had proposed it in the last days of the 1995 budget negotiations. They would start popular tax cuts now and dare Democrats not to renew them when the time came.

The Speaker's suggestion did not sit well with us, and not principally for political reasons. If we were going to all this trouble, why should we agree to plant a potential time bomb in the budget? Nor were we sure if his politics were right. It was not clear that voters would choose a little extra money in their pockets over the preservation of programs such as Medicare and education that carried significant political weight with the electorate. But, of course, the real danger was not that we would have a debate about national priorities and then make the hard choices between taxes and spending. It was that we would take the easy way out and run up the deficit again.

Finally, to make the budget deal work, Gingrich proposed that the CPI be adjusted downward. But Gingrich wanted to place a buffer between his members and any political fallout from a direct vote on the adjustment itself, so he proposed a deus ex machina. A commission would spit out the size of the CPI adjustment, which would then be plugged into the budget. That way, his members would not have to take a perilous political vote on the size of the hit. Gingrich offered the White House the great honor of appointing the commission, an honor we quickly declined. If we were going to touch the CPI, both parties would have to hold hands all the way.

THURSDAY, FEBRUARY 20, 1997

The Republicans were wasting no time. Lott was talking up the two-bill strategy in public. He was letting it be known that Republicans were considering separating the budget and tax bills. And in wonderful Lott fashion, he was open about the reason—the party did not want a replay of the "Mediscare" that had hurt it so badly two years earlier.

Lott was also building up the size of the tax cut, claiming the president's budget contained $160 billion of tax increases that could be used to pay for cuts in other tax rates. He had more than double counted the president's proposals, but, of course, the White House was not his audience.[1] It was conservatives who needed to be enticed into the wisdom of a separate tax bill. Combine those revenue raisers with whatever could be saved on the spending side, and you could have a whopping big tax cut. And if those big numbers happened to be lowered as part of the negotiations, Republicans would simply blame Democrats.

IT WAS THE Speaker calling again. On the tax bill, he was already talking deal. The president would get his HOPE scholarship and other proposed education tax pieces, Republicans would get a cut in capital gains, and both parties would agree to a $500 per child tax credit. The child credit had support from both Republicans and Democrats. It was in the Republican Contract with America and was the centerpiece of the Christian Coalition's tax program. A less expansive version was contained in the president's budget, but it was still expensive. But, of course, the Speaker had a suggestion about that too: if a balanced budget got in the way, he said, just start the child tax credit now, phase it in over time, and sunset it if necessary.

THAT EVENING, THE weekly political meeting ran late. When it was finished, we still needed ideas on the suggested CPI commission, so it was back to Erskine's office. Gene Sperling, the designated worrier, was raising all the appropriate red flags. Millions of voters would be affected by this adjustment. Bob Rubin reminded us of what happened to House Ways and Means chairman Dan Rostenkowski when seniors went berserk over the 1988 catastrophic health care bill.[2] Thinking it was doing the rational thing, Congress had based seniors' catastrophic premiums on their ability to pay, a move that had sent politically active well-to-do seniors over the top. They had mobbed Rostenkowski's car in Chicago, flopping all over the hood. It was great theater, but it didn't stop there. By the time seniors had fully expressed themselves, Congress was clamoring to repeal the measure, which it did expeditiously.

Gene felt we should run our CPI ideas past key interest groups. Why not start early to see if we could defuse the resistance? It was a tough call. A near-universal political fact is that getting things done is tougher than stopping them. Power is distributed not only between the executive and legislative branches but, more important, within Congress. Interest groups—especially those with deep pockets—have easy reach into the legislative power centers where decisions are made. And given the distribution of power in Congress, interest groups have multiple shots at stopping any effort to change the status quo—in subcommittee, full committee, the rules committee, the leadership, or even with a single powerful member drawing a line in the sand. Given this, the trick is not so much how to use the interests groups as how to deflect their stopping power.

MONDAY, FEBRUARY 24, 1997

It was one month to the day since we initiated our quiet diplomacy with Domenici. A lot had happened. The president's budget had been successfully launched and arrived alive on Capitol Hill. Congressional leaders had come to understand the broad outlines of the budget challenge and some of the large pieces that would be needed to fill the deficit hole. The president was fully engaged, consulting with Democrats and talking budget agreement with both Republican leaders. The discussions were becoming more concrete: economic and budget projections, a CPI adjustment, the two-bill strategy, and suggestions about the tax package were all on the table. And we were working with Domenici toward a hoped-for compromise on spending.

The White House budget team's first job today was to bring the vice president up to speed. We quickly outlined where things stood. The federal government faced an $80 billion deficit in 2002 if CBO deficit projections were used and each side achieved its policy objectives. That was why interest in a CPI adjustment was so high—an adjustment would bring in big money, and the technical case for making it was strong. But, of course, the politics were awful. That was why we were trying to launch a commission to deflect the howls of those who would be negatively affected.

Gore knew that Representative Gephardt would likely challenge him for the Democratic presidential nomination in 2000, and this budget agreement would have some sharp political edges. But the vice president never flinched. If a CPI adjustment was what was necessary to balance the budget and achieve the president's domestic policy objectives, then he was for it. That was that. On the CPI, Gore urged us to consult with organized labor and groups representing seniors, particularly the American Association of Retired Persons (AARP). He wanted to know if these groups could be brought on board in support of a CPI commission and, if so, could help structure the process.

LATER THAT DAY, during a budget team meeting with the president, conversation turned back to the CPI. The president thought Senator Daniel Patrick Moynihan should play a lead role on the issue. The Democrat from New York was rightly seen as one of the key protectors of the Social Security system. He had opposed all attempts to privatize Social Security, fearing it would undermine the intergenerational contract Americans had with each other.[3] And he was out front on the need for an adjustment to the CPI. Apart from balancing the budget, Moynihan saw the adjustment as the right thing to do—a way to extend the solvency of the trust fund and a way to hold back calls for privatizing Social Security.

On the two-bill strategy the president was open to splitting the deficit reduction and tax bills, but he wanted to delay making a decision. It was still early in the process, and he knew the right tactic would likely present itself. And, of course, even though two separate votes might be engineered, the bills would be inextricably linked. From a numbers perspective, the deficit reduction bill would have to overshoot a balanced budget in order to fund a net reduction in taxes.

More important, the two bills would take their shape as part of the same negotiation. The trades necessary to find a compromise did not always respect a neat division into spending and tax components. If the Republicans wanted a reduction in the capital gains tax rate, we would insist on tax policies like the HOPE scholarship. But we would also insist on getting things on the spending side of the ledger—including children's health care, environmental protection programs, and the like.

TUESDAY, FEBRUARY 25, 1997

Domenici had been out of town and wanted to confer with Frank Raines and me before a scheduled meeting with Lott and Gingrich. He was upset with them. He had a tendency to grind his jaw when troubled, and the tension was evident across his face. His presumption had been that he and the White House would work out a budget agreement—then worry about shepherding it through Congress. But the leaders had jumped out front, going public with their two-bill strategy even before we had the outlines of an agreement.

Domenici also had a problem with a CPI commission. He wanted to plug a 0.5 percentage point downward adjustment in the CPI into whatever budget was agreed to. That would be that. There could be a CPI commission if we liked, but Domenici wanted its mission to be long-term and any recommendations to be reported at some distant date that would not affect this year's budget agreement. He wanted to forge ahead quickly without the benefit or political cover of a CPI commission. He had been told to reach a budget agreement and strongly believed the CPI adjustment needed to be part of it. Why risk all the public back and forth a commission would incite? Just do it.

THE PRESIDENT HAD invited the House Democratic leadership as well as their ranking committee members to a meeting in the White House residence. Erskine and I asked minority leader Gephardt to come early to discuss the budget with the two of us.

Leader Gephardt viewed the budget deficit as a challenge, but a challenge only for Republicans. He wanted them to slog through the regular order and produce their own budget. His caucus was almost uniformly against tax cuts; their priority was balancing the budget. That was the White House priority as well, but even if we eliminated the president's tax cuts, the deficit could still be $75 billion in 2002. Gephardt made clear he would oppose any CPI commission whose recommendation went beyond the recommendation of the Bureau of Labor Statistics (BLS) — the official CPI arbiter. He believed that going one step beyond the BLS would politicize the issue. He would agree to asking the BLS to review the CPI index quickly. But that was as far as he would go.

Almost thirty House Democrats were in attendance that evening. The president was in good form, giving tours of the historical rooms on the second floor of the White House residence. By 7:30, everyone was seated in the Yellow Oval Room. It is a good room for meetings—large enough for private conversations, but small enough to make speaking and listening easy when a group is assembled. People usually found themselves at ease in this comfortable and relaxing room, which is part of the president's home.

The president began, as he normally did, in a quiet and subdued way, letting the story and his voice build as he went along. "We all know the public trusts the Republicans more on taxes. And Democrats have to work hard to stay even on the deficit and the economy. On the other hand, the public trusts us more on things like education, the environment, health care, and other family issues."

The president freely admitted that if Congress could balance the budget this year, everybody would get credit—including the Republicans. Everybody's poll numbers would go up, and the country would benefit from a good budget package. And if that caused continued economic growth, then even better. But it would be to the Democrats' disadvantage if the budget debate got partisan and fell into gridlock.

The Democrats' best strategy would be to reach a budget agreement this year, Clinton said. If Democrats waited until 1998, an election year, to get an agreement, the Republicans in the House would be in prime political position to claim credit for the agreement—a replay of 1996. Passing a balanced budget in 1997 meant that by 1998 Congress would have moved beyond the issues that tend to favor Republicans—taxes and the budget—and cleared the way to address Democratic strengths. The Democrats' messages on education, health, and the environment would be more credible because they would be within a balanced budget. Democrats no longer could legitimately be called the tax-and-spend party

Clinton felt that with fiscal issues off the table in 1998, the Republicans would return to the social issues that swing voters, particularly women, found troubling. Not only were Republicans fractured on social issues, but Democrats had found a way to trump them on values issues—those that go to the heart of people's day-to-day lives—crime, welfare, family leave, TV content and advertising, teen smoking, and on and on.

It was a good statement well delivered. Clearly, many in the room had not thought the politics through this way. They were intrigued but difficult to move. The battles over Medicare and tax cuts were still fresh in their minds. These were battles the Democrats had won, and many thought a confrontational replay would be to their advantage.

WEDNESDAY, FEBRUARY 26, 1997

The next day I filled in Daschle and his leadership staff on the previous night's meeting, as well as on the state of play on the CPI commission. Daschle was fine with a commission but wanted to head in yet a different direction. He wanted to reassert the primacy of the BLS in setting the CPI, but since the bureau could not finish all its revisions in time for this year's budget, he agreed that the commission should provide the number. And when BLS finished its work, Congress would make whatever changes were necessary to realign the value of the CPI index with the BLS revisions. And, Daschle reminded me, the president would have to be way out front on the CPI adjustment to give the political cover needed for any of this to work.

THE SPEAKER WAS back in town, where visions of CPI commissions were dancing in several heads. Erskine and I needed to see if we could find a meeting of the minds. We outlined the most recent positions for Gingrich. Domenici wanted to just do it, plugging a CPI adjustment number into the budget agreement. Daschle wanted to dress up the adjustment in BLS garb, but give Congress the freedom to make the adjustment based on a commission recommendation. And Gephardt was intent on staying under the safe umbrella of the Bureau of Labor Statistics and not going a penny or percentage point beyond whatever it would bless.

Gingrich went off in a totally different direction. He wanted to pass a law establishing the commission and providing that its recommendation on the CPI adjustment be automatically plugged into government benefit formulas—all without his members taking a direct vote on the adjustment number itself. Congress would vote only on the process, not directly on the adjustment. He suggested Alan Greenspan, chairman of the Federal Reserve, and five economists for the commission. He wanted both chambers to consider the enabling legislation before the next congressional recess, which was only weeks away.

Wow! This was different. Maybe it would work in the House where the Speaker could instruct the House Rules Committee to preclude amendments to the bill. But the Senate was a very different story. Senators had freedom to introduce amendments, which meant that a bill establishing a CPI commission could involve many difficult votes. Appointing a commission—an administrative act—already required the president and congressional leaders to stick their necks out on this sensitive issue. Gingrich's approach would force many senators to do so, too.

Erskine and I kept our silence for a moment, hoping the idea would somehow vanish. It was Arne Christenson, Gingrich's chief of staff, who spoke first. "Just let me play devil's advocate," he began. "How could members vote on a process, the end result of which was largely unpredictable?" "A pig in a poke," I added. Christenson pointed out that the range of the adjustment could be anywhere from 0.2 percentage points to 2.0 percentage points. And the policy and political implications were vastly different depending where the commission came out.

Erskine and I told Gingrich the vote would be tough on Democrats, and we did not think there would be much support. How many Republicans would vote for it? Gingrich said he didn't know, but he was certain that Republicans would never vote on the actual number, no matter what political protection the commission offered.

ERSKINE AND I were scheduled to return to the White House, but instead of taking a right out of the Speaker's Capitol office, we veered left toward the Senate and walked into Senator Daschle's office unannounced.

Daschle was in a meeting in his main office, so we settled in with Pete Rouse, his chief of staff. Within moments Daschle had joined us, and we were explaining Gingrich's idea to both men. They confirmed our judgment. It was a nonstarter. Not even a third of the Senate Democratic caucus would give it serious consideration, they said. No member would agree to a pig in a poke. And the notion of Greenspan leading the commission would make many Democrats uneasy. He was already on record in favor of the adjustment and would not be seen as impartial. From the viewpoint of many Democrats, he was a very political Republican Federal Reserve chairman.

THAT AFTERNOON MARK PENN, the White House's lead pollster, presented his latest findings at the weekly political meeting. We were surprised—but should not have been—that the public liked the commission approach to the CPI adjustment. When asked if experts should inform important decisions, most people said yes. Penn also reported that the strategy to separate the budget and tax bills was a clear winner with the public. Putting deficit reduction first had great appeal. Eat your vegetables, then comes dessert.

It was clear in listening to the president that he had been talking to Lott quite a bit. And Lott had been making headway on the presidential guilt factor. Erskine and I had been treated to the speech a couple of times. Lott said that he and key Republicans had courageously led by advocating establishment of a CPI commission but the president was silent. Where was the president? Where was the presidential leadership Congress needed?

The president was still trying to get comfortable with the CPI commission, again stressing the importance of getting Senator Moynihan out front on the issue. With Moynihan's help, the adjustment would be about greater accuracy, but it would also be about extending the life of the Social Security trust fund.

That was a message that Clinton thought would go down well with Democrats. The president was rehearsing aloud all the arguments he would use to convince himself as well as others.

THURSDAY, FEBRUARY 27, 1997

Majority Leader Dick Armey was number two in the House Republican leadership. Trained as an economist, he was a pro-business conservative. His day job was to oversee the business of the House, trying to make sure the trains ran on time. Over the past year, his star had risen within the Republican caucus, both because of Gingrich's missteps and because of his own close relations with many House conservatives. From the White House viewpoint, he was straightforward to deal with. Impeccably friendly at a personal level, he would tell you what he thought in a forthright manner. And his policy views were usually quite different from ours.

On the CPI commission, he was cautious. He had a slogan, born of the tough battles he had fought for more than a decade: "If you demagogue it, you own it." It meant that Republicans would not be leading on the CPI issue. They had been burned on Social Security in the 1980s and Medicare in 1995 and were not about to go three for three. But the Republicans in the House might follow if the public were thoroughly convinced that the CPI adjustment was the initiative of the president and Democrats in Congress.

Armey was worried that Gephardt and other House Democrats would transform the CPI commission into an issue about Social Security—an easy transition to make. To go along, House Republicans would need an ironclad guarantee that Democrats, including Gephardt, would be fully on board and would not criticize the commission or its recommendations.

Erskine told Armey that would be impossible because Gephardt was opposed to the commission. On the Democratic side, the president would take the lead, and Daschle and many Democrats would likely follow. But the president would need Republican support. Bowles made a strong case for House Republicans to stand with the president to do the responsible thing. Armey held his counsel, a polite but telling silence.

THE BUDGET TEAM had asked Gephardt to pull together several prominent House Democrats to talk budget strategy. Erskine Bowles, Frank Raines, Gene Sperling, and I were to meet with Gephardt, Spratt, Charlie Stenholm of Texas, Marty Sabo of Minnesota, Dave Obey of Wisconsin, Nita Lowey of New York,

George Miller of California, and Vic Fazio of California. It was a good cross-section, including both liberals and moderates.

After several others had spoken, Gephardt started to pull together the common threads. Both the left and right wings of the Democratic caucus were united against tax cuts. He said Democrats should wait the Republicans out and let the process go forward. If the Republicans faltered, Democrats could step in and try to peel off their moderates, passing a Democratic budget. It was the same suggestion he had made to the president in the Oval Office, but this time he had a receptive audience.

Gephardt then turned to the CPI. He cited Spratt's belief that the Bureau of Labor Statistics might make as much as a 0.3 percentage point downward adjustment in the CPI. However, if Congress went beyond the BLS number and legislated a larger CPI adjustment, the process would become politicized. Nita Lowey followed quickly; why cut COLAs and hurt our constituents to help Republicans pass a budget that contained tax cuts? Where was the fairness of that? Spratt closed with a fair-minded suggestion that seemed to be in the middle but would still leave a budget gap. Perhaps, he suggested, a commission could be established to advise the BLS and "superintend" their efforts, focusing resources and attention and moving the process along. But like Gephardt, Spratt said he would support the BLS recommendation and not a penny more.

LATER THAT DAY, Erskine and I got an earful from Senator Lott. He was upset at the White House. He said he had been out front on the CPI commission for a week and there had been nary a peep from the White House. Where was the president?

Lott was in a big hurry on the budget. As emphatically as I had ever heard him, he declared that there would be no balanced budget agreement this year unless it was bipartisan and had the president's involvement. The Republicans would not, under any circumstances, produce their own deficit reduction package. They had been down that perilous road before and were not about to do it again.

Instead, they would take a pass on deficit reduction and simply move the appropriations bills that kept the government funded. After all, there was no legislated requirement to reduce the deficit. If both parties and the president worked together, Lott said, then they could do what was right for the country. If they couldn't work together, then the hell with it.

Then he started drawing imaginary circles on the table. The solution to the budget was an ever-expanding set of circles, he said, and at the center was the

CPI adjustment. Once that was in hand, the numbers would work for our priorities and theirs. That would allow the next circle, an agreement on spending reductions with Domenici. Then the circle could be widened further, bringing in committees and the caucuses. But the CPI was the innermost circle.

FRIDAY, FEBRUARY 28, 1997

The last day of February and the Democratic leaders were at the White House for one of their semi-regular meetings with the president. The discussion eventually turned to the CPI commission. Daschle took the lead and was encouraging. He laid out the approach he had offered in his office. Democrats would seek political shelter under the cover of the BLS. But as part of the budget agreement, an interim CPI adjustment could be made, based on the recommendation of an impeccable panel of experts.

But Gephardt remained adamantly opposed to a CPI adjustment determined within a political and budgetary context. It would be impossible for the commission's report to be seen as apolitical. Democrats should not move beyond the BLS, no matter what the substantive case. Like Armey, Gephardt feared making his members vulnerable to a political attack. And organized labor presented a big problem. Wages had just now begun to rise after being nearly stagnant for two decades. The commission's conclusions on the CPI would feed into almost every labor negotiation and contract, working against those who were just now seeing their real compensation rise.

The meeting ended amicably, but later that morning, the letters started coming in—AARP and organized labor were weighing in against the CPI commission. Gephardt and his staff had not wasted any time after the White House meeting. They had moved quickly to brief the most sensitive and powerful groups, easily getting them spun up against the commission. Representative Gephardt had decided to preempt the president.

MONDAY, MARCH 3, 1997

Janet Yellen, the chair of the Council of Economic Advisors, was the White House point person with the Bureau of Labor Statistics. She had numerous conversations with BLS commissioner Katherine Abraham. There was good news and bad news. Yellen was optimistic that if the commission was structured appropriately and given credible members, the BLS would not criticize it. On the adjustment itself, it looked like the BLS would make a 0.15 percentage point downward adjustment for free—in time for this year's budget. But any further adjustment would not be decided upon in time to affect our deliberations.

Our budget group had been expanding, not only through Yellen's work on the CPI, but also with the addition of the deputy secretaries of Treasury and OMB, Larry Summers and Jack Lew. Summers, Bob Rubin's sounding board at Treasury, was a brilliant economist who also had a natural knack for policy. Lew had spent years in the House and was expert on the budget. He also had a good personality for negotiating: knowledgeable, fair, and tough when he needed to be. What the White House schedulers had named the group of five had now grown to a group of eight.

MEETING WITH THE budget team, the president anticipated just about everything we had to say. He and congressional Democrats would be attacked for cutting COLAs in order to pay for a tax cut, even if the spending and tax bills moved separately. Our counterargument was that any COLA adjustment would extend the life of the Social Security trust fund. We were slipping into the trust fund arguments the Republicans had used to shield their Medicare cuts from political attack—arguments we had crushed in 1995.

The president was weighing the alternatives. Even though he was worried about the commission idea, he saw the CPI adjustment as the right thing to do. The president suggested that perhaps the adjustment was best made as part of a budget agreement. Evaluated in a vacuum, the CPI adjustment pitted accuracy against many soon-to-be-upset constituents. Not a fair fight. But within the context of the budget, the adjustment might seem preferable to other means of balancing the budget, such as cuts in Medicare, Medicaid, and other important programs.

On the commission itself, the group coalesced around the idea of using former heads of the Council of Economic Advisors. A mix of Democrats and Republicans would be appointed, and if they agreed to a recommendation, they would be articulate defenders of their conclusions. Finally, we would run interference on our left and see how bad it might get. The next day Erskine and a few others would meet with the AARP, then organized labor.

TUESDAY, MARCH 4, 1997

Both the AARP and organized labor were locked and loaded. The meetings were civil but direct. The groups were dead set against a CPI commission. AARP was represented by John Rother and Marty Corey. The three of us were friends, having been on the same side of many issues. But this would not be one of them. Rother and Corey went through the litany we had heard from House Democrats. The BLS had to make the call; otherwise the result would be politicized. In fact, the BLS already had advisory commissions in place, they noted, and there was no need for outsiders to superintend them.

Anything done this year would be seen as motivated by the budget, they continued. If there were to be a commission, it would need to report in a future far beyond the current one. And it should be focused on the broad issue of saving Social Security, considering adjustments to the CPI along with other policies to aid the solvency of the Social Security trust fund. AARP would strongly oppose the CPI commission and would work openly and aggressively against it.

The representatives of organized labor were even more adamant. Anything the BLS did was fine; it was technical and below the radar screen. Their membership would not even notice. But the recommendation of a CPI commission could affect up to 60 million working men and women. A lower CPI would immediately become the basis for the next round of labor negotiations, and management would try to drive wage increases to the new lower number.

The labor unions were particularly incredulous that the White House would support the CPI route as a means of finding budget savings. If the federal government needed to save money on COLAs, why didn't Congress just cut COLAs? Why go the more general route of adjusting the CPI and hurt a lot of hard-working men and women. To the union representatives, the issue was not the accuracy of government measures or even the budget deficit. It was a simple matter of dollars and cents for those they represented. Don't hit us; hit somebody else. Labor made it clear the unions would mobilize their troops against the CPI commission, using every weapon in their arsenal. They would fight it from day one and would try to discredit the commission before and after it reported.

WITH THESE BODY blows, the CPI commission was on life support, but not yet dead. Its passing would occur that afternoon in a meeting with Daschle and a group of Democratic Budget Committee members—Lautenberg, Barbara Boxer of California, Kent Conrad of North Dakota, Patty Murray of Washington, and Ron Wyden of Oregon.

This was the day the Senate would vote on a constitutional amendment requiring a balanced budget. The Republican-backed amendment was going down to defeat again. Democratic senators Bob Torricelli of New Jersey and Tim Johnson of South Dakota were voting no, a reversal from their previous votes on the issue while members of the House. The amendment would receive only sixty-six votes, one short of the two-thirds majority required for passage for the amendment. A perennial top priority of the Republicans was going down to defeat again, and they were angry.

Lott, Gingrich, and Domenici—and Kasich in a separate venue—held press conferences that day.[4] They let their anger get away from them, and it spilled over into the real budget. They unleashed their rhetorical barbs against the president's budget, calling it disingenuous and fraudulent. The very same budget that had arrived alive a month earlier was now the object of their derision. They were calling for the president to submit a new budget.

As expected, these attacks stirred up the ire of Democrats. How dare the Republicans criticize the president's budget?[5] They had not even offered a budget plan of their own. The congressional Democrats knew easy pickings when they saw them and had scheduled a press conference to hammer away. Our meeting that had been intended to be a thoughtful discussion of the CPI commission had turned into a partisan pep rally. As Daschle was leaving for the press conference, we asked him about the CPI commission. "Why should we bail them out when they do this to us?" he responded tellingly. Our thoughtful ally was also overtaken by events. The CPI commission was dead. To launch it now would drive a wedge between the White House and congressional Democrats, not to mention the interest groups that were cranking up their opposition.

WEDNESDAY, MARCH 5, 1997

Members of the budget team were already scheduled to see Gephardt and other House Democrats again the next day to consult on the CPI commission. Gephardt's conference room was packed with over a dozen House members and twice as many staff. Knowing that the CPI commission had died the day before allowed the White House team a high degree of detachment, easing the tension. We kept our counsel and listened.

The agenda had been well planned, covering every substantive and political side of the issue. David Bonior of Michigan, the Democratic whip, echoed organized labor's concerns. An adjustment would hurt the working class, Bonior said, those who were just beginning to benefit from the booming economy. How could the White House even consider such a move when the results were likely to be tax cuts for the wealthy? Gephardt repeated his views, and almost all the others spoke. Not a single member spoke in favor of the CPI commission. Even those members who were ready to step up and consider a CPI adjustment were opposed to a commission. They did not need a commission to tell them what to do. They would just do it.

Returning from the Hill, we updated the president. Gene Sperling started with the understatement that we had heard about what we expected. But as the particulars cascaded out, the hopelessness of launching the commission was obvious. We guessed that the BLS might produce a small adjustment in the CPI that would help balance the budget. Anything above that would have to be legislated as part of a budget agreement. But there would be no CPI commission.[6]

CHAPTER FOUR

The Handoff

With the CPI commission no longer an option, all we in the White House could do was ramp up our meetings with the four lead congressional budgeteers as quickly as possible. We were far along with Domenici, with Spratt close behind. But we would need to intensify our efforts with Kasich and Lautenberg. We had been talking strategy and big picture with them but needed to get deeper into the budget muck. We would also reach out to House Democrats beyond Gephardt's leadership circle. If he mediated all of our interactions with the Democrats in his chamber, it would be a very long year.

Tuesday, March 11, 1997

Frank Raines and I were back at it with Kasich. Perhaps predictably, he was upset about our proposal for "saving" the Medicare trust fund by moving a good portion of home health care expenses out of Part A of Medicare into Part B. He said he would never, ever, ever agree to that. To him, it was a sleight of hand that did not solve Medicare's long-run problems. We repeated the arguments we had made to Domenici: the policies necessary to keep the current trust fund solvent went well beyond the politically possible, and members would not vote to cut Medicare unless the life of the trust fund was extended as part of the bargain.

But he was undaunted. If the federal government could not afford to do more, Congress would make just enough cuts to extend the trust fund a couple of years. No budget gimmicks for him. We reminded him that the Republican Contract with America budget had also reconfigured the trust fund. He ignored us and kept hammering away—now attacking our entire Medicare proposal. CBO had reestimated the savings in the president's Medicare proposal at $82 billion, rather than the $100 billion estimated by OMB. To Kasich, this number was pathetically low—even the Democratic Blue Dog budget had $120 billion of savings. True, but we reminded him that the Blue Dog budget extended the life of the Medicare trust fund by using the same home health transfer gimmick as the president's proposed budget. That took Kasich by surprise. Well, he said, "if the White House had that level of savings, then maybe we could look at the transfer" of home health care from Medicare Part A to Part B. In ten minutes he had gone from a nonnegotiable point of principle to the reality of putting an acceptable budget together. We needed him to make that transition a few more times, notably on using the OMB deficit projections rather than the CBO projections.

SPRATT WAS ALREADY deep into the substance. His House Budget Committee staff had been test-driving their own budget model. They had zeroed in on the arcane economic assumption that drove CBO's projections of corporate profits and the resulting impact on tax payments.[1] Like the Republicans, Spratt understood that this assumption might need to be revisited.

On Medicare, Frank and I told him the budget would need to end up with more than the current $100 billion of savings, probably as much as $115 billion. The administration experts were comfortable with the policies that produced that number, but, of course, we would have to win agreement for those policies as part of the negotiation. Spratt absorbed it all and then turned to Democratic priorities. He wanted to narrow the focus to three or four key items. At the top he put education—the HOPE scholarship and the tax deduction for the costs of postsecondary education. Next was children's health. He knew Democrats would enthusiastically support the president's proposal to provide health care coverage to an additional five million children. Finally, he insisted that the 1996 welfare bill be amended to undo the harm it did to legal immigrants.

WEDNESDAY, MARCH 12, 1997

Frank Lautenberg was not as far along in his thinking about the budget as Spratt was. Lautenberg was the new ranking member on the Senate Budget Committee, succeeding Senator Jim Exon of Nebraska, who had retired. But the Senate committee staff was fully up to speed. Sue Nelson, of the Senate Budget Committee staff, had been working closely with the White House for months, coordinating with Daschle's staff, particularly Larry Stein, Daschle's policy director, and Randy deValk, one of Daschle's top policy analysts. Without these three individuals, our work in the Senate would have been many times more difficult.

At my meeting with him, Lautenberg said he was eager to get started. He was an experienced legislator and a fierce advocate on behalf of his state and his beliefs. Principal among those was the importance of going after the tobacco companies and anyone or anything that encouraged smoking. He also believed in spending lots on transportation, particularly mass transit, and as a member of the Appropriations Committee, he was in a strong position to see that get done.

Thursday, March 13, 1997

Bill Hoagland, the Senate Budget Committee's Republican staff director, was calling. The two of us could be fully open with one another, having developed a strong working relationship when I served as Democratic staff director on the committee in 1989 and 1990. We regularly shared budget options on a confidential basis, being forthright about what our sides could and could not accept. On this day, Bill was cautionary about our prospects. The political back and forth on the budget was on full public display, and it was all negative. Republicans were demanding that the president submit a new budget proposal, and Democrats were deriding the Republicans for not offering a budget of their own. Fearing that his negotiations with the White House might get derailed, Domenici was moving in two new directions, Hoagland said.

On one track, Domenici had asked to meet with members of the Breaux-Chafee group, a bipartisan group of approximately a dozen moderate Senators who had come together after the 1995 budget collapse. Led by Republican John Chafee of Rhode Island and Democrat John Breaux of Louisiana, the group had offered a centrist budget in 1996, splitting the pain of spending reductions between entitlements and discretionary spending. Their plan also contained $105 billion in tax cuts and called for a half percentage point downward adjustment in the CPI. It had received forty-six votes in the Senate—a surprisingly strong showing, although the vote was a throwaway for some senators who knew it would not pass.

Domenici was smart to reach out to this group. If negotiations between Domenici and the White House failed, he would try to reach an agreement with these senators, forming a bipartisan coalition to pass a budget that the White House would have trouble opposing in the light of day. Fortunately, the

White House had an excellent relationship with Breaux. He was close to the president, a moderate by inclination, and someone who loved to be in on the action—always happy to be the emissary to the other side. He would give a good read on Domenici's initiative.

Domenici's other track was to get the Senate Republicans to agree on an exit strategy that balanced the budget. If another collapse was imminent, they wanted to make sure they held the high ground. There was a consensus emerging. If forced to the wall, Senate Republicans would propose a budget without tax cuts. They would use CBO numbers, stay within the political bounds for cutting Medicare and other sensitive entitlement programs, and adjust the CPI as much as the Bureau of Labor Statistics would allow. To make it all add up, they would cut the hell out of nondefense discretionary spending but exempt politically sensitive programs, such as education.

This would be the answer to Democratic taunts to produce their own budget. The Republicans would not repeat the mistakes of 1995. This time, their spending reductions would balance the budget rather than pay for tax cuts. And if this politically smart budget did not provide enough cover, they always had the option of last resort—just pass the appropriations bills and get out of town.

But as smart as this was, it was still an exit strategy. And an exit was not at all what the Republican leaders wanted. They wanted an agreement that balanced the budget and gave voters a tax cut. That result could be had only through an agreement with the White House.

DESPITE HIS PUBLIC venting, Kasich was intent on pressing ahead with private budget discussions with Frank Raines and me. In a rather surreal setup, Kasich had assembled key members of his House Budget Committee staff in another room—somewhere. Frank and I sat with Kasich in his office, and all we could discern were their voices on the squawk box. These disembodied budgeteers would walk us through their suggested policies and politely and knowledgeably respond to questions. Since no names were used, Frank and I had no idea to whom we were talking. But we knew that the staffers on the other end of the line would play a key role in shaping any agreement. In these negotiations, every policy and program beneath the numbers was thoroughly analyzed and scrubbed. Each camp would develop its preferred policies, run the traps with colleagues and interest groups, and then take the positions into negotiations. Each side had its trusted policy experts who would engage as part of the principal-level negotiations, as well as on their own at the staff level.[2]

Kasich's Medicare proposal was definitely in the ballpark. The $113 billion of savings was close to what we could ultimately agree to and, with a few prominent exceptions, was not too bad on policy. Kasich had also proposed that the Medicare Part B premium be higher for individuals with higher income. It made some policy sense, and we were not about to rule it out at this stage. We just didn't know if it would fly. Congress had been forced to repeal the catastrophic health care bill because of opposition to a similar means-tested premium.

Then Kasich moved to the earned income tax credit. The EITC program was created in 1975 during the administration of President Gerald Ford as a means to encourage work by reducing the tax hit on the working poor. By increasing the take-home pay of low-income workers, the EITC reduced the need for welfare payments. It also made sense on economic and political grounds as an alternative to increasing the minimum wage. The argument was that a high minimum wage would discourage employers from hiring. Although workers with jobs would receive the higher minimum wage, fewer people would be employed.

The solution to increasing the minimum wage was the EITC. Low-income workers would get a tax credit toward their income taxes, allowing them substantially more take-home income. In addition, in many cases, the benefit called for under the EITC formula was greater than the worker's income tax liability. In that case, the worker received the difference as a check from the Treasury. The combination of their own wages and the payment from the Treasury was designed to lift the working poor out of poverty—all without influencing employers' hiring decisions.

The EITC had been one of the government's more successful programs, keeping millions of low-income workers out of poverty. Unfortunately, a program that began as a bipartisan initiative under a Republican president had come under political stress. Democrats had become the program's key supporters, expanding the EITC in several rounds of legislation, including the 1993 Democrats-only budget package.[3] At the same time, most Democrats had continued to support increases in the minimum wage, arguing that many workers failed to take advantage of, or fell outside, the EITC.

For their part, many Republicans had come to view the program as a kind of welfare, even though the beneficiaries held jobs. Republicans had no problem with the working poor paying less in taxes. But many Republicans considered the refundable part of the credit—the check written by the Treasury—to be spending, rather than a tax break. And the final straw in their eyes was the fact that the EITC had failed to weaken Democratic interest in the minimum wage.

Kasich wanted to cut back the EITC program by including more sources of income in calculating eligibility for the credit—not necessarily a bad idea but one that required careful scrutiny. He also wanted to deny the EITC benefit to childless workers, however, a policy Democrats strongly opposed. It went in exactly the wrong direction from the president's welfare-to-work proposal. If the idea was to move people from welfare to work, why undermine a key means of supporting the working poor? Childless workers were the poorest of the poor.

Frank and I ended the meeting by defending the OMB economic and budget projections. With the demise of the CPI commission, the difference in deficit projections had taken on huge significance. Under CBO's deficit projections, there was not enough room to balance the budget while allowing both sides to meet their political and policy objectives. Kasich was still adamant about using CBO numbers, but in a revealing moment, he said, "Well, I'll just load up my shotgun, and Lott can load up his, and we'll see who wins." He was admitting that there were Republicans—powerful ones—who were not necessarily with him on that important issue.

WHAT A BUSINESS. Progress with Kasich, and now we were sliding sideways with Domenici. Frank and I encountered only bad news in our meeting with Domenici and Hoagland later in the day. They were still way over the top on Medicare, wanting $141 billion in cuts over five years. That translated to a whopping $190 billion in Medicare cuts over six years, tens of billions more than they had wanted when negotiations over the Contract with America budget broke down in January 1996 and way beyond our policy and political tolerances.

Then another spoiler. Domenici had already let us know that he hated the enforcement mechanism that brought the president's budget into balance in 2002. The fact that CBO had judged it acceptable did nothing to reduce his ire: he was opposed to a mechanism that did the balancing so late in the budget window and that had taxes as part of the solution.

Now the senator put forth a radically different approach to making the budget balance if the projections turned out to be wrong. He would "trigger up." The president would not get his program expansions, including the $62 billion of new entitlements Domenici disliked, unless the budget deficit was tracking expectations. If the budget was properly headed toward balance, there would be enough room for the president's priorities. From our viewpoint, his proposal was a complete nonstarter. The White House was not going to let the president's policy initiatives be the only hostages in any agreement with Congress.

Domenici announced that he was off to meet with the Breaux-Chaffee group: he wanted the White House to appreciate that he had other options. And by the way, he added, if there was not going to be a budget this year, the Republicans had their exit strategy figured out. They would exit waving a balanced budget plan with no tax cuts, no CPI adjustment beyond the BLS recommendation, and very tight domestic discretionary spending.

Friday, March 14, 1997

Reaching Senator Breaux the next morning, I learned that Domenici's outreach to the Breaux-Chafee group had not gotten far. There was too much dissonance between their plans. The Breaux-Chafee group had been out front on the CPI adjustment not only to pay for a tax cut but also to reduce the cuts that would be needed in Medicare and domestic discretionary spending. That did not align well with Domenici's call for deep spending cuts. And Domenici's scorched-earth exit budget had even less appeal to this group. The Breaux-Chafee group was still on its own, ready to talk, but not signing on to anybody's plan yet. But it was still the middle of March, and a lot could change.

MEANWHILE, TROUBLING DEVELOPMENTS were brewing inside the White House. At Wednesday's weekly political meeting, both the vice president and Gene Sperling had started to advocate the partisan path that Gephardt and the House Democrats wanted to follow. Undoubtedly, the triggering event was the Republican demand that the president resubmit his budget. Arriving late to the meeting, I tried to balance the discussion by pointing out that congressional Democrats were far out front beating up the Republicans. But that was different from the president's role. He had to be above the fray, be the leader who drew the sides together. He needed to be bipartisan and constructive.

Having missed much of the discussion at the political meeting, I needed to check with some of the moderates in the White House, so I arranged a Friday lunch with Mark Penn, Rahm Emanuel, Bruce Reed, and Don Baer. In 1996 Penn, the White House pollster, had been instrumental in keeping the campaign in the political middle, actively focused on all those "values" issues that had proven so successful. Rahm Emanuel did politics, but he also was a mover and shaker in his designated policy areas—crime, drugs, and a few others.

Rahm could deliver. If he said he'd do it, it got done, whether the job was winning over an influential member, finding the right presidential appointee, staging an event, working the grassroots, or steering the president. His instincts were constructive even though he was very partisan. He liked getting things done. Bruce Reed was head of the White House Domestic Policy Committee. His policy views were largely in sync with those of the centrist Democratic Leadership Council. He had been the point man on welfare reform and typically took the lead on domestic policies for which economic issues were not at the fore. Finally, Don Baer ran White House communications. His moderate leanings lined up well with the president's preferences. His shop did a remarkable job getting the message out.

Over lunch, I described the budget situation and our need to get to a bipartisan handoff. To jumpstart the process, it was clear that the president would need to play an active role. Bruce suggested the president call the congressional leaders to Camp David. It would show leadership, spotlight the issue, and create an incentive for them to agree to a process before the Easter recess, which was scheduled to begin in a week. It was a good idea but not perfect. Gephardt was a problem, and it was the budgeteers in Congress that needed to do the work, not just the leaders.

We turned to the issue of the vice president. Penn said his major task was to convince the vice president to run a general election campaign in 2000, rather than one focused on the primaries. In Penn's view, it was wrong to think the path to the White House lay in competing with Gephardt on the left. Gore would be far better off maintaining the moderate base that had carried President Clinton into office. Veering left would simply isolate him and reduce support. Penn would talk to the vice president.

THAT AFTERNOON, SUE NELSON, of the Senate Budget Committee staff, did a quick run of the numbers to see what the Republican budget exit plan would look like. She began with CBO projections, took out all the spending initiatives and tax cuts, threw in a possible BLS-sanctioned 0.3 percentage point CPI adjustment, and cut deeply into domestic discretionary spending in politically nonsensitive areas. She faxed the answer in an hour. The Republican plan computed; it was a viable exit.

MONDAY, MARCH 17, 1997

One Democratic group that had offered a budget plan was the House Blue Dogs. Representative Charlie Stenholm was the driving force behind this group of House moderates. These budgeteers were for the hard medicine, and Stenholm was serious about deficit reduction. The Blue Dogs had gone public with their budget the week before.[4] It sought no tax cuts, and actually increased a few taxes by declining to renew some expiring tax provisions. The budget had no program expansions, was tight on entitlements and discretionary spending, and had a very large 0.8 percentage point downward adjustment in the CPI.

The Blue Dog budget was about as sparse and pure as a budget could get. And it achieved a remarkable result. The proposal balanced the budget without counting the Social Security surplus. To meet that larger challenge, their budget did not get to balance until 2005. But their task was about $170 billion tougher in 2005 alone.

But even if the Blue Dog budget were fully enacted, an "if" that was all but impossible, it would not cover the looming budgetary problems brought by the retirement of the baby boomers. In several years, simply balancing the budget without counting the Social Security surplus would not be enough. Once retiring baby boomers began to draw their Social Security benefits early in the next century, the surplus would turn to deficit. The rest of the budget would have to generate enough of a surplus to cover the shortfall in Social Security if the budget were to remain in balance. Additional spending cuts or tax increases would be needed. Even the austere Blue Dog budget was only a partial solution to the major fiscal challenges the nation was approaching.

DEMOCRATIC SENATOR KENT CONRAD was a long-serving member of the Budget Committee who was also serious about balancing the budget.[5] Meeting in his office, he told me he wanted a budget agreement, but he wanted the Republicans to produce their own budget first. He believed the Republicans should be forced to reconcile their conflicting goals before sitting down. He wanted to give them the opportunity to screw up. He also wanted them to get their act together. The latter was not necessarily a good idea.

In 1990 Democrats had been in much the same position as Republicans were this year. A Republican—George H. W. Bush—was president, and the Democrats controlled both chambers of Congress. The Republican administration and its OMB director, Dick Darman, were anxious for a bipartisan solution to the budget. Democrats were, too, but they were wary of a president who had campaigned so vigorously on a "no new taxes" pledge. If deficit reduction was only about cutting spending, Democrats were not interested.

At that time, Senator Jim Sasser of Tennessee was chairman of the Senate Budget Committee. He and his Democratic colleagues were responsible for getting the budget process moving, but President Bush was calling for a quick sit-down. From the Democrats' perspective, there were at least three things to worry about. The first was arriving at a unified Democratic negotiating position. The second was getting revenues on the table. The third was having an exit plan if the bipartisan negotiations broke down.

Sasser astutely chose to rally the Democrats on his committee to pass a congressional budget resolution.[6] That allowed Senate Democrats to consolidate their views and establish their plan as the starting point for negotiations. Equally important, it gave the Democrats a means to quickly restart the congressional budget process if bipartisan negotiations broke down. The House Democrats under Budget Committee chair Leon Panetta did the same thing, moving their budget out of committee and passing it on the House floor. The demonstration that Democrats could move a budget by themselves gave additional leverage in any future talks.[7] In an extraordinary meeting with Democratic leaders George Mitchell, Tom Foley, and Gephardt, President Bush agreed to put taxes on the table as a condition for starting the bipartisan negotiations. After a tumultuous six months, a massive deficit reduction bill was signed into law, one that contained both spending reductions and tax increases.

Now Conrad and many other Democrats were arguing that they should beat up the Republicans and force them to get their act together. To a large degree that was already happening. Republicans in the House and Senate were coalescing around a very smart exit strategy—a budget without tax cuts. But, of course, a collapse of negotiations, with both sides waving exit budgets, was not what the Clinton White House wanted. We wanted to complete the job of balancing the budget, and that meant getting a bipartisan agreement.

TUESDAY, MARCH 18, 1997

In separate news appearances, Gingrich and Lott floated two ideas favorable to the White House bipartisan efforts.[8] Gingrich suggested that the tax cut could be delayed until after the budget was balanced. Balancing the budget, he said, was a "moral imperative." This approach was different from the previously floated two-bill strategy in which the budget and tax bills were separate but moved in tandem. Gingrich was for balancing the budget first and then seeing if a tax cut was affordable.

It was a smart move, at once conciliatory to Democrats, but also aligned with the exit strategy Republicans had been cooking up. From the White House viewpoint, it was the former that was important.

Senator Lott's contribution was equally helpful. He stated that the economic assumptions were on the table, and perhaps the two parties could compromise somewhere in the middle. He was telling all parties that there was enough room to balance the budget and achieve the policy objectives of both sides.

How should the White House respond to these overtures? Gene and I were puzzling it over with Erskine in his office. The president had rejected the idea of a leadership meeting after the Easter recess—that would be almost three weeks away. He wanted to engage more quickly and grab an opportunity to force the pace. We also worried that a leadership meeting might be counterproductive. With both Gephardt and Armey in the room, it might be hard to agree to a constructive process. Moreover, we did not want to look like we were trying to convene a budget summit, although we were. Many Democrats would be upset about a call for a summit; they would see it as pulling the Republican cart out of the ditch. They wanted the Republicans to have the chance to self-destruct in public. As for the Republican leaders, a summit at the White House would revive painful memories of failure.

Then it hit me. It was obvious. The president should invite the leaders of the budget committees to the White House, not the congressional leaders. The meeting would not be a summit, and the handoff would be at the appropriate level. The guys who understood the budget would take the first crack. Such an approach would solve one problem that had contributed to the failure of the 1995 negotiations: Domenici and Kasich would be in the lead, not sitting in the back room, waiting for a glimpse of white smoke. And if a solution were reached, they and Spratt and Lautenberg would be invested in the process and would help carry the agreement through their committees and in the House and the Senate.

A meeting with the budget committee chairs would also meet the president's desire to accelerate the action. The four budgeteers and the White House could work over the Easter recess and report their progress to the leadership after Congress returned. With Congress out of town, the people who knew the budget would have two relatively quiet weeks to get started. And with any luck, the process would have taken on a life of its own by the time everyone else got back to town. Erskine saw that it would work. This was the handoff!

But we needed to act immediately, and we were nearly out of time. It was past three in the afternoon, and the news window would close in an hour and a half. We would have to make the calls to the leadership and budgeteers and draft the president's statement. We had about an hour.

Erskine and I began the calls from his office. We started with Gingrich and Lott: they would be the easiest. We told each Republican leader that the president wanted to respond in kind to their flexibility and was ready to move forward. We thought it best to use the budgeteers in the first stages and build from there. They both jumped on the idea. We forgot to ask Lott to tell Domenici, but Gingrich said he would talk to Kasich.

The Democrats had to be approached differently. We emphasized to them that Gingrich and Lott had shown flexibility on two key issues, potentially helping to get an agreement Democrats could support. Now we had an opportunity to "lock in" their flexibility on tax cuts and budget projections. Daschle saw the merits of the case and agreed. We varied the tone for Gephardt; rather than ask for his approval, we politely informed him of what the president intended to do. He was courteous but warned of the risks of bailing the Republicans out.

Next it was the Democratic budgeteers. We had the call to Spratt ready the instant we ended with Gephardt. We wanted to be the first to talk to him. He was quickly on board and affirmed the decision. He volunteered that we were moving just in time and had risked getting marginalized. Having throttled back the call for tax cuts, the Republicans were reaching out to the House Democratic Blue Dogs. Next we placed a call to Lautenberg, who also went along, following the logic of locking in the Republican overtures.

We were about out of time. As Gene was drafting the president's statement, we started to divvy up the rest of the calls. I would call Domenici, Kasich, and Raines. Gene would talk to Bob Rubin. I started with Domenici, telling him that unlike 1995 we were going to do it right this time—beginning with the budget chiefs. They were the ones who could forge an agreement with the White House. He was good to go, but in typical Domenici fashion, cautionary. He wanted the president to understand we would have to make cuts in entitlements. He was already practicing his speech.

Kasich was genuinely excited. Gingrich had gotten hold of him and had already received his clearance. He was ready to go.

The president went live at 4:15 p.m., starting with the announcement that Tony Lake had withdrawn his name as the nominee to head the Central Intelligence Agency. Then he turned to the budget and made the pitch. The handoff was about to happen.

Wednesday, March 19, 1997

The meeting with the congressional budgeteers began at 3:00 p.m. on Wednesday. We had only ten minutes of prep time with the president. Gene went over the president's talking points for the opening: he was personally committed to reaching a balanced budget; it was critical to act this year for the good of the country; he cared about his priorities but would be flexible; the budgeteers would need to narrow the options in the key budget areas; decisions on the high-profile political pieces—the size of the tax cut, the economic assumptions, any CPI adjustment— would be left for later.

I rated the participants. Spratt and Lautenberg would be good. Domenici would push on entitlement spending and would not be afraid to criticize the administration's budget. Kasich was Kasich. He was excited about the prospect of moving forward together but might go off somewhere by himself. Kasich was the last holdout on splitting the difference between the CBO and OMB deficit projections, and that topic should not be raised in this meeting—his leaders had already figured that one out. Finally, I reminded the president that Domenici and Kasich felt the 1995 deal failed because they had been on the back bench. This time he needed to acknowledge their importance.

The president's remarks were right on target. He pledged to try to achieve a balanced budget. He would be flexible and asked the same of them. He wanted to get the job done; he was not interested in scoring political points. He said that an agreement that was good for the country was in reach. This was the group that could get that agreement, and we needed to start working together now.

He asked Domenici to speak first. Domenici was still thinking about the Breaux-Chafee group. He told the president there was a bipartisan group of senators interested in an agreement. The president's budget had not done enough to cut entitlement spending and, of course, the CPI. The president needed to do more, or our efforts could be supplanted by others. We all knew that was extremely unlikely.

After this false start, Domenici got back on track. First he emphasized that we could not have a reprise of 1995 when he and Kasich were left out of the negotiations. Then Domenici turned to tax cuts and told the assembled group that he wanted to clarify what Gingrich had meant to say when he had suggested passing the tax bill after the budget bill—that got a huge laugh. Domenici thought the tax cuts should be worked out as part of the negotiations, but he would leave it open until later whether a tax bill would move in tandem with or later than the budget bill. Finally, he put on both his budget and appropriator hats. If discretionary spending, which had already been declining as a share of the budget for years, was to be spared further reductions, entitlement spending would have to be cut further.

The president asked Kasich to go next. Kasich said the budget needed to be balanced and the best way to start was to deal with Medicare first, passing that agreement as a stand-alone bill. It was an amazing proposal, particularly since the White House team had told every Republican that a separate Medicare bill was a nonstarter. The most charitable interpretation of Kasich's proposal was that he had promised someone he would ask.

Then he was off on the CPI, expressing his disappointment that the president had not gotten more out front on this issue. And he wanted the president to lead on Medicare, show public leadership, meet the test.

The president stopped him cold: "If you keep creating public tests for me, I'll fail them all." He said the two parties had to do this together for it to work. The Republicans could not demand that he go it alone. Kasich got the point and turned constructive. He said he thought the two sides were close on Medicare. That prompted the vice president to step in and make plain that there would be no separate Medicare agreement—a position that was quickly echoed by Spratt and Lautenberg. That one was settled, and we wondered why it had been raised in the first place.

Lautenberg and Spratt followed in their turn. Lautenberg went out of his way to compliment Domenici, which was acknowledged and appreciated. His and Spratt's remarks were positive and constructive. They were ready to get to work.

The president was out of time. He was off to Helsinki that evening and needed to prepare for his summit with Russian president Boris Yeltsin. As the meeting broke up, Nancy Hernreich, the chief of Oval Office Operations, came in with a gift from the president for John Kasich's upcoming wedding. It was the perfect touch.

THE HANDOFF HAD been accomplished. We were publicly under way with the support of the nation's elected leaders. Five-sided negotiations had been agreed to. The rhetoric would surely continue to fly at many levels: Democrats wanting to shake Republicans out in the open; Republicans upset at their own Speaker for suggesting that tax cuts might be delayed; and the press wanting everything to be played out in the open. It was all part of the process. But we were hopeful this Wednesday afternoon. The key players who knew both the substance and politics of the budget had been brought together successfully. No one could predict the many turns in the path ahead, but we had a very good starting team, and it was bipartisan.

CHAPTER FIVE

Staking Out Territory

Under the leadership of Erskine Bowles, and Leon Panetta before him, the White House staff worked issues to death. Every policy and tactic was thoroughly examined, discussed, and analyzed again. The same was true on the budget—even more so. Our team spent hour after hour after hour in the chief of staff's office doing the policy and political drills from all angles. Every negotiating position was put together, taken apart, and put back together again to make sure the numbers, policies, and politics lined up. Formal and off-line discussions with congressional Republicans and Democrats were evaluated and integrated daily. It was time-consuming and at times exhausting. But everyone was on the same sheet, and the sheet usually made a lot of sense. That harmony of purpose in 1997 was in large measure due to Erskine Bowles's leadership skills.

The key budget negotiators would be out of town for the first week of the Easter recess. That was good; all sides needed time to prepare for the upcoming engagement. There would only be staff meetings for the first week, with policy experts from the White House and cabinet agencies meeting with Republican and Democratic congressional staffs, marching through the competing positions, raising red flags, noting flexibility as well as recalcitrance, and gauging where the compromises might lie.

As for negotiating strategy, the White House expected the Republicans to try to settle their politically sensitive issues early, particularly Medicare. They would try to get the president to lead the way on a CPI or COLA adjustment. They would try to hold to the more imposing CBO deficit projections, forcing the negotiators to find larger savings in both discretionary and entitlement spending to pay for the president's spending initiatives. And ultimately they would want the final trade to be between tax cuts and the economic assumptions driving the deficit projections. Their home run would be to get the tax cuts that they desperately wanted in exchange for accepting rosier economic assumptions. In essence, it was the same trade that was made in the Reagan fiscal implosion of 1981. The double sin in 1981, however, was that many of the spending reductions that were supposed to pay for the tax cuts were not real. Back then, the negotiators had plugged in a magic asterisk, pledging to find the savings somewhere, sometime. Sixteen years later Congress and the White House were still trying to find the savings. But there was a fundamental difference between then and now. In 1997 both sides were determined that the spending cuts would be real and that the deficit hole would actually be filled.

TUESDAY, APRIL 8, 1997

Once the principals got back to town, the official budget negotiations began. Our bipartisan team of budgeteers had agreed to consult first with the chairmen and ranking members of committees having jurisdiction over the major budget components—Medicare, Medicaid, discretionary spending, and others.

As a prelude, I went over to the Capitol to meet with Domenici and Kasich. The two Republican budget committee chairmen started by laying out their plan for getting an agreement. As expected, they were intent on driving the deal to completion and taking their solution to the president and congressional leadership for ratification. This was impossible for two reasons. First, the president and the congressional leaders were intent on sharing the credit for any budget deal. More important, a handful of big, politically sensitive issues—such as the CPI adjustment, taxes, the president's priorities, and the deficit projections—would require direct involvement from the leaders. I tried to cast the mission of the budgeteers as getting as far as possible, cataloguing both agreements and remaining differences, and then taking those to the White House.

That suggestion triggered the ghosts of 1995. Domenici said he wasn't sure they would go to the White House under those circumstances. If the two sides had not reached an agreement on Medicare by then, the president might make an offer the Republicans would reject and then Democrats would blame them for wanting to cut Medicare too deeply, a replay of the 1995 budget confrontation that led to the government shutdowns. Moreover, Domenici and Kasich worried that even if the White House was dealing in good faith, there might be a Gephardt ambush.

Not wanting the sour mood to wash into the next meeting with members of the health committees, I decided to reveal our hand on Medicare: the administration was willing to increase Medicare savings from the CBO-scored $82 billion to $100 billion. This was a major concession by the administration, not only accepting the CBO's estimate of the president's Medicare savings, but upping the total amount of savings to $100 billion as scored by the CBO. But Domenici and Kasich started to push back immediately, without even a thank you. They simply wanted to pocket the money and ask for more. Domenici was still promoting a totally unrealistic five-year Medicare saving of $140 billion—down from the $158 billion he had started with but still far beyond what even Kasich thought was feasible. They held forth on the inadequacy of our move for a few minutes and then ran out of steam. They knew that at the end of the day, the White House would make the call on Medicare. They could only push.

IT WAS QUITE a health care crowd—Representatives Bill Archer of Texas and Charlie Rangel of New York, chair and ranking member of the House Ways and Means Committee; Republican Bill Thomas of California and Democrats Pete Stark of California and Sherrod Brown of Ohio from the House health sub-committees; and Senator Bill Roth of Delaware, chairman of the Senate Finance Committee. It was standing room only as the White House and committee staffs joined an already-full room of budgeteers to talk Medicare.

OMB's Nancy Ann Min walked through the president's proposal, amplified by the new $18 billon of Medicare savings.[1] There were no real surprises for any-one in this group. Medicare spending had been rising rapidly for years, and the containment strategies were well known. They had been thoroughly defined and debated in the budget battles of 1995. That failed effort actually made the job easier this time. Everyone in the room knew how the dials could be tuned to hit a Medicare savings number. We all also understood what Medicare savings numbers would take us beyond the political and policy tolerances.

Embedded in the president's budget proposal were several new initiatives in Medicare, all paid for as part of his balanced budget proposal. The Repub-licans had no problem with the president's proposed screening and preven-tion programs. But they hated the Alzheimer's respite care proposal, not on policy grounds but because it was a potential budget buster. For the same reason, they opposed the proposal to reduce the amount of deductibles paid by Medicare recipients, a move that would cost $48 billon over ten years.

At the end of the meeting, the group assembled a list of issues needing fur-ther clarification and work by the policy experts. As we broke, everyone in the room was sworn to secrecy—no talking to the press. But Rangel slipped and let the press know the White House had offered to raise our projected Medicare savings to $100 billion as estimated by the CBO. That gave us a green light to get in front of the story. The White House press people got a good story in the *New York Times*, which reported our proposal to be a serious move on Medicare.[2]

Back at the White House, Erskine and I went to see the president. He only had a few minutes—the state dinner honoring Canadian prime minister Jean Chrétien was that night. We walked Clinton from the Oval Office to the residence. He was on crutches after breaking his knee tripping on golfer Greg Norman's stairs in Florida.

Having just come from separate follow-up meetings with Domenici and Kasich, I explained our extremely delicate position on the consumer price index adjustment. Although the commission was dead, we needed to keep the CPI adjustment in play as part of the budget negotiations. Throwing it overboard at this time would be a disaster. Domenici and Kasich would be much less willing to compromise on the CBO budget projections. And that would compound the numbers problem. The Republicans would drive harder on entitlements and discretionary spending, squeezing the president's priorities. Despite the loud earfuls we had gotten from Democrats and interest groups who hated any CPI adjustment, we would be undermining our own negotiating position if we backed down now.

By the time we finished, we were in the president's upstairs dressing room. He looked down at his socks, asking if they were blue or black. He could not move well enough to take a good look. We told him blue, and he reached into his sock drawer for black. It was time to leave.

THAT EVENING CHRIS JENNINGS, the senior White House health adviser, called with an important development. A significant number of Republican senators were cosponsoring the Kennedy-Hatch health bill, which called for increasing the tobacco tax to expand health coverage for children. It even looked like it might have enough votes to be reported favorably from the Senate Finance Committee.

This one had a lot of sides. Most Democrats loved beating up on the tobacco companies, and a tax on tobacco products would be a great way to pay for the president's initiative to provide health care to five million uninsured children. But Republicans and tobacco-state Democrats did not like it at all. And Trent Lott strongly opposed the proposal. If the bill got legs, it could have a major impact on the budget negotiations. Depending on what happened, the tobacco tax could either help pay for health care or sink the agreement.

WEDNESDAY, APRIL 9, 1997

With work on health care under way, the second bipartisan budget meeting focused on domestic discretionary spending. The budgeteers began with OMB director Frank Raines painting the broad picture. Domestic discretionary spending had been declining for years, both as a percentage of the budget and relative to the size of the nation's economy.[3] It had fallen from more than 4.5 percent of gross domestic product in the mid-1970s to 3.3 percent of GDP in 1996. Under the president's proposal, it would fall further until in 2002 it would be only 2.9 percent of GDP.

The president's budget cut some $58 billion below the inflation-adjusted baseline in nondefense discretionary spending. The baseline measures what current domestic programs would cost if their funding were increased at the rate of inflation.[4] To make way for the president's priorities, the White House had squeezed nonpriority programs, reducing their funding by 15 percent in inflation-adjusted terms.

Domenici responded on a conciliatory note. He understood the president had important priorities and would need some assurance that they would be protected in the appropriations process. He asked us to name seven or eight priorities, the Republicans would throw in a few, and the two sides could then see what they could agree to protect.

This suggestion immediately brought howls from Kasich. The thought of Republicans piling on top of Democrats' spending requests set him speechifying. He wanted to "cut everything." All this money was being wasted. The agencies that got all this money were just using it to "beat up on people." The government needed to spend less and "let Americans have more money in their pockets." It was easy to see how Kasich had become budget leader of the House Republican class of 1994.

But then Domenici and Kasich started a playful back and forth, with Domenici suggesting he be allowed to add a couple of spending items to ours, but Kasich would not get to add any. He would just tell us how to cut them all.

IMMEDIATELY AFTER THIS meeting, our group of White House and congressional budgeteers convened with the powerful leaders of the appropriations committees. Appropriators know the government and its programs. Their job is the meat and potatoes of keeping the government provisioned and functioning. Give them a pot of money and they know how to spend it. They had become quite accustomed to taking the big number from the budget resolution and divvying it up, first among the subcommittees of jurisdiction and then among the respective programs. The appropriations process is more workmanlike and less partisan than the work of other committees. By hook or by crook, the government funding bills need to be passed every year, ideally by the beginning of the new fiscal year on October 1. The essential need to keep the government running year after year is a good discipline, one that can foster cooperation.

Representative Bob Livingston of Louisiana was chair of the House Appropriations Committee; Dave Obey of Wisconsin was the ranking Democratic member. Their counterparts in the Senate were chairman Ted Stevens of Alaska and Democrat Robert Byrd of West Virginia, represented at this meeting by his trusted staff director, Jim English.

Livingston was ready for "tough numbers" as part of this agreement. The country would have to live within its means. Obey jumped in on the Democratic side, saying that the infatuation with low numbers without adequate consideration of the consequences for people and programs was killing the appropriations process. In his view, the budgeteers tended to make up "anonymous numbers" without knowing the real consequences. He suggested that the budget negotiators start from the president's budget and decide what was needed and what could be restrained. That prompted Livingston to assert that there was no restraint in the president's budget, an assertion that Obey rebutted with equal force.

In contrast, Stevens took a hands-off position. He basically wanted Congress to reach an agreement on the budget and give him his pot of money. He would take care of the rest. He and his committee had work to do. The budgeteers needed to finish theirs.

Domenici, himself a member of the Appropriations Committee, informed his colleagues that the president and congressional leaders would be agreeing to fund certain areas and programs. The appropriators would need to honor the agreement and protect certain priorities. That was not the ideal message to send to powerful people who liked to run their own show. But Domenici tempered it just right. The budget agreement, he promised, would have "fundamental entitlement reform." Those budget savings would help free up more money for the appropriated accounts, both now and in the future.

THAT EVENING THE White House budget team met again with the president and vice president. I reported that we were in a good position but not nearly there yet. We had accomplished a good handoff—Lautenberg and Spratt were engaged and proving themselves to be team players. The meetings during the Easter recess had helped clear the underbrush, and now the principals were marching through the major budget categories. Domenici and Kasich were being positive in the negotiating room and in all their public statements.

But congressional Democrats were generally unhappy about the White House moving so quickly. They still wanted to wait the Republicans out, forcing them to produce their own budget. The White House had been able to contain Democratic unhappiness by constantly reasserting two themes: the president would only make an agreement that Democrats would support; and in the event that negotiations broke down, the Republicans would be far behind schedule and in a jam.

On the budget agreement itself, I reported, the Republican leaders were open to trading the president's priorities for tax cuts. Their first, second, and third priorities were all the same: a reduction in the capital gains tax rate. In addition, the negotiators were moving toward splitting the difference between the CBO and OMB deficit projections. The uncertain element was the CPI adjustment. Lott, Domenici, and Kasich wanted to do it, but only if they could hide behind the president. Gingrich and Armey were much more circumspect, knowing where Gephardt stood and doubting that presidential leadership would do much to immunize them from Democratic attacks. Our position was that the president would lead on the CPI if the Republicans would move away from those tougher CBO numbers. We would just have to see who flinched first.

Gene Sperling described how far the president could go on Medicare savings. Our health experts believed we could reduce spending by $115 billion over five years without undue harm to the program. The bulk of the additional savings above our current offer of $100 billion would come from dropping two of our spending initiatives, Alzheimer's respite care and the proposed reduction in deductibles paid by Medicare recipients. And we could find additional savings in Part B of Medicare by requiring some beneficiaries to share more of the cost.

The vice president was the first to jump in. He said that we should press ahead and conclude an agreement quickly. It would be good for the country and good for Democrats. But we needed a "risk management strategy" in the event the negotiations came up empty. He also wanted to be sure we knew that we had the votes in both chambers before the White House stuck its neck out.

These were the right questions. Our response was that we would quietly shop the deal on both sides before going public. Quiet outreach would allay

Republican and Democratic fears. We had built enough trust to deal openly with both sides.

THURSDAY, APRIL 10, 1997

When the subject is taxes, everybody shows up. It was time for the budgeteers to consult with the powerful tax-writing committees. On the Republican side, that meant Bill Archer, chairman of the House Ways and Means Committee, and Bill Roth, chairman of the Senate Finance Committee. On the Democratic side, the ranking members were Charles Rangel on the House side and Daniel Patrick Moynihan on the Senate side. Including the full staff contingents, there were well over fifty people in Domenici's office of several hundred square feet.

By mutual consent, these budget meetings had until now avoided staff-level discussions on taxes. Taxes were the most political piece of the puzzle. Many congressional Democrats were displeased by the shared desire of the Clinton White House and the Republican Congress to cut taxes. From the White House viewpoint, however, tax cuts were both a useful tool to achieve policies such as the HOPE scholarship as well as concessions to be traded for things we wanted. But the size of those trades could not be calculated until sufficient budget savings to foot the bill had been identified.

Convening the meeting, Domenici called on Treasury secretary Bob Rubin for a brief overview of the president's tax proposals.[5] The policies were familiar to everyone in the room: the HOPE scholarship and a $10,000 postsecondary education tax deduction; a child credit proposal that spent less money than the Republican one; an expansion in individual retirement accounts; and a capital gains tax break for homeowners. Each of these proposals would likely be a part of the final agreement. But the Republicans disagreed vehemently on the specifics of each of the president's suggested policies as well as their size. Their proposals were more sweeping and therefore more costly.

Roth was the first to speak. He said that Senate Republicans would need a significant tax cut. The president's was too small to win Republican support for a budget agreement.[6] Archer chimed in to make the same point, and he warned that of the $76 billion of suggested revenue raisers in the president's budget, his committee could do at most $5 billion, in addition to an extension of the airline ticket tax that everyone agreed was needed The message was clear. Archer wanted a large tax cut, but his committee was not going to be much help in coming up with offsetting revenues to help pay for it.

In response, Lautenberg argued that balancing the budget and making targeted investments should take priority over sweeping tax cuts. To garner Democratic support, any capital gains tax cut would need to be targeted and tight. Rubin added that there was no economic evidence to support a capital gains tax cut. That statement was like throwing a match on gasoline, setting off a conflagration of assertions and counterassertions. Soon, not only the capital gains tax but also the estate tax was being forcefully debated along well-known and well-worn lines. An hour and a half passed, with each side staking out its territory, before Domenici closed, as he usually tried to do, on a positive note. Despite the bitter debate that had just taken place, he told the overflow crowd that Congress and the president had a rare opportunity for a bipartisan agreement.

THAT EVENING CLINTON and Gore hosted Daschle, Lautenberg, Gephardt, and Spratt at a meeting in the White House residence. Gephardt was intent on repeating his message on the budget: Don't deal with the Republicans until they pass their own budget resolution. Force them to show their extremism. They were disorganized and in disarray. Republicans were still internally divided on tax cuts versus balancing the budget. They would be unable to pass a budget resolution and would fall into further confusion. Once that happened, the Democrats could pick off a few Republican moderates and pass a Democratic budget.

Gephardt's strategy sprang from a heartfelt belief that letting the Republicans share credit for balancing the budget in 1997 would undermine the Democrats' chances to regain control of the House in 1998. The White House also wanted a Democratic House, but none of us on the budget team thought gridlock was the solution.

In contrast to his House counterpart, Senator Daschle supported the president's approach. If the two sides could negotiate an agreement that a majority of Democrats would support, then they should do it. And if the negotiations broke down, the Republicans would be late in the cycle with little room to maneuver.

That brought Gephardt back to his main theme. He suggested that the White House negotiate for another week and then break off talks, trying to make Republicans produce their own budget. The president pivoted around Gephardt's suggestion by asking him what would happen if a bipartisan agreement passed with a strong vote in the Senate. Wouldn't Republicans in the House be under pressure to support it? "No," Gephardt quickly answered. This assertion flew in the face of the White House team's political judgment.

If a strong bipartisan majority in the Senate lined up with the president in support of a balanced budget, Republicans in the House would be under enormous pressure to support it. In fact, their failure to do so might just deliver the House to Democrats. But, of course, Speaker Gingrich was too smart to let that happen.

The one thing Gephardt managed to do was scare Gore. The vice president was full of questions. What would be the end game if there were no deal? Would Congress go to a continuing resolution to fund the essential services of government?[7] What about this new "no shutdown" provision that was threatening to become a part of the supplemental appropriations bill now moving through Congress?[8] What if it was in force when a budget crisis erupted?

The no-shutdown provision was indeed problematic for a lot of reasons. A direct result of the shutdowns in 1995, the provision would guarantee that the ongoing functions of government would automatically be funded in the event of a budget crisis. The prime sponsor was Arizona Republican senator John McCain who had become very upset in 1995 when the Grand Canyon was closed.

Politically, the no-shutdown provision had several sides. Taken as a way to avoid future disruption to essential government services, the provision appeared sensible on the surface. But there was more to this seemingly high-minded provision than met the eye. Like all budget process proposals, it was laden with politics and policy. If government funding were to go on automatic pilot, how would the controls be set? What would stay open and what would close? At what level would the government be funded? How these questions were answered would determine whether the provision lined up more closely with Republican or Democratic preferences. And if one were quite happy with the settings on automatic pilot, why try to work out differences inside the regular legislative process? It could actually be an inducement to gridlock. Why bargain and compromise when simply walking away turned on the automatic pilot at funding levels one might be very happy with?

FRIDAY, APRIL 11, 1997

At Domenici's Capitol office, the budgeteers were convening early—members were eager to head for their home states and districts to work over the weekend. The meeting was the administration's opportunity to describe the president's initiatives. Chris Jennings explained the president's health initiatives, OMB's Ken Apfel followed with welfare, and Gene Sperling spoke on education.

The Republicans were restrained. They knew these were wins the president needed to have and that he was on strong political ground. Not a single Republican spoke against the president's education proposals. But as expected, Kasich pushed back on the welfare proposals. Republicans might agree to reverse the denial of benefits to legal immigrants who were in the country before the new welfare law was adopted, he said, but why should the government help immigrants who came into the country despite the new, tougher rules? And on food stamps there was no give. Kasich had championed the provision of the 1996 welfare law that denied food stamps to childless workers after three months, no matter what. In areas of the country where there were few jobs or no government training or work slots, that provision could hit hard. But Kasich was adamant—he believed states already had plenty of flexibility for special cases.

FIVE O'CLOCK FRIDAY afternoon is not the greatest time to be giving new assignments—but that was the nature of the business. The feedback from the week's meetings needed to be assimilated and fed into the White House negotiating strategy. We expanded the ongoing analysis of possible savings in discretionary spending that would still make it possible to meet the president's priorities. The president needed to see not only what $10 billion off his budget proposal would mean programmatically, but also what $20 billion, then $30 billion in cuts would do.

The Treasury team was assigned to analyze tax packages, factoring in the White House proposals and what the Republicans would want. Treasury would first run the numbers for a net tax cut of $75 billion; then they would look at $100 billion. Meanwhile, the CPI group was working up the justifications for adjusting the CPI more than whatever the BLS recommended—and coming up with offsets to shield the lowest-income beneficiaries—if it came to that.

And these big items just scratched the surface. We needed to draft legislative provisions to make sure that what we agreed to in negotiations actually got enacted in law, find a way to bridge the divide with Kasich on food stamps, rank entitlement spending to determine what could be reduced further, identify possible defense savings, repackage the welfare-to-work proposal, come to a compromise on Medicaid funding, and on and on.

MONDAY, APRIL 14, 1997

The budgeteers were talking Medicaid.[9] The committees of jurisdiction were also well represented, by Senator Roth and Representative Michael Bilirakis of

Florida on the Republican side and Representatives Sherrod Brown and Henry Waxman of California on the Democratic side. Helping to represent the White House position was Health and Human Services secretary Donna Shalala.

It was a strange meeting with strange alliances. The state governors had done their work. They had convinced Roth and Bilirakis to line up against the administration's proposal to limit Medicaid payments to a state based on the number of Medicaid recipients in that state. The Republicans would have preferred maximum flexibility for the governors, ideally, through a block grant each state could use as it wished.

The two Democratic legislators also opposed the White House proposal, but for different reasons. They wanted Medicaid to be a full-blown entitlement and were against the suggested spending restraint. Waxman's view was that Congress should close the loopholes that the governors had opened, get rid of any fraud and abuse in the program, and then fully fund the medical needs of the poor. What if health care costs rose faster than the per capita cap? What kind of safety net was that?

The hard part was that both Republicans and Democrats had legitimate concerns. The White House had proposed giving states new flexibility to bargain with providers for better deals as well as greater freedom to move recipients into managed care.[10] But the governors wanted even more, including the freedom to determine which medical services would be available to which recipients. The administration was caught in a tough spot. We had to do something to curb the abuses and rapidly expanding costs of the program. At the same time, we were trying to ensure sufficient funding for qualified recipients. Our policy tried to steer a delicate course between curbing costs and serving the legitimate purposes of the program. Nobody was particularly happy.

BACK AT THE White House, Mark Penn's polling was confirming our own political judgment. A hypothetical budget agreement that balanced the budget, cut $100 billon from Medicare, invested in education and health care, and reduced capital gains taxes was approved by a margin of 61 to 30. Even more interesting was the congressional analysis. A Democrat who supported the package would have a twenty-point advantage over a Republican challenger. If the Democrat opposed the package, she or he would be at a fifteen-point disadvantage.

TUESDAY, APRIL 15, 1997

Another meeting with Lott: he was also thinking political strategy, his focused on the rollout to announce the agreement. This leader was way out in front. He said that once the agreement was reached, the two sides should hold separate press conferences to announce it—the Democrats at the White House and the Republicans on the Hill. That would be better for his conservatives. Everybody had internal politics to juggle.

In my coat pocket I happened to have two floor passes from the 1996 Democratic convention. On the back of one, I made two columns, labeled Republican and Democrat. In the Republican column I listed their budget "wins." They would get entitlement reform—significant cuts in Medicare that would put the experience of 1995 behind them—and the president would take the lead on the CPI adjustment, another long-term entitlement saving. Republicans would also get their key tax cuts, including capital gains. In the Democratic column I listed the HOPE scholarship and other education initiatives, the kids' health program, the welfare fixes, and the president's other domestic initiatives in domestic discretionary spending. And, of course, both sides would share the credit for balancing the budget.

On the back of the other convention pass, I also made two columns, listing what each side would hate about the agreement. Republicans would hate the new program "start-ups," particularly those they would characterize as entitlements. And they would hate all those new initiatives in domestic discretionary spending. But the Democrats would hate the CPI adjustment and several parts of entitlement reform such as charging some Medicare beneficiaries higher premiums. And for many Democrats, tax cuts were a big problem, particularly when it came to capital gains.

THURSDAY, APRIL 17, 1997

Senate Democratic leader Daschle worked hard at keeping his members informed and wanted us to do the same, so we went over to the Hill to brief Democrats on the Senate Budget Committee. The meeting began with Barbara Boxer of California and others making the case for waiting the Republicans out. Unlike other Democrats who endorsed this strategy, this group had a legitimate territorial interest. The Senate Budget Committee was responsible for producing the overall blueprint of the federal government in the form of a congressional budget resolution. Our negotiations would, in effect, bypass the regular order. If the talks succeeded, the committee would be presented with a bipartisan compromise all tied up and ready to roll. But not all of the members were happy with this prospect. Some of them wanted to use the regular order to help the Republicans self-destruct.

It was clear that this group of Democrats did not know what their Republican colleagues were planning. I told them that the regular order was no longer an option. If the negotiations broke down, Domenici and Lott were not going to convene the Budget Committee. I reminded the Democratic senators that the Republicans had already placed two budget resolutions on the Senate calendar—the exit budgets Domenici had devised. If negotiations broke down, the Republicans would proceed directly to the Senate floor and pass their budget on a party-line vote.[11] This time their budget would avoid the traps the Republicans had stumbled into in 1995.

The room was silent. I went on to describe the Republican exit strategy. The Republicans did not have to reduce the deficit by a penny this year. And if they took a pass on deficit reduction, it was easy to produce a budget that was safe from political fire. In fact, their only intention would be to pass the appropriations bills and get out of town.

Against this possibility, we were in good-faith negotiations to balance the budget and win on important Democratic priorities. The negotiations were the only route to balance the budget and achieve a Democratic agenda in education, health, welfare reform, and the environment. As Frank Raines said, we were "pleading guilty to a strategy of thinking we could get a better deal through negotiation rather than confrontation."

Paul Sarbanes of Maryland got it immediately, saying, "We might rue the day we broke off negotiations." But, he correctly said, "Democrats need a process of inclusion to stay in the loop." Daschle stepped in and asked the administration to meet every other day with Budget Committee Democrats. It was the perfect solution to a tough situation. If the Republicans were not going to open up the normal budget process to his members, Daschle would make sure they were part of the process right there in his office. It was that kind of thinking that had made him the Senate Democratic leader.

Then Patty Murray of Washington raised the key political issue. If Congress was headed toward a compromise that balanced the budget and had major wins for Democrats, how did members get out in front of it and take the credit? We agreed to meet a couple more times in Daschle's office and then bring the senators to the White House for a meeting with the president. They would tell him what they wanted as part of a budget agreement, drawing lines in the sand in the party's areas of strength and then get out front defining and defending the Democratic position.

CHAPTER SIX

Offer and
Counteroffer

Hours of consultation and positioning—and years of budget battles—had
made evident to our group of bipartisan budgeteers the fault lines between the
parties. Now we had to close the gap, inventing a middle that was acceptable
to both sides and to the American people. Our challenge was to thread the
political and policy needles with hundreds of moving parts and powerful
players swirling around.

THURSDAY, APRIL 17, 1997

Pete Domenici was calling; he was upset. He had just learned that Trent Lott
was meeting with the president the next day, and he was worried about what
they might do. The meeting was news to me as well; I'd have to get back to him.

Erskine confirmed that Lott was indeed coming the next day. The topic was
the chemical weapons convention. But it was hard to believe they would pass
up the opportunity to talk budget. Domenici had good antennae.

I called Domenici: "False alarm, it's the chemical weapons convention."
But we quickly agreed to meet early the next morning: I'd bring Raines and
he'd bring Kasich. It was time to accelerate our drive toward an agreement.
Time and our leaders might not wait.

FRIDAY, APRIL 18, 1997

Friday is getaway day. Congress typically works into the night on Thursdays
so members can get to their states and districts for the weekend. That means

85

the Capitol and congressional office buildings are usually very quiet on Fridays—no votes, no hearings, and very few members in attendance. The four of us met in the quiet and privacy of the Energy Committee library, adjacent to the hearing room.

It was clear that Domenici and Kasich had not been able to resolve their differences. There was no budget proposal from the Republican budgeteers. But Kasich was eager to talk about the Republican "trigger-up" budget enforcement proposal. He and his colleagues wanted to hold the president's spending initiatives hostage to a year-by-year certification that the budget was on track to balance. We rejected his proposal; the president would not bet on the come.

Furthermore, we believed that the budget enforcement mechanisms adopted with bipartisan support in 1990 were just about ideal.[1] Under the current regime, budget enforcement rested on twin pillars. The first was designed to hold spending by the appropriations committees in check. It set dollar limits, or caps, on the amount of spending in discretionary programs, with separate overall dollar limits for defense, domestic discretionary, and international spending. The second enforcement mechanism was called pay-as-you-go, or PAYGO. It required that the budgetary effects of any tax cuts or increased entitlement spending be offset and paid for with other budget savings, thereby neutralizing the overall impact on the budget. These procedural roadblocks had proven remarkably workable. We told Kasich we saw no need to mess with success.

THE WHITE HOUSE budget team's next meeting was with the Democratic members of the Senate Budget Committee. As it was a Friday, only six senators were in attendance. We had agreed to meet as often as the Democrats liked, probably twice before next week's meeting with the president. By then, they would fully understand the White House priorities and positions and, we hoped, become convinced they were worth fighting for. We very much wanted the lines they would draw in the sand to be ours.

Senators are accustomed to overviews, high-level descriptions of issues and positions. Given the breadth of their responsibilities, they must understand a very large number of issues. They typically deal at the level of concept, not detail. The detail that validates the concept is left to the policy and political experts who advise them. But here we were, responding to Senator Daschle's request to load them up on budget minutiae.

OMB's Nancy Ann Min marched the assembled senators and staff through our Medicare position, including the details behind our current $100 billion savings number. The presentation was good, and the discussion even better.

But it was also the start of a long weekend, and senators' schedules are very busy. After another meeting, their demands for inclusion would have turned into requests for staff-level briefings. The gist of those briefings would be conveyed to senators, and by the time they met with the president, they would have figured out the lines in the sand they would urge upon him.

WHEN ERSKINE AND I checked in with the president late Friday afternoon, he showed us the budget offer Lott had given him that morning during the meeting that was advertised to be about the chemical weapons convention. Lott had proposed a method for negotiating the key components of an agreement. His proposal was to start by finding enough savings to balance the budget under the tougher CBO deficit projections. There would initially be no CPI adjustment, no tax cuts, and none of President Clinton's initiatives. Under these conditions, it was straightforward to get a balanced budget with reasonable cuts in Medicare and other entitlements, along with savings in discretionary spending. In fact, the viability of this approach had already been demonstrated—it was the exit plan Domenici had already put on the Senate calendar.

The next step of Lott's plan was to get money on the table to pay for the things each side wanted. Lott proposed three sources of funds: the extra room gained by moving away from CBO deficit projections halfway to those of OMB; the CPI adjustment; and revenue raisers. Given that pot of money, the two sides would trade dollar-for-dollar additions of what each wanted and would stop when the money was gone.

The president asked what Erskine and I thought. I told him this approach would produce a decisive win for the Republicans and a loss for our side. Congressional Democrats would be very upset. Consider what the Republicans would want to add back, I said. They could get their key tax priorities, reductions in capital gains taxes, an expansion of IRAs, and a good start on the child tax credit, for around $60 billion over five years.[2] What did we need? To fund the Democrats' domestic discretionary initiatives, we would need to add back between $40 billion and $50 billion over five years. And our entitlement expansions could cost as much as $40 billion. On the tax side, the HOPE scholarship and education deduction were another $35 billion. Starting from Lott's suggested base, the president's initiatives cost about double those of the Republicans. A dollar-for-dollar exchange would leave us short. The Republicans would get their tax cuts, but the president would lose many of his initiatives.

We urged the president to give our process more time to work. We were expecting an offer from Domenici and Kasich. He should go slowly with Lott for a few days and just tell him the White House team was considering his proposal. But he should not raise any alarms that would cause Lott to blow back into the Domenici-Kasich process. Don't accept or reject Lott's proposal. Just be nice, we advised, and slow.

MONDAY, APRIL 21, 1997

Bill Hoagland was calling: Domenici and Kasich wanted to present their offer. Hoagland warned that we would not like it—the domestic discretionary number would not move far above a hard freeze at last year's spending amounts. He asked us not to blow up—it could be worked out, he said; the offer was just a start.

Frank, Gene, and I received the Republican offer in Domenici's Hart Building office. There was some good news, but mostly bad. On defense, Domenici and Kasich had smartly shifted the spending path to help us balance the budget in 2002; it was close to what we had been discussing at the White House.[3]

On Medicare, they were at $125 billion in savings, a marked improvement over Domenici's previous proposal of $140 billion. They had hit Medicare Part B beneficiaries as expected, both by increasing and indexing the deductibles, as well as by implementing an income-related premium. But they still had not included the home health transfer needed to extend the life of the Part A Medicare trust fund.

We pushed back hard on the trust fund. No member would want to vote for Medicare spending reductions without getting credit for extending the trust fund past the turn of the century. Moreover, Bill Thomas, chairman of the Ways and Means Health Subcommittee, was proposing the same transfer. No one was pure. I asked Domenici and Kasich to think ahead to the not-so-distant future when the Medicare Part A trust fund would be going belly up. Payments to hospitals and other Part A service providers were already going to be cut deeply in this budget round. But the Republicans believed the key to controlling Medicare costs was to make senior beneficiaries absorb a larger share of the cost, thereby creating incentives not to overuse health services. With the Medicare trust fund being emptied, the natural pressure would be to squeeze providers, not beneficiaries. By refusing to make the home health transfer now, Republicans were creating a future dynamic that would lead to the opposite of what they desired on policy grounds. Domenici got it. It was clear that Kasich was the problem.

The great divide continued in domestic spending. On domestic discretionary spending, they had come up only $25 billion above a hard freeze—still about $40 billon short of the president's budget proposal. And they only offered $15 billion on our entitlement programs. They had agreed to fund child health care but at way too low a level. On the plus side, they would restore benefits to disabled legal immigrants who had been in the country before passage of the 1996 welfare law.

To balance the budget while paying for their tax cut, they had gone toward OMB deficit projections by accepting OMB's assumption of higher corporate tax revenues. But the price for that accommodation was a 0.5 percentage point downward adjustment in the CPI.

After taking us through the remaining pieces of their proposal, they asked if we could respond by 9:00 p.m. that night. We laughed out loud. We had expected their proposal at Friday's meeting, and here it was three days later. And we were supposed to turn this around in half a day? Not only would the proposal have to be analyzed by the White House, but we would need to consult with congressional Democrats. We'd be back to them.

WEDNESDAY, APRIL 23, 1997

The Senate Budget Committee Democrats were gathered again. Having marched through Medicare on Friday, this meeting was supposed to be about Medicaid. But as usual, the group could not get down to a policy discussion without rehashing the politics. Members like to do this: it is their strong suit and more fun than the nitty-gritty of policy proposals. Those who disapproved of the White House negotiating strategy were especially willing to spend the entire meeting in the political back and forth. These particular senators were reluctant to move from political calculation to a substantive discussion, for fear that once they rolled up their sleeves and grappled with policy choices, they would become a part of the process.

Eventually, Chris Jennings was allowed to present the president's proposal on Medicaid. It was amazing how little homework the staffs and members had done. The proposals had been in full public view for six weeks, but some acted like they were hearing it for the first time. Some even acted like we were springing it on them. But Jennings plowed along and the protestations started to subside. The arcane details of the budget can be a powerful sedative.

THAT EVENING THE president met with Democratic members of the House leadership and Budget Committee. In the Yellow Oval Room, Clinton began in his normal muted tone. He thanked John Spratt for his efforts and reemphasized his desire for an agreement that a majority of Democrats could support. He made the by-now common political and substantive arguments. Democrats should finish the job we began in 1993. We had won against the Contract with America budget and should implement an agreement that would validate Democratic values.

Then he addressed what had become an article of political faith for him, one that had been confirmed by his own success. He said that elections are about the future. The candidates who win elections are those who present the most compelling vision of the country's future. To move the national debate to the Democratic vision, the party needed to put the Republican-leaning issues of the deficit and taxes behind it. Democrats would then be free to run on education, health care, and a fair and just society. These were Democratic issues and Democratic candidates could win on them. He said that the Republican agenda was sterile and divisive and would fail once Democrats had dealt with the deficit and tax issues.

But there would be a price for this agreement. The Republican majority would have to have their wins. Finally, the president said he hoped his listeners would leave the meeting talking about Democratic priorities. He felt those who were opposing an agreement were making a profound error. It was a strong statement—and convincing to anyone who was truly listening. Many were.

SCHEDULES HAD GOTTEN in the way of an earlier meeting with Gingrich, but Kasich had called to say the Speaker could meet with Erskine and me at 8:00 p.m. that evening. Kasich, by intent or inadvertence, also revealed a critical piece of information: the House Republicans were not behind him on the CPI adjustment. He told me that he had tried and tried; that he had berated and implored his colleagues to support the 0.5 percentage point CPI adjustment, but that he had found few takers.

We had suspected that this day was coming. The Republicans' fear of the AARP, organized labor, and particularly House Democrats had forced them to fold. Now this meeting with the Speaker had taken on enormous significance. The quid pro quo that Domenici and Kasich had demanded for moving toward OMB's deficit projections was about to be taken off the table by Republicans.

I related the call to Erskine. He and I agreed that we would continue to say that the president was willing to "take the spear" on the CPI adjustment. We would be insistent on our desire to go forward; the president was ready to show courage and lead on the CPI adjustment. He would be steadfastly good to go.

AT 8:00 P.M. WE met in the Speaker's Dinosaur office, so named because of the enormous skeletal head of a *Tyrannosaurus rex* that dominated one corner of the room. Kasich was already there. While waiting for Gingrich, the three of us traded golf tips. Erskine was a natural, and he just had to keep a loose grip. Kasich was trying to keep his left foot down. He also had some convoluted way of pointing his right thumb toward his ear on his backswing. We resisted the temptation to draw any parallels.

When the Speaker arrived, fresh from discussing budget options with some of his colleagues, the four of us started on our list of wins for both sides. First, we would balance the budget, a win for both parties and for the country. Then the White House needed wins in education, health, environment, and welfare. And since many of our initiatives were in domestic discretionary spending, we would need to have the president's priorities protected right through the appropriations process.

The Republicans' win list was substantial; Erskine said he would rather be selling the agreement to the Republican caucus than to the Democrats. Republicans would win major entitlement reform in Medicare, Medicaid, and other mandatory programs. They would get tax cuts. The president needed his tax initiatives, but Republicans would get a capital gains tax cut, something on the estate tax, and the child tax credit. Finally, and perhaps most important, the president would take the spear on the CPI adjustment. He would stand up and tell the world the adjustment was the right thing to do. He would ask Congress to approve it. He would take the lead in the most public and visible way.

The Speaker did not miss a beat. Although House GOP members hated many of our initiatives, he understood that "the president's win list was the price of admission" to get the major entitlement reform and tax cuts they wanted. He assured us everything could be worked out. But, he said, there was a problem. His guys, as he called them, could not legislate a change in the CPI. Republican House members could not be put in a position of having to vote on a measure that would cut cost-of-living adjustments for Social Security and other benefit programs.

Erskine and I paused, looked at each other, turned toward the Speaker, and gave him our best possible incredulous looks. "What?"

The Speaker was poised. He said this was not a show of bad faith. The two sides could still get an agreement, but his members would not subject themselves to the political ads that AARP, labor, and the Democrats would run against them. He said he had warned us early on that Republicans would not vote to change the CPI number. He would do anything at a managerial level to get a change in the CPI, but there would be no vote on a number.

We countered that this was one of the foundations of the agreement. It was the right thing to do. The president was willing to lead and provide the political cover. Then we stretched the truth. We said we could deliver a majority of Democrats in both bodies (we didn't say dead or alive). With large numbers of Democrats voting for it, and with the president out front, it would be impossible to attack. We urged the Speaker to hold his ground.

But the Speaker wasn't buying it. He said a conservative Democrat like Charlie Stenholm might vote for it, but no one would run campaign ads against him. It would be the Republican in the next district who would face the wrath of labor and AARP, supported by Gephardt and David Bonior, the minority whip.

Erskine and I kept at it, looking disappointed and disbelieving. How could we get an agreement without the CPI? The numbers simply did not work. We all knew that.

The Speaker pushed back. He would work with us on the numbers. Then he came up with one of those fanciful, unrealistic ideas of his that could be so disorienting. He offered to place a provision in the supplemental appropriations bill giving the president the authority to fire the director of the BLS. He suggested that the current director, Katherine Abraham, be replaced with Michael Boskin, who had chaired the commission that had recently proposed trimming the CPI by 1.1 percentage points. We all knew that such a transparent and heavy-handed move would create a firestorm on the left, guaranteeing there would be no CPI adjustment at all.

Kasich broke in, saying Congress and the president would have to find a creative solution. He wanted the deal to work and was genuinely disappointed that his side could not carry the CPI adjustment. The Republicans would be flexible on the numbers. That's what we needed to hear John Kasich say.

AFTER WE LEFT the Speaker's office and were safely out of range, Erskine and I looked at each other with big grins—and did a high-five. We felt we had carried the day on the CPI adjustment. Erskine laughed and said, "Throw me into that CPI briar patch." We knew we had passed a critical threshold. The Republicans had pulled the plug on our most politically difficult issue and taken the responsibility. Our deficit projections were on the table and looking better all the time. And, perhaps most important, the Speaker was up and running and wanting an agreement.

THURSDAY, APRIL 24, 1997

In the morning, the president met with the Democrats on the Senate Budget Committee. He made the political and substantive case for our strategy as well as anyone could. It was go time.

Later, Frank, Gene, and I met with Lautenberg and Spratt to walk through Domenici and Kasich's offer. But that offer had been partially overtaken by events: House Republicans had blinked on the CPI adjustment. There would be no CPI change beyond whatever the BLS proclaimed. John Spratt breathed a huge sigh of relief.

Then the three of us began to put forward a possible counteroffer. That's when trouble began. In the White House, we had been at it so long and intensively that we had moved beyond the frame of reference of our Democratic budgeteers. They were not yet at the same level of engagement or in the same hurry as we and their Republican counterparts.

Spratt said he was uncomfortable with making a counteroffer that moved off the president's $100 billion number for Medicare. He was also intent on convening his House Democrats to vet the proposal. He would have to run the offer past his leaders before he could move. On the Senate side, Lautenberg was of the same mind—consultation would be required.

After the meeting, I found Daschle coming off the Senate floor. He was taken aback that we had gotten an offer so quickly from the Republicans and uncomfortable that the White House would consider responding so soon. While the White House could not control the timing of a Republican offer, his big concern was how Senate Democrats would react. He thought many in his caucus would be very unhappy now that an agreement was moving from the hypothetical toward the real.

The Senate would be in session until late that evening, voting on the chemical weapons convention. Daschle decided to gather a large group of Democratic senators and have the White House budget team brief them. He asked us to describe only the Republican proposal and not venture into a possible response. That would be too much, too soon for the system to handle.

It was after 8:00 p.m. when senators started to assemble in Daschle's office. Frank and Gene were running late, and Daschle asked me to start without them.

We were pledged to confidentiality with the Republican negotiators. But more than fifty people were crammed into Daschle's meeting room, and there was a good chance that one of them would leak the Republican offer to the press; some in attendance would like to see the negotiations derailed. Nonetheless, we had to go ahead. Daschle began by saying that we had received a Republican offer that afternoon and the White House was seeking their input and guidance.

I said that the Republican offer was not a serious one but rather a positioning move at the start of the process. I tried to reassure the Democratic senators that the White House had no intention of making a bad deal. We were pledged to an agreement that Democrats would support. Walking through the offer, I characterized the pluses and minuses without mentioning precise numbers. Kent Conrad kept interrupting, asking for numbers, particularly on Medicare. I would only say their proposed five-year Medicare savings were around $125 billion.

Frank arrived and started to walk through the offer sheet. He tried to waffle on the numbers but finally confirmed the Medicare number. I warned about confidentiality, and that precipitated a ten-minute round-robin on leaks, politics, and anything else senators wanted to talk about.

Frank started through the offer sheet again. I was sitting near Daschle and Paul Sarbanes of Maryland, and we agreed to avoid getting into the details lest they all be leaked. Sarbanes interrupted the presentation, saying senators did not need to know each and every number but did need to discuss strategy. That was a green light for each senator to restate his or her position. And away we went. John Kerry of Massachusetts was particularly negative. His view mirrored Gephardt's—he wanted to fight last year's battle, not realizing that the Republicans had learned their lessons. He was also demanding a budget settlement that was blind to the reality that the Republicans controlled Congress.

But other senators came to our defense. We had asked moderates John Breaux, Bob Kerrey of Nebraska, and Wendell Ford of Kentucky to attend the meeting to offset the "blow it up" leanings of some of the liberals. They argued that the Democratic budgeteers should press ahead and get the best agreement we could. Lautenberg admitted that the process was "lame," but said there was no other process and the senators had to realize that.

Daschle whispered for me to describe the Republican exit strategy. Kerry tried to cut me off, but Daschle wouldn't let him. We were able to make all the political and substantive arguments to this larger group of Democrats that the president had made with members of the Budget Committee.

Finally, Lautenberg stepped in. He said, "We are where we are. We can make an agreement that is good for Democrats. But that means dealing with the Republican majority. Anyone suggesting an alternative strategy must not be able to count. They have fifty-five votes and can do what they want on the budget. We are a minority in Congress led by a Democratic president. He is the only one who can deliver a Democratic victory." His forceful words carried the day, taking us across a critical threshold with Senate Democrats.

The previous twenty-four hours had made one thing clear. A negotiation based on a series of offers and counteroffers was unworkable. There was neither the time nor the political coherence to run the gauntlet multiple times. If each stage had to be explained, argued, reconsidered, and assessed in large group settings, it would be impossible to reach and hold an agreement together. The negotiators needed to focus on bottom lines.

FRIDAY, APRIL 25, 1997

At the White House, Erskine had received an update from Vic Fazio, the chairman of the House Democratic caucus. The news was not good. House Democrats were not "in a mindset for a deal." We had not really expected otherwise. Gephardt and his circle were flat out against an agreement. And even though Spratt wanted an agreement, he was in an extraordinarily difficult position. Spratt said everyone needed to respect the process, including the need to consult and let members be heard. But the deck was stacked against us because his leaders were out to undermine our efforts. In the Senate we had the strong and steady hand of Tom Daschle. In the House the leaders were doing their best to get in the way. It was clear that we needed to increase our outreach to House moderates.

MANY OF THOSE moderates were part of a coalition called the New Democrats, a group whose politics closely mirrored those of the Democratic Leadership Council (DLC). Started in the mid-1980s by a group of moderate-to-conservative Democratic members of Congress, the DLC sought to shift the locus of Democratic politics toward the middle by offering a center-of-the-road alternative to both the ascendant Republican right and the descendant Democratic left. DLC participants tended to be from swing states and districts. At the core of their philosophy was the notion of individual responsibility. The legitimate role of government was to ensure opportunity, not outcomes. Collective action should be anchored in the community, and local challenges should be met through local innovation. This intellectual foundation of responsibility, opportunity, and community found a ready advocate in the governor of Arkansas, William Jefferson Clinton. Not only was he the most eloquent spokesman for the view, but many of his policies in such areas as education and welfare reform reflected these core beliefs.[4]

The White House was intent on keeping close to the New Democrats and their leaders, Representatives Tim Roemer of Indiana, Cal Dooley of California, and Jim Moran of Virginia. In our meetings with them, I outlined the elements of a possible agreement. We would erase the red ink in a balanced way, spreading the pain among entitlements and discretionary spending. But we would also make room for investments in education, health care, and the environment. We would use targeted tax cuts to make education affordable, allow homeowners a capital gains preference, and encourage employers to hire more workers. It was an easy sell. They were already there and ready to support the White House.

OUR NEXT MEETING with the budget negotiators on both sides was subdued and workmanlike. We were going through a process that we knew had to be altered. After Kasich and Domenici left, we were open with Lautenberg and Spratt about our political assessment. We would lose the opportunity for an agreement unless we changed tactics. The back and forth would kill us. We needed to try for a final settlement.

Spratt and Lautenberg understood the problem. But the politics of their caucuses limited the ability of the two men, particularly Spratt, to move quickly. Senate Democrats were at least pointed in the right direction, but the resistance of the left-leaning House leadership put Spratt in a very tough situation.

The White House was left with only one alternative. We would take a hard run at the Republicans, trusting that we could win quick agreement. Everything would be directly communicated to Lautenberg and Spratt—even if they could not be publicly associated with our proposals—and together we would assess the odds that the Democratic caucuses would support the agreement.

SATURDAY, APRIL 26, 1997

Domenici and Lott were leaving for New Mexico on Saturday afternoon. That left Saturday morning to make substantial progress. Frank, Gene, and I met with Domenici, Kasich, and Hoagland at Frank's house at 8:30 a.m. Our side started with the counteroffer the White House had prepared.

Our offer on domestic discretionary spending barely moved off the president's proposal, cutting $11 billion but then adding back $8 billion in a separate account for highways and the president's literacy program. Domestic discretionary spending was where we were determined to prevail. Domenici had indicated flexibility, but Kasich was still arguing for deep cuts. We knew this one would go to the wire.

On Medicare we went to savings of $105 billion against their $125 billion, indicating an obvious settlement at $115 billion. The Republicans were open to the home health transfer to extend the life of the Part A trust fund but were demanding a significant hit on Medicare beneficiaries as the price. Chris Jennings was working on a compromise in which a large portion of home health care expenses would be transferred and subjected to the existing 25 percent Part B premium, but the full premium would be phased in over a long period.[5] And to protect low-income Medicare recipients, we would ramp up existing subsidies to the poor.

On the president's entitlement expansions, we had trimmed the five-year number from $62 billion to $43 billion. But on the children's health initiative, we had moved our five-year number from $16 billion to $20 billion in order to bring more children under Medicaid. Domenici and Kasich accepted the goal of getting five million more kids covered but were hard set against spending $20 billion to do it.

On taxes the Republican negotiators had lowered their net tax cut from $100 billion to $92 billion, which amounted to a gross tax cut of $142 billion. That position was not too bad. It made room for the HOPE scholarship, a capital gains tax cut, their original estate tax provision, the child tax credit, and the president's "brownfields" tax incentive for environmental cleanup in urban areas.

It had been an intense few hours as we pressed each other, probing for where the middle might lie. The decibel level had risen at times above any previous threshold, but the negotiators were moving in the right direction. We all agreed to continue working on several fronts. Jennings would continue his shuttle diplomacy with both sides on the home health transfer and the children's health initiative.[6] The Republican budgeteers would work with the deputy Treasury secretary, Larry Summers, on some acceptable revenue streams, and I would talk to Senator Byrd about our desire to shuffle highway funding.

MONDAY, APRIL 28, 1997

Meeting again with Lautenberg and Spratt, Frank, Gene, and I gave an overview of the Saturday meeting with the Republican negotiators. Spratt was relieved the CPI had fallen away as a political issue. But given the loss of savings that a large adjustment in the CPI would have created, he urged us to go easy on sugarcoating our economic assumptions. That request would be a tough order to fill. He concluded the meeting by saying, "We can't get it straight by this week." We were determined to prove our friend John Spratt wrong.

CHAPTER SEVEN

An Agreement

The clock was ticking. Our bipartisan negotiators needed to quickly reach an agreement on the big budget pieces that would be memorialized in a congressional budget resolution. Having worked with the Republican negotiators and our Democratic allies for months, we had come to understand the wins each needed and the losses that could not be absorbed. We had probed and debated hundreds of policies in an effort to find the center both sides could support. Now we needed to seize the moment, reach across the aisle, and agree to that middle.

TUESDAY, APRIL 29, 1997

The president and the vice president gathered the budget team to settle on the key elements of a possible compromise before Frank, Gene, and I reconvened with the Republican negotiators. I suggested that if we found $115 billion in Medicare savings, dropped $25 billion from the president's original proposal on nondefense discretionary spending, and added in our less high-profile savings, we could balance the budget and invest $32 billion in the president's initiatives on children's health, benefits for legal immigrants, and other key policies while leaving room for an $85 billion net tax cut.

But Bob Rubin objected to my number for reducing the president's request on nondefense discretionary spending. He thought $20 billion should be the limit. Others joined in on his side, and the president's negotiating position moved to $20 billion.

RICHARD GEPHARDT WAS out to stop us. In an effort to put pressure on the White House, Gephardt had asked Erskine and the rest of the budget team to a special meeting of the entire House Democratic caucus at 5:30 p.m. in the Armed Services Committee room. In anticipation, we put our legislative affairs team into overdrive. Throughout the afternoon, Janet Murguia, our top House legislative affairs person, and her team of Peter Jacoby, Dan Tate, Andy Blocker, Al Maldon, and Lucia Wyman, along with legislative affairs chief of staff Tim Keating, contacted our moderate allies, briefing them and asking— imploring—them to come to the caucus and defend the president's position. Liberals dominated the House Democratic caucus, and their loud and some-times rancorous discussions tended to overwhelm the moderates, some of whom had simply stopped attending. But we desperately needed them that afternoon.

Vic Fazio, chair of the caucus, was the moderator—a good break for us. Erskine began. He said the president wanted an agreement, but only one a majority of Democrats would support. The president would insist on wins on domestic discretionary spending, education, kids' health, benefits for legal immigrants, and the environment. But the Republicans would need their wins as well, notably on entitlement savings and tax cuts. It was the only way to reach an agreement.

Erskine asked me to describe the outlines of a possible deal. I covered the Medicare and the welfare provisions, including those that would reverse the hit on legal immigrants. Then Frank Raines described the other pieces of the package. Just as he was finishing, Erskine had to take a phone call from the president. When Fazio told the caucus that Erskine had to take a call from the only person he had to answer to, Representative Barney Frank yelled out, "John Kasich." He got a huge laugh.

Then the members lined up behind microphones on each side of the floor to offer their comments. In Erskine's absence, it was my job to listen and respond. Fazio did a remarkable job of limiting each speaker to one minute. And he was a master of civility, keeping the tone the best it could have been under the circumstances. Generally he let four or five members speak before asking me to respond. It was ideal from our viewpoint. I did not have to address each member or topic individually but could zero in on any openings for pushing our message.

First up were Representatives Maxine Waters and Jim McDermott, who both voiced hard opposition to any agreement. But then Tim Roemer made a strong statement urging us to press ahead. Looking at the lines behind the microphones I could see moderates were well represented. The cavalry had arrived. Steve Rothman and Henry Waxman opposed our plans, but then Cal Dooley punched back, helping to make our case, along with David Minge, Allen Boyd, and Charlie Stenholm. Then it was Marty Sabo, the former budget chief and a voice respected across the ideological spectrum. He said he did not like the process but would give us the benefit of the doubt. The caucus should hold its judgment until it saw the outcome. That was the turning point.

Then followed John Tanner, John Baldacci, Gene Taylor, and Ellen Tauscher in support—offsetting those in opposition—Jerry Nadler, Rosa DeLauro, Dave Obey, and Barney Frank. It was the split decision we were hoping for: the caucus had not rallied behind Gephardt. We had survived and were moving ahead.

I found Erskine in the cloakroom off the floor of the committee room. The president had talked to Lott about an agreement along the lines we had just outlined. For once it seemed as if the White House, the Republicans, and a substantial number of congressional Democrats were moving together toward the middle.

WEDNESDAY, APRIL 30, 1997

Wednesday was a crucial day to bring our allies along. Representatives Roemer, Dooley, and Spratt assembled the New Democrats. We were a go with this group of House moderates. Then it was back to the Democrats on the Senate Budget Committee for an update. Medicare savings would be $115 billion, and on the net tax cut we hoped to end up between $80 billion and $90 billion. Lautenberg, who had taken on a lot of the heavy lifting, was terrific with his members. He had his Democrats lined up to support a bipartisan deal.

I CIRCLED BACK to meet Hoagland in Domenici's Capitol office. I described a "possible settlement" that would allow us to reach a compromise in which the last moves would be deficit neutral. On the savings side, we would go from $105 billion to $115 billion on Medicare; we would reduce our entitlement-like initiatives to $32 billion; we would reduce domestic discretionary to $20 billion below the president's budget proposal. Those moves on our part would allow a net tax cut of $80 billion. The last problem was nondefense discretionary spending. We had no more to give; they needed to come to our number.

LATER THAT AFTERNOON, Frank, Gene, and I convened with the Republican negotiators. Not only did we need to preserve the president's position on non-

Table 7-1. *CBO Estimates of Nondefense Discretionary Spending under Various Scenarios, 1997–2002*

Billions of dollars

Scenario	Projected amounts by year						Cumulative 1997–2002
	1997	1998	1999	2000	2001	2002	
Inflation baseline	280.3	288.5	296.9	305.3	313.0	321.5	1,525.2
President's proposal	282.1	287.3	295.4	296.2	292.0	293.3	1,464.2
Difference from inflation baseline	+1.8	-1.2	-1.5	-9.1	-21.0	-28.2	-61.0
Freeze baseline	280.3	280.3	280.3	280.3	280.3	280.3	1,401.5
Difference from president's proposal	-1.8	-7.0	-15.1	-15.9	-11.7	-13.0	-62.7
Difference from inflation baseline		-8.2	-16.6	-25.0	-32.7	-41.2	-123.7

defense discretionary spending, but we also needed to invent a presentation that would bridge the political divide and allow both sides to declare victory.

The difference between the president's nondefense discretionary budget proposal and a "freeze" at fiscal 1997 levels was approximately $63 billion over five years (table 7-1). But that was not the only "freeze" baseline we could draw on for presentational purposes. If the baseline were frozen, but allowed to rise, not with inflation, but because of technical factors such as the rates at which beneficiaries took advantage of government programs, the difference between that freeze baseline and the president's proposal would fall to $53 billion. The House Republican rank and file gauged spending restraint relative to a freeze baseline whose details were largely a mystery to them. We could use the higher freeze baseline to close $10 billion of the perception gap.

But we still needed to move the freeze baseline even higher to allow both sides to declare victory while accommodating our goals. Bill Hoagland and Frank Raines found the answer in the fine print of the Section 8 housing program, which subsidized housing for low-income families. We could "freeze" spending under Section 8 by freezing the number of units of housing that were made available to beneficiaries, rather than the dollars that were spent. This approach would yield a much higher "freeze" baseline. Now we could square the political circle.

It came to this. Over five years, the difference between the president's non-defense (domestic and international) discretionary spending proposal compared with the hardest of the hard-freeze baselines was $62.7 billion. We were willing to take $20 billion off the president's request, leaving a gap of approximately $43 billion. The Republicans had already offered $25 billion above a freeze, leaving a difference of $18 billion. Using our alternative freeze baselines, the Republicans could agree to the additional $18 billion of discretionary spending without appearing to move beyond $25 billion above a "freeze." The president would be able to fund his initiatives, and the Republicans would be able to claim to have held the line. Domenici and Kasich agreed to the increased funding that the president desired as well as to our concocted presentation that could be sold to two very different caucuses. Most important, they understood the bottom line: it all added up to a balanced budget.

Having reached agreement, we wanted to ensure that appropriated spending actually hewed to these amounts. The negotiators agreed to use the reconciliation bill to legislate the maximum amounts that could be spent on defense and nondefense discretionary programs over the five years of the agreement, thereby guaranteeing that the needed budget savings in discretionary spending would actually materialize.

OUR NEXT MEETING was with the Blue Dogs at Representative Gary Condit's office. Same good result: they were ready for the agreement. Then back to the White House for a meeting with the group of eight. Today our job was to make sure all the big pieces of the package were in place. I wrote four lines on a small sheet of paper and asked Erskine if the president could sign off on these: $115 billion in Medicare savings, an $85 billion net tax cut, $20 billion off his domestic discretionary spending request, and $30 billion for entitlement initiatives. He nodded yes. We were ready to try to reach an agreement that night.

WE WERE SCHEDULED to meet with the Democratic budgeteers at 9:30 p.m. But first we needed to confer with their Republican counterparts to make sure there would be no deal-breaking surprises. So Frank, Gene, and I convened with Domenici, Kasich, Hoagland, and Kasich's staff director, Rick May, at 8:30 p.m. in Domenici's office.

In a tense but largely preordained meeting, the three of us reached agreement with the Republican budgeteers on the big pieces. Over the many, many hours we had all spent together—stating our positions, probing for flexibility, separating the posturing from the true needs—we had arrived at a consensus solution that would meet both parties' political and policy requirements.

We agreed to Medicare spending reductions at $115 billion, a net tax cut of $85 billion, a reduction of $20 billion in the president's request for domestic discretionary spending, and $31 billion of new money for the president's entitlement initiatives, as well as the remaining smaller pieces needed to fill the deficit hole. It all added up to a balanced budget, setting right the fiscal ledger of the United States government.

IT WAS 10:00 p.m., and Frank, Gene, and I were running late for our meeting with Lautenberg and Spratt in Domenici's Capitol office. But when we got there, the office was closed, and Lautenberg and Spratt were not there. I was able to reach Lautenberg's staff director, Bruce King, to explain the tentative agreement and asked him to brief Lautenberg as soon as he could. We found Spratt in his Longworth office and briefed him at 10:30 p.m. He was remarkably tolerant of the late hour and the delay.

THURSDAY, MAY 1, 1997

The next morning we briefed Daschle and confirmed the specifics of the agreement. But Gephardt had called a caucus for 2:30 p.m. in a last effort to delay or kill the agreement in the House. Once again the White House went into full gear, bringing together House moderates for a briefing on the agreement before the full caucus met.

The moderates gathered in a small room in the Longworth Building. It was an overflow crowd. They liked what they heard and were ready to show up in force at the caucus. But during the meeting we received word that the full caucus had been cancelled because the White House meeting with the moderates was "in bad faith." We pushed on. We would have been incompetent not to. Then the word came that the caucus was back on for 4:30 p.m., but the White House would not attend. Then the final message. We were invited after all.

NEXT STOP: A briefing with Democratic senators. Barbara Boxer and John Kerry tried to slow the pace by proposing that a majority of Democrats approve the next steps before entering a final agreement. But we stood firm, arguing that this agreement was one that Democrats could easily support. And Senators Harry Reid, Kent Conrad, Dianne Feinstein, and Bob Kerrey supported our case.

After the meeting, Daschle told the press that he believed a majority of Democrats would support the agreement. It was nice to have that out there publicly. Daschle had a wonderful sense of when to make the call.

NOW BACK TO the Republican side. I went to see Senator Lott to begin locking down the major tax policies. But he said the president and he had worked it all out. There would be limits on the size of the tax cut over both a five-year and ten-year horizon. In addition, the Republicans would not attempt to cut the earned income tax credit, which subsidized the working poor. He claimed that was the entire extent of the agreement on taxes. I told Lott that such a proposal was a nonstarter for the White House. We would need to agree to the specifics of the major tax policies and work together to shepherd them through committee, all while making sure the tax cuts did not explode in the outyears.

Sitting in Lott's office, I called the president and told him that Lott's "solution" was completely unacceptable. The president agreed and asked Lott and me to try for an acceptable compromise.

In the next few minutes, Lott and I were able to agree to several things: the Republicans would back the president's education proposals, including the HOPE scholarship; there would be no poison pills; and the Treasury and the Joint Committee on Taxation would cooperate on estimating the revenue effects of any tax cuts. In addition, limits would be set on the overall size of the tax cuts, not only over five years, but for ten years as well. Lott was willing to compromise at $250 billion on the ten-year revenue loss, but I knew Bob Rubin wanted to push lower. I called the president to update him and to lock down the size of the five-year net tax cut at $85 billion. While I was on the phone, Lott came over and said that he and the president had agreed to the $85 billion two weeks ago. I knew he wasn't kidding.

After Lott and I had finished, I received a call telling me that Bob Rubin had just finished with Finance Committee Democrats. Rubin and I met in Daschle's office, along with Daschle's key staff, to review the outlines of the agreement on taxes I had sketched out with Lott. After updating them, I returned to Lott's office. Sitting there, I received a page from Martha Foley at the White House.[1] She had good intelligence that the CBO was changing its budget projections. What in the world could that mean?

MARTHA'S PAGE WAS completely disorienting. The CBO could not possibly be revising its deficit projections. It was May 1, and the CBO only revised its projections twice a year—in January for the *Economic and Budget Outlook,* and in August for the midyear update. There must be an error. This could not be happening.

But it was happening. Martha indicated that the CBO now believed that revenue flows to the Treasury would be $45 billion greater each year for the next five years than had previously been projected. And the CBO was so certain of this new projection that it was announcing now that the new numbers would appear in the August revisions. Bill Hoagland was in Lott's office, and we got on the phone together, trying to reach the CBO director, June O'Neill. We got Jim Blum, her deputy, instead. Bill and I had known Jim for years. He was a career professional and about as straight a shooter as there was. He would not be playing political games. We asked about the revisions. He said it was true. Revenues were coming in high enough and consistently enough for the CBO to revise its projections upward. The CBO had been wrong.

Bill and I looked at each other. We knew this surprise could kill the deal. We had spent months figuring out the policy and political compromises that would fit into the budget box. And now the size of that box had changed: it had gotten significantly larger. This was good news that could kill the agreement. Who would want to take the hard medicine if they didn't have to? Why cast a hard vote for spending cuts if there was the prospect of a free ride? It was time to assemble the troops and figure out how to handle this CBO surprise.

The group was growing in Lott's office. Hoagland had been joined by Kasich and Domenici, along with Lott. I received a page to call the White House. I needed to return immediately for an emergency meeting—the deal was falling apart. Cynics argued that the Republicans had known about the CBO revisions for days and had suppressed the information so that they could drive us into making deeper spending reductions. It had all been a set-up.

I looked at Lott and asked him when he knew of the new CBO numbers. He said, "Today, same as you."

WALKING INTO THE chief of staff's office, I confronted a firestorm. The shouting was in full swing. Frank Raines was leading the injured party category. He said the Republicans had tried to trick us. We should call off the deal and see what the new numbers meant.

Coming in late, it was hard to get my bearings. Martha Foley was agreeing with Frank. They were both in blow-it-up mode. But their voices would not be the decisive ones. I needed to know where the senior White House people were. It was hard to tell. Erskine, Gene, Rahm Emanuel, and Ron Klain, the vice president's chief of staff, were keeping their counsel even as the decibel level kept rising. People were mad. It was hard to get past the anger and figure out the right thing to do.

I listened for a few minutes, but the answer was obvious. The agreement had to hold. If we faltered now, the White House would lose its best chance of achieving the long-sought goal of a balanced budget. But we would have to move quickly. The projected new revenue would energize the opposition on both the Democratic and Republican sides. Democrats would want to reduce the hit on Medicare, while Republicans would want to up the ante on tax cuts.

I told the group that walking out on the agreement would be totally incomprehensible to the average American. "If the American people knew the White House staff was considering blowing up a balanced budget agreement because the numbers had gotten easier, they would have us hauled out there," I said, pointing to Erskine's patio, "and summarily shot." I said that abandoning the agreement would be catastrophic for the president's second term. If we lost the deal, it would validate the president's worst critics. That precipitated another round of rejoinders and heated expressions.

In the verbal melee, I was able to get a side conversation with Klain. He agreed we needed to push the deal to completion. I lip read across the room with Emanuel; he nodded that we needed to go forward. Then Gene weighed in. He said we had to be truthful about the revision, but that could not be an excuse for inaction.

But Frank kept trying to press the charge of bad faith. Bob Rubin asked the Treasury's revenue estimators what they thought of the CBO revisions. Treasury had doubts that revenue inflows would be as strong as CBO was now saying and warned that we needed to be cautious about the budget office's optimism.

Then it was Erskine's turn. He said we should interpret the new CBO numbers as a vindication of the administration's stewardship of the economy. We should not treat the new estimate as some event upsetting the world order. We should press ahead. Then the investment banker in him clicked in. He said we should go back to the Republicans and use some of the new money to shore up the deal, not destroy it. We would not blow up the agreement; we would use the found money to make it better.

That carried the day decisively. But we had precious little time. The easy part would be taking the rough edges off the agreement. Spending money is easy. The hard part would be shoring up the twin pillars that held up the agreement—Medicare and taxes.

I went upstairs to my office and relayed our decision to Bill Hoagland. We would need to add back about $25 billion in spending to take the political edges off and secure the votes. But we would hold to the central agreement on Medicare and taxes and find some way to lock away the new-found money for deficit reduction. When we were done with our rejiggering, there would not be a free penny left to attack or undermine the balanced budget agreement.

At 11:00 p.m. the White House team placed a call to Lott's office. By that time, the Republican negotiators, including Lott, had assembled. We repeated our line. Kasich got it and was ready to start dealing out the $25 billion. But

Domenici was not sure about reopening the package. He started arguing about our list of add-backs.

I told them that the add-backs were not the issue. The new money could blow the entire agreement. Over the five-year period, CBO had just put over $200 billion on the table. We were in danger of losing the Medicare savings if we did not press forward. And if the Democrats forced us to restore Medicare spending to higher levels, then the Republicans would want to up the ante on tax cuts. To save the agreement, we had to act decisively: we would hold to the agreed-upon Medicare savings if they would hold to the agreed-upon tax cut; we would use $25 billion to cover our political flanks; and we would lock away the rest so that those who opposed the agreement could not use the new-found money to undo it. That was the right course, I said, and we had less than one day to pull it off. They all got it and agreed. These were responsible guys.

Friday, May 2, 1997

Almost no sleep and back at the White House by 6:30 a.m. I wrote down the key points for Lott and Gingrich and then phoned Gene at home, waking him. We had to be square on the list of add-backs before I ran them past the Republican leaders. Then I reached Erskine, went over the list, and got his approval to go for it with Gingrich and Lott.

I tried the Speaker at home at 7:00 a.m. and managed only to wake his wife. He had already left for the House gym. The congressional telephone operators had him on the phone in five minutes. His first words were, "I hear you guys want to spend some more money." Kasich and Domenici had spoken to him. We were not starting from scratch.

I told Gingrich that new, higher revenue estimates would be in the CBO August budget revisions. Those seeking to delay or blow up the deal now had the perfect excuse—they would want to wait for the new numbers before acting. I warned the Speaker that the Medicare savings would be the first target, with the total likely to fall from the agreed-upon $115 billion to less than $80 billion. As a consequence his guys would never agree to the home health transfer needed to extend the life of the Medicare trust fund. In short, both the Republicans and the Democrats would still be in the Medicare soup. Once his guys caught on to the new money, they would want deeper tax cuts—way beyond the tolerance of the president or congressional Democrats. The balanced budget agreement was hanging by a thread. Congressional leaders and the White House needed to act now to affirm the budget agreement, I said, or there would be no balanced budget agreement.

Then I addressed the foundation of the agreement. We would hold to our Medicare savings if the Republicans would hold to the size of their tax cut. The two sides had arrived at an amazing moment. No two issues had been more closely associated than Medicare and taxes. That linkage had been the main point of contention in the virulently partisan budget wars of 1995. Democrats had mercilessly excoriated the Republicans with the charge of cutting Medicare to pay for tax cuts. The Republicans had stood their ground, and together the parties had reached an impasse of historic proportions, forcing the government to shut down.

Now, in contrast, I continued, after three months of quiet talks and trust-building, the leadership of both parties had reached an agreement to balance the budget. We were reaching out to each other to do the responsible thing. Medicare and taxes would be linked once again. But this time it would be to save the balanced budget, not destroy it. The Speaker agreed immediately.

NOW THE NEGOTIATORS needed to shore up their flanks. We would put some money back in so no one could trump us with a better package. And we would lock up the rest for deficit reduction, taking it out of the hands of anyone trying to use free money to defeat us.

Bill Hoagland and I recommended that the budget switch completely to CBO deficit projections rather than the OMB assumptions the White House had imported to lower the deficit projections. That would reduce the extra money to just over $100 billion over five years. Of that, $25 billion would be spent, and the balance dedicated to deficit reduction.

To ease passage of the deal, Gingrich and I agreed to spend some of the $25 billion by throwing away the per capita cap on Medicaid. Every governor hated the cap, and it was not clear that the committees of jurisdiction would vote to retain it. If we didn't get rid of it, someone was likely to do it for us. Next, we agreed to raise the defense number a little, bringing it closer to what the Joint Chiefs of Staff wanted. That would help with moderates like Democratic representative John Murtha of Pennsylvania and with the members of the Armed Services Committees. Third, we agreed to put several billion more into transportation. The transportation coalition was powerful, and with a transportation authorization bill up for renewal later in the year, we would need to leave room for maneuver. Finally, we would add $4 billion to the president's priorities. I told Gingrich the money would be dedicated to programs that would win votes for the overall budget agreement or at least lessen resistance.

I asked him to call Lott and then I would follow. I also asked Gingrich if he had written down the numbers. He hadn't and made light of his own poor staff work. He got a pencil and we went through the numbers again.

After the Speaker reviewed the new agreement with Lott, Lott called me. He was good to go. The clock was ticking.

AT 8:00 A.M. I asked Betty Currie, the president's personal assistant, to put me through to the president. He was in physical therapy for his knee. I went through the add-backs and the central trade that had to hold on both Medicare and taxes. He agreed to everything.

I told him we had not yet reached agreement on the tax pieces that we had been working on before the CBO surprise. Lott had agreed to the HOPE scholarship and the higher education deduction. He was fine with a process of consultation between the Treasury and Joint Tax Committee to make sure Congress and the White House were using the same numbers. And he would not use the tax bill to mess with controversial provisions that Democrats cared about such as the earned income tax credit, the low-income housing credit, and anything to do with pension reversion.[2] But we still needed to settle on an overall ten-year figure for revenue lost to tax cuts to ensure that the tax cuts did not explode in the years beyond the budget horizon. The Republicans were talking a revenue loss limit of $288 billion over ten years, and Treasury was at $212 billion. Lott was in the middle at $250 billion.

By 8:30 a.m. our group of eight had assembled in the White House. I relayed the new agreement that had been reached with the Republicans. They would hold on the tax cuts if we would hold on Medicare. And they had agreed to the $25 billion of add-backs.

Next I needed to bring Democrats up to speed before we started the negotiation to finalize the agreement. A lot had happened in the fourteen hours since CBO dropped its bomb. I began with a call to John Spratt, who argued that "we need to slow down, absorb the new development, and see where the House Democratic caucus is."

I told him that if negotiations were not completed today, the agreement would fall apart. Not only would the Democrats lose the entitlement reforms he cared so deeply about, but more important, the Republicans would want to increase the size of the tax cut. The Democrats would be throwing away an agreement that actually balanced the budget. If things got out of control, it could be 1981 all over again. I said that anyone outside Washington would think Washington politicians were insane. They get good news that makes the job easier and their response is to do nothing or go in the other direction. It would confirm every negative notion that the average citizen held of Washington politicians.

I described the $25 billion of add-backs that were designed to shore up support for the package among Congressional Democrats. Spratt was troubled by the increase for defense, but he agreed it was probably necessary. Then I went through the key trade-off that had to hold. The Republicans would stay with the agreed-upon tax cut, even in the face of billions of found money, if the Democrats would hold to their Medicare number. Spratt agreed with that central component but remained unconvinced that the agreement needed to be reached today. It was hardly surprising. Spratt was in the most difficult position of all. He was on the president's side and had always wanted to do the right thing. But he also got daily earfuls from House Democrats opposed to the agreement. In his first year as the ranking Democrat on the Budget Committee, he had been asked to pull off a virtuoso balancing act in a Democratic caucus that was deeply divided.

WE WERE SCHEDULED to meet with the full team of budget negotiators at 9:45 a.m. but needed to arrive early to get square with members of our own party. It was clear that we would need reinforcements to carry our message to House Democrats. I placed calls to Representatives Stenholm, Tanner, and Roemer. But Roemer was on a plane to Indiana, Tanner could not be reached, and Stenholm was at the top of the Capitol Dome, taking a group of constituents around. White House budget experts Barbara Chow and Martha Foley and I took a car to the Hill and headed to Domenici's office.[3] As we were descending the stairs, Stenholm was right in front of me, talking to a reporter. If ever providence shone on us, this was the moment.

I pulled him aside and explained the situation. He immediately saw the logic of holding the package together. He agreed to call as many moderates as possible and rally support.

And then another lucky break. John Spratt came around the corner just as Stenholm and I were finishing. We brought him over and double-teamed him, arguing for the absolute necessity of finishing today. We would face a catastrophe if we lost our nerve, we said. Spratt was listening and starting to believe.

DOMENICI'S CAPITOL OFFICE was packed and chaotic. And it was all Democrats. Frank Raines was going through the $25 billion of add-backs and getting hit hard on the defense increase. Worse, an earlier conversation with Spratt had put Frank Lautenberg in a slow-it-down mode. As I came in, Lautenberg was venting his anger at the new CBO development, just as some of the White House team had done the night before. Lautenberg was suspicious about who knew what when. Sometimes it is hard to judge if surprises were cooked-up or real. The CBO surprise was real.

Just then Domenici, Kasich, and their team pushed into the room. We asked for a few more minutes, and they waited in the hall. I listened as Spratt and Lautenberg continued to spar with Raines but then went outside to talk to Domenici and Kasich. They had just come from a meeting with their leaders, and they were empowered to deal.

I told them that we were in trouble—some of our Democrats were pressuring to slow-walk the agreement. If an agreement was not reached in the next few hours, it could be lost. This bipartisan group of negotiators was the center, and the center had to hold. If this group could announce an agreement today, it could preempt those who would use the new numbers to undermine the foundations of the agreement.

THIS WAS THE decisive meeting, and Kasich went first. He was the most emotional I had ever seen him. He was groping for words to express his thoughts and emotions. Gathering himself, he said that our bipartisan group had to push ahead and conclude the agreement. If we failed today, all would be lost. The right wing of his party would demand a $300 billion tax cut bill. And the Democrats would demand that the entitlement savings be taken down. He said this was a defining moment—we had to conclude the agreement for the good of the country. He asked us to do what was right, to do what we all believed in. Finally, he said, "Guys, I'm asking you, no, I'm begging you, I'm begging you to conclude today and balance the budget—for our country—I'm begging you." He placed his head in his hands, at the point of emotional exhaustion.

Domenici went next. He said, "I'm not going to beg you, because I know and trust you will do the right thing for our country." Turning to Spratt and Lautenberg, he said, "You are two of the most decent people I have ever dealt with and you have been a tremendous part of this effort. I know you will do the right thing."

Then the lifesaver. Bill Hoagland had his little portable magic marker board. It showed the sequence of numbers necessary to conclude the agreement. But more important, it showed how to lock out anyone who tried to come behind us.

The finesse was to go completely to the new CBO deficit projections and throw away the OMB assumption on corporate revenues that the bipartisan negotiators had used to give more room.[4] The CBO adjustment added a steady $45 billon to the pot each year, in contrast to the OMB corporate revenue projections, which grew over time. This meant that the difference between CBO and OMB revenue projections declined in the later years, leaving less of a windfall to be dealt with. If the spending add-backs were done right—and they could be—the budget would just balance with no room to spare in 2002. Anyone trying to raise spending or cut taxes beyond our agreement would throw the budget out of balance in 2002. Their budget would not balance. They would be locked out.

In a strange twist, we were back to CBO numbers. After having argued for months on the validity of the administration's economic projections and agreeing to use some of the OMB assumptions to give ourselves extra room, we were now back to those "pure" CBO numbers that now gave us even more room—more than we desired at this critical juncture.

The negotiating group went through the add-backs. The Republicans agreed to $4 billion more for the president's initiatives, as well as latitude to place the new money in categories by common agreement. That meant that none of the add-backs would cross politically charged lines; we were out to shore up the agreement, not create problems. Kasich said he would agree to additional work slots for food stamp recipients. He wanted the package to work and knew the issue was important to many Democrats. He was willing to put aside his strong preference for the good of the agreement.

While we were hammering out these details, I received a call from Stenholm. He had talked to Representatives Dooley and Tanner, as well as the staffs of several moderate members. They all favored closing the deal today. I asked him to keep working, focusing on moderates in the Democratic leadership such as Fazio, Steny Hoyer, and Barbara Kennelly. He said he would stay with it. I announced the Stenholm report inside the room. Spratt was listening carefully.

The next interruption was a page asking me to join Erskine in Lott's office, where they were going to work out the tax piece. As I was rising to leave, Spratt asked that we hold firm on taxes; it would be critical to his Democrats.

ARRIVING AT LOTT's office, I found only Erskine, Lott, and Gingrich. All the others had been asked to leave. Erskine was methodically reciting the White House position on the tax issues, and after each point the Republican leaders would respond. They agreed to have Treasury and the Joint Tax Committee consult on the revenue estimates of various tax policies and were willing to put that assurance in writing. On the president's tax policies, they would guarantee the HOPE scholarship and higher education deduction at $35 billion.

They would also block attempts to insert poison pills in the provisions governing the EITC, the low-income housing tax credit, and pension reversions. And they assured us that our smaller tax items—the brownfields tax incentive to clean up polluted industrial sites and the work opportunity tax credit to help employers hire former welfare recipients—would be protected. But unlike their pledge on the tax estimates, they were resisting putting their commitments on the president's tax policies into writing.

They were unwilling to accept any restrictions on the form or amount of the capital gains and estate tax provisions, other than to agree that the final provisions, along with everything else, would fit into the overall limits on the tax bill. And on that score, they would not go below a $250 billion ten-year revenue loss. It was the level Lott had indicated the night before, and they were holding firm.

By noon, Erskine and I were heading back to the White House. We needed to brief the president on the outcome of the meetings, including the need to settle on a figure for the ten-year revenue loss.

The president was still at the dedication of the new Franklin Delano Roosevelt Memorial, so we went to Erskine's office. I placed a call to Daschle and briefed him on the spending agreement. Then Erskine took the phone and began to walk Daschle through the tax provisions. I called Lautenberg in his Hart office, where he was meeting with John Spratt. They had gotten to closure on the major spending issues and were trying to reach Daschle to explain the agreement. We did a little Keystone cops routine: they said they could not talk because Daschle was on the other line; I said that couldn't be—Daschle was talking to Erskine, who was sitting right in front of me. Finally we got it all straight and they were good to go—just as we received word that the president had returned and was ready to see the team.

In the Oval Office with the president, vice president, and budget team, Erskine asked me to begin. I said that we had concluded a successful negotiation on the basic package. I went through the $25 billion of add-backs, all of which had been accepted by the Republican leadership and negotiators. It was an agreement that balanced the budget while investing in America. We would be able to achieve substantially all of the president's policy goals as laid out in his budget proposal. This was clearly an agreement worth consummating. But there were two outstanding issues—getting in writing our verbal tax agreement with the Republican leaders and locking down the ten-year revenue loss from the tax bill.

The president asked me what we should do. I recommended that he try to push Lott lower than a $250 billion revenue loss, but cautioned that the revenue loss limit should not be a deal breaker. The agreement was a major victory and we should move forward. As for the tax agreement, we had secured commitments to protect the president's priorities. If those understandings were not honored, we had the veto threat and the certainty of a veto-sustaining margin. I also said we had to consider the kind of tax bill we would get if this agreement were not completed. With the new CBO money on the table, we would not be worrying about a tax bill that spent $250 billion over ten years but one that went well beyond that number.

Bob Rubin went next, indicating his displeasure with the $250 billion tax revenue loss, which he felt was too high. He wanted the president to try to push the number down. Importantly, however, he said the overall agreement was worth supporting.

The vice president interjected strongly. He said that if the talks broke down, there would be more money on the table, and the Republicans would be able to put together a budget with a larger tax cut. He pointed out that they could do so without being forced to make deep cuts in spending. Politically, they would be less vulnerable, and it would be harder to push them back. His comment went right to the political heart of the matter. The conflict with Republicans that the House Democrats were seeking was predicated on tough numbers. But the CBO revisions had delivered a way out for the Republicans. If they were smart, they would be nearly impossible to attack politically.

The vice president strongly recommended that the president accept the agreement. He said we had won on our priorities, all within a balanced budget. He agreed that the president should push Lott on the tax number, but we should go ahead with the agreement no matter how that came out.

After listening to his advisors and his vice president, the president did what we expected. He accepted the agreement.

We agreed that the president should call Lott from the Oval Office and ask for two more commitments: a letter memorializing the agreement that we had struck on the tax bill, and a limit of $240 billion on the ten-year revenue loss. The tax letter would make it more difficult for the Republican-controlled committees to walk away from the agreement. Frank Raines suggested that the president act upset about the CBO number surprise, using that as leverage. But that was not the president's style.

Far from being hostile, the president was his friendly self on the phone with Lott. He dutifully went through all the points. The president managed to secure the critical pledge to put the verbal agreement on taxes policies in writing. Lott focused on the limit on the ten-year revenue loss. After listening for a moment, the president covered the phone and whispered loudly to the group, "This guy is good." We laughed out loud. Lott was telling him he would be glad to lower the ten-year revenue loss to $240 billion if the president would agree to reduce his education tax cuts from $35 billion to $25 billion. It was time to call it a day. We had our balanced budget agreement; the final pieces were a letter reflecting our broad agreement on tax policies and a ten-year revenue loss of $250 billion.

Once the president had finished his conversation with Lott, the topic turned to the announcements and briefings. Clinton would make the announcement at a Senate Democratic retreat scheduled to be held in Baltimore later that day. We would helicopter key House members to Baltimore to join the president and senators for the announcement.

It was 1:30 p.m. on Friday afternoon, May 2, 1997. We had beat the clock and held the agreement together. We had dodged death from good news. Erskine and I shook hands, and I left the Oval Office and the White House. I went home, mowed the lawn, and drank a few beers.

During the course of the afternoon and into the evening, the congratulatory calls came in—from Domenici, Kasich, Bill Hoagland, Gene, Erskine, and then, at 10:00 p.m., the president. We laughed and shared the moment. It was a great day for the country.

CHAPTER EIGHT

What Was That
We Agreed To?

We had pushed ourselves past the point of exhaustion. A weekend would not be enough time to recuperate. All those involved in the negotiations would need a few days to gather their strength. We had come an enormous distance in slightly more than three months—from quiet forays through partisan political barriers to the handoff and then to an agreement that had survived death from good news. Most important, our contingent had stood together when it counted; we were learning to act like partners.

MONDAY, MAY 5, 1997

The first official act would be to memorialize the agreement in a congressional budget resolution. In the regular order, the budget resolution had only three sets of hard and fast numbers. The first set was total revenues, total spending, and the deficits of the federal government over the five years of the agreement. The second set was the total amount of funds allocated to the appropriations committees. To reduce the deficit, the pot of money going to the appropriations committee in each chamber had to be below the baseline amount. The third was a numerical deficit reduction target assigned to the authorizing committees expected to contribute to deficit reduction.[1] If each committee hit its individual savings target, then the overall revenue, spending, and deficit amounts would be met. Traditionally the authorizing committees had nearly complete freedom to determine the package of policies that would hit their assigned deficit reduction number. But this year it needed to be different; committees that were accustomed to doing their own thing would have to be led, induced, cajoled, threatened, and sometimes overridden in order to enact the policies that were part of the agreement.

THURSDAY, MAY 8, 1997

Unfortunately, the CBO surprise had not left our negotiating group time to agree on all these important policies. In our Friday flurry to save the agreement, we had together taken a leap of faith that we could quietly agree on the many specific issues that remained unresolved or unexamined. By the time the budgeteers reconvened the following Thursday, OMB had produced a draft memorandum incorporating what the White House wanted locked down as part of the budget agreement. It was far more detailed than anything that had been discussed or that the Republicans would agree to. We had over-reached by a mile, including explicit protection for hot button issues such as legal services, family planning, advanced technology initiatives, and the National Endowment for the Arts. The OMB list was so brazen that depending on your perspective, it was laughable or offensive.

John Kasich definitely thought it was the latter. He called it a "stick it in your eye" list—a reasonable description from his perspective. To avoid confrontation, we asked Bill Hoagland to run through the document, pointing out the areas in contention that would have to be settled before the budget resolution could move forward. It was time to roll up the sleeves again.

NOT ONLY THAT, but problems were looming on taxes. House Ways and Means chairman Bill Archer said he was not about to have the White House or even his own leaders tell him how to write major elements of his tax bill. This dispute had to be kicked upstairs and quickly. On Thursday, Erskine, Bob Rubin, and I convened with the Republican leaders and their tax chairmen.

Representative Archer said he was committed to a balanced budget and would be sensitive to the needs of the White House, but he would not allow the administration to specify the provisions in his committee's tax bill. He said he would write the bill in a bipartisan manner and would consult with Democrats, including the White House. He even indicated that he had talked to the president, who had agreed that Archer could write his own tax bill with one exception—although he did not say what that was.

Archer's statement was extremely worrisome. In the two years of Republican rule in the House, Archer had done very little consulting with Democrats and had flat run them over with the 1995 Contract with America budget. Furthermore, his rendition of his conversation with the president did not ring true. It sounded like what he wanted to hear, not what we knew the president would have said.

Chairman Roth of the Senate Finance Committee went next, mirroring Archer's comments. But his claim to bipartisanship was largely true. The Finance Committee had reported the 1996 tax bill with unanimous support.[2] Roth said he would respect the numerical limits set in the budget resolution, but he would not commit to protecting particular provisions the White House wanted. His committee would consult and listen, but it would write the tax bill.

Gingrich followed, initially backing up the chairmen's push for consultation only. He suggested that Bob Rubin sit down with the committees and get some reassurance that the tax bill would be one the president could support. But, importantly, he said that if the White House insisted, it could "exercise its legal option" for a letter from Lott and him laying out the specific tax policies that they had agreed to on Friday. This veteran legislator knew what would be needed to hold the agreement together, and he was doing his part. As it turned out, that responsible act largely cleared the way for a successful tax bill.

Then Archer came back, undermining his own previous assurances on the tax bill. He indicated that the president's critical educational initiatives "weren't coming out of committee." I pressed him on the number, even putting aside the particular policies. Would he adhere to $35 billion for education? If he at least set aside the money, we could fight over the policies as we went along. Archer said that "it would be hard to fit the $35 billion into the bill." But he offered that whatever they came up with in education, they'd name it "HOPE." Now that was reassuring.

Gingrich went back to the four main components of the tax bill: the HOPE scholarship, the child credit, the estate tax, and capital gains relief. He made the pitch for consultation but again repeated that the White House had a "lien" on Lott and him for what they had agreed to.

Then majority leader Armey spoke. He was a regular-order man. He said the bill would be better if the leaders and the White House did not try to dictate to members. The letter would be a "bowneck" around the members and could threaten support for the deal. It could be a "stink bomb that could blow everything up." He talked of his and Gingrich's different personalities and their different approaches to leading the House. Gingrich was the outside guy and he was the inside one. "Hunter and skinner," Erskine interjected.

The meeting closed with Archer and Roth saying they wanted the agreement to work, and in particular they wanted to balance the budget.

Erskine, Bob, and I rode back to the White House together. It was obvious we needed the Republican leaders to intervene; Archer and Roth were not going to get it right on their own. We immediately began preparing drafts of the tax letters. The first was about the big pieces of the agreement, the size of the tax cut, the HOPE scholarship, and the other policies that needed to be part of the tax bill. The second letter addressed cooperation between Treasury and Congress's Joint Committee on Taxation, the legislative branch's official estimator for the budgetary effects of tax policies. I sent both drafts to Arne Christenson, the Speaker's chief of staff, early the next week. His response was pretty close to our position. He said the tax bill would cost no more than $85 billion in revenues over five years, and $250 billion over ten. On education, the Republican leaders wanted to pledge that "up to $35 billion" would be provided in the form of "a tax credit, deduction, or both," which was not bad. As part of the tax break, however, the Republicans wanted to give parents the ability to save, and not just pay, for education. That set off alarm bells; we worried that they would fund an education IRA and say tough luck to the HOPE scholarship.

TUESDAY, MAY 13, 1997

The bipartisan budget negotiators were continuing to make progress—filling in the holes that remained after the Friday sprint to save the agreement. Negotiators agreed to set aside $1.5 billion to protect low-income Medicare beneficiaries from the effects of subjecting home health care to the 25 percent Medicare Part B premium, and to reinstate Supplemental Security Income and Medicaid benefits to legal immigrants who had entered the country before the passage of the 1996 welfare bill.

The toughest fight was over the administration's desire to explicitly protect the president's priorities in nondefense discretionary spending. This was the hot button for John Kasich and many other Republicans. The White House negotiators were pushing the limits of their tolerance. Finally Kasich had had enough; he started grousing and left the room. After about half an hour, Domenici said that Kasich must be upstairs with the Republican leadership. He had a sense for these things. At 6:00 p.m. a call came from Gingrich's office. They wanted to see me.

Kasich had taken his unhappiness with the White House to the Speaker. Gingrich told me he wanted to be clear about what they would and would not protect in nondefense discretionary spending. He would protect our policies in education with the exception of Goals 2000.[3] The increase in Head Start funding was fine, as were our worker training programs, funding for the Environmental Protection Agency, community development block grants, and even the president's COPS program aimed at increasing the number of cops on the beat by 100,000. The Speaker was being generous.

But he said there was no way he would agree to protect our programs in energy conservation, Amtrak, mass transit, and particularly national service. It was a bit of a mystery why the Republicans were so opposed to the national service program, which rewarded students doing community service by providing them with financial help for education. It was not a budget buster, it was a great way for young people to help others and themselves, and it smacked of the volunteerism that was part of the Republican view. Our best guess was that they felt the president was encroaching on their territory. Some of the biggest fights are over the middle, with both parties constantly trying to grab and hold the political center. Bill Clinton fully understood this, and he had shown an uncanny ability to grab and hold the middle, whether on welfare reform, education, tax cuts, or national service. And that alone was enough to make the program contentious.

On the numbers, it turned out that our budget negotiations had overshot on the spending side on that frantic Friday, and committee staff were juggling the numbers to make it all add up. They were still short, and Gingrich was asking for a billion each off defense and nondefense discretionary spending in 2002. I was relieved that he was asking for so little. More than $25 billion had just been added to numbers the administration could have lived with, and the giveback was only $2 billion.

But there was a new problem on the horizon that went right to the heart of the politics of the budget. Everyone had signed on to the two-bill strategy in which the bill to balance the budget would be voted before the tax cuts. Everyone in the White House, from the president on down, had told every Democrat in Congress that was the way it would be. But there was a procedural problem in the Senate. Because the tax bill would be largely funded through the spending cuts contained in the budget bill, the tax bill would not fully pay for itself; considered alone it would increase the deficit. That would trigger a point of order under the Senate's so-called Byrd rule, which required sixty votes to override.[4] That meant that the minority Democrats could band together to kill particular provisions like cuts in the capital gains and estate taxes. And that prospect had the Republicans very worried. I said we would work on it.

WEDNESDAY, MAY 14, 1997

The full Democratic congressional leadership was meeting with the president for the first time since the announcement of the agreement. In the prep meeting, we warned the president that some Democrats might try to draw lines in the sand on the tax bill, urging the president to veto it if it did not fit their political views. We warned that any talk of veto would get amplified by those opposed to the agreement. We needed to settle critical spending issues, and it would be counterproductive in the extreme to upset Republicans with talk of vetoing the tax bill.

In the meeting with the legislators, the president said that Democrats should take credit for the nation's strong economy since 1993. The current agreement balancing the budget was possible only because of Democrats' responsible actions in 1993 and beyond. He urged them to claim the mantle of economic growth and fiscal responsibility. On the agreement itself, he said that Democrats had clear and decisive wins. Even the tax bill was much better than advertised. President Clinton said that the 1981 Reagan tax cuts had tallied $2 trillion in lost revenue over ten years; the current tax bill was one-eighth that size. And within the tax bill, we had locked in $35 billion for education. The president said he thought the Christian Coalition would drive the child tax credit to around $70 billion. That would leave only about $30 billion for everything else in the first five years. It was a tight tax package.[5]

Then the president recited a partial agenda for the future after a balanced budget had been achieved. Even after our expansion of children's health coverage, another five million children would still be without health care. We could fight for better schools by funding school construction and pushing for tougher educational standards. There were crime issues from juvenile justice to guns that needed to be addressed. We could do much more on the environment. And we should be for campaign finance reform, even if the Republicans killed it. Emphatically, he wanted Democrats to claim victory, something he said the Republicans were better at doing.

Gephardt returned to the budget agreement, citing the lack of trust in the House. He said the administration would have to lock the deal down in writing if it was going to happen as we planned. He said there would be "adequate" support for the agreement among House Democrats. Inside the White House, we had wondered what there was left to oppose in the budget bill. The CPI adjustment was gone, AARP was on board with our policies on Medicare, and the agreement included several key Democratic policy initiatives. We felt House Democrats would support the balanced budget bill in large numbers— far beyond "adequate."

It was all going very well until the president started down a dangerous road. He began by recounting a conversation he had had with Bill Archer. He said he had told Archer that Democrats would work hard to pass the agreed-upon tax bill. And Archer had offered that if the tax bill went beyond the agreement, he would expect the president to veto it.

Gephardt jumped on the opportunity the president had created. He urged the president to veto a bad tax bill. The president said, "I will." Rather than leading the conversation toward getting a tax bill he could sign, he was letting himself get led into the rhetoric of confrontation. Erskine and I looked at each other. Less than ten minutes ago we had warned Clinton about this very trap. David Bonior, the Democratic whip, would not let go. He urged the president to play hardball on taxes. The president pledged again to veto a bad tax bill. He even suggested that that was the reason for the two-bill strategy— so he could sign the balanced budget bill and veto the tax bill if he had to. Erskine and I were directing our most telepathic stares at the president, hoping to bring him back to reality. But he was off and away.

After the fourth invocation of the president's veto power in less than five minutes, the vice president stepped in. He reassured the attendees along the lines the president had pursued, but also let them in on the delicate matter of concluding the spending side before raising the veto flag. The president had gotten so far off track that we were reduced to divulging the innards of our tactics. And, of course, that was dangerous in another way. We were handing over the instruction book on how to blow up the deal. If they could just get the veto talk out soon enough, the Republicans would balk and the whole deal could come undone. But it was all the vice president could do at this point. As he was speaking, a light went off in the president's head and he put his fist to his forehead. He knew he had erred.

But providence was with us once again. There was a vote in the House, and there would be no time for the House delegation to talk to the press as they left the White House. They had to leave immediately, without facing the cameras in front of the West Wing. But Daschle stayed behind and talked to the press. He did it perfectly, right on message. It paid to be lucky and have good smart friends.

Immediately after the meeting, Erskine and I walked with the president to the Oval Office. Erskine shut the door and would not allow anyone else in. He said to the president, "You know I love you like a brother, but you just screwed up!" We jumped on his case, telling him he had raised the veto flag four times. Then we repeated the mantra he had to stay with: "I want a tax bill that stays within the agreement. I expect Democrats and Republicans to work together to produce a tax bill I can sign." Don't stop saying that!

THURSDAY, MAY 15, 1997

Early the next morning, Erskine and I went to the White House residence to discuss the remaining issues that had to be settled before the budget resolution could be enacted. The president was in shorts and a tee shirt, trying out different walking canes.

We would try to lock in funding for the country's international obligations, but the Republicans might balk at paying our arrears at the United Nations. They would likely resist some of the president's, and particularly the vice president's, environmental initiatives. And they would fight us on the funding for the national service program. They knew that they would ultimately be forced to yield in the appropriations process as we turned up the heat and glare of public scrutiny. But they would not agree to protect national service funding as part of this agreement.

The president agreed that the issue of separate budget and tax bills was absolutely critical. We simply could not walk into a meeting of Democrats and tell them that there would be only one bill after promising them two. Our credibility would be completely undermined. In the negotiations that day with the Republicans, we would reassure them that the president would sign the tax bill if it stayed within the agreement, and we would provide Democratic votes in the Senate to overcome the Byrd rule if it became an issue.

Finally, Erskine took out the draft tax letters. Our first concern was shoring up the education tax cuts. We were willing for the letter to read "roughly $35 billion" but not "up to $35 billion." The president said that "up to" could mean anything, but that "roughly $35 billion" would be at least $33 billion, an acceptable outcome to him. And the education tax cuts had to help families "pay for education," not "save for education." We could not let the tax writers turn the education tax cuts into an IRA. Finally, our education money had to be directed to the postsecondary level and not be made available to fund secondary school vouchers, which were anathema to Democrats.

As Erskine and I were leaving, the president asked what time we thought we would finish. The meeting was scheduled to start at 9:45 a.m., so I said we'd return around 11:00. It was exactly right to the minute, but off by twelve hours.

LOTT, GINGRICH, AND Armey were waiting for us in the Dinosaur room. They began by passing out a new document. They were no longer using ours. We would have to cross-check everything; this was going to take a while.

On the front page of their sheet was the key political issue—the separate budget and tax bills that would have Congress balance the budget before giving tax cuts. We told them this was a "drop dead" issue for the president. I went through the list of safeguards to ensure they would not get screwed. We were working in good faith to enact the agreement, and many of the president's top priorities such as the HOPE scholarship would be part of the tax bill that everyone wanted passed. If the president or anyone else tried to play games with the tax bill, the Republicans had all our spending initiatives to hold hostage in the appropriations bills that would come later. The three men took this all in but were still very worried. It was not really an issue of the Byrd rule being used to kill the entire bill, they said. Their fear was that the Byrd rule would be used to knock out provisions like capital gains or the estate tax.

Gingrich and Armey were still seeking some kind of assurance, so I offered up new language for the agreement: "the two-bill approach would depend on good faith efforts by all parties to assure the success of this legislative outcome." This was code for our concession that they could wrap the bills together if they were about to get screwed on the tax bill, as they could do in any event. Gingrich tweaked the words a little, and they accepted it. The big political issue that could have killed the agreement was resolved. There would be many more hours of haggling with billions of dollars and important policies at stake. But the political and procedural foundations of the agreement were still secure.

THE FIVE OF us proceeded through the administration's list of protected initiatives. Almost every item invoked a marvelous speech from Lott or Gingrich, and they were gifted speechmakers. In the confines of the room, they had license to be both direct and blunt, but in a good-natured way. We had all heard each other's talking points many, many times, but the freedom to let it rip added a wonderfully comic and relaxing feel to these critically important deliberations. Erskine and I disagreed with virtually everything they threw at the wall and would respond in kind. But the back-and-forth was actually productive. The discussion was proceeding at two levels; one was how they really felt about some of our "shit," but the other, and ultimately dominating, level was what each of these responsible leaders knew had to be done to carry the budget agreement. The rhetoric was the salve they applied as they agreed to protect many of our policies with which they strongly disagreed.

But the president's national service program was not one of those. Lott went off about what a total waste of money the program was, claiming it was ineffective to boot. His guys hated it, and he would not lend his name to support it. He admitted that his liberal members would break with him, and the president would get his money in the end, but he was not going to protect the program. The Republicans leaders were dug in.

Then on to other programs they did not want to protect—some of the vice president's environmental initiatives, Amtrak, mass transit, energy conservation, Goals 2000 in education. We gave on Goals 2000 in exchange for the president's "America Reads" program.[6] The five of us were getting deeper and deeper into the detail, at a level that was beginning to have no meaning to the three Republican leaders. We started throwing issues to staff in another room and out to policy people by phone.

We had been at it all morning. Domenici and Kasich had been in and out of the room intermittently, pacing like expectant fathers worried the doctors were going to screw up. There was tension written all over Domenici's face. He wanted to convene his committee to begin marking up the budget resolution. He and Lautenberg were up to speed and ready to go. But he knew he had to wait until we were finished. To Domenici, it was always important to get it right. He was worried that the agreement on which he had been so instrumental might slip through his leaders' fingers. Right before noon he came in and said, "I want to shake everyone's hand and wish you all good luck and hope we can get this done." It was straight from the heart.

Kasich was jumpy. The day before, he had announced a House Budget Committee meeting at 2:00 p.m. to consider the budget resolution that would memorialize our agreement. But it was evident that our meeting with the leaders would not finish by then. The best he could do was to take these decisions, plug them into the rest of the agreement, and convene the committee late at night. The pressure was showing; he was pacing, a little threatening, but mostly feeling helpless and worried. He had put all of himself into this agreement, and like Pete Domenici, did not want others to fail him.

WE WERE FORCED to break at midday to brief Senate Democrats on the agreement. We were back at the Speaker's office by 2:00 p.m.

When we reconvened, Lott was still upset about associating his name with this bundle of protected programs. He did not mind the administration getting the money; he just did not want to be singled out as the guarantor of all these policies he didn't like. We suggested he could remove his name if the three leaders would agree to a simple declarative sentence as part of the agreement: "Funds will be provided at the president's level." He agreed. He was on the hook, but not personally identified as such.

Next was the critical issue of the tax letters. Erskine went through our requirements for the two letters. By this point the Republican leaders were becoming extremely exercised. They agreed to the president's education proposals being funded at "roughly $35 billion." But that was it. They would not agree that the funds should be used exclusively for postsecondary education; nor were they about to rule out the creation of an education IRA. Gingrich was headed toward a sit-down strike. He said we could keep asking and asking, but he was done giving. He said that he would not agree to a single item more, even if it meant no deal. He seemed convincing, and as our concern started to show, he winked. But he was close to being tapped out.

Erskine and I phoned the president, seeking his permission for a "take it or leave it" offer to close out the negotiations. We told him that on our domestic priorities, we had everything we needed, but the Republican leaders absolutely refused to protect the funding for national service. The president said he was willing to leave it out of the protected package and do our normal digging in and fighting in the appropriations process. But we would have to lock in the "roughly" $35 billion to pay for postsecondary education.

Erskine and I reconvened with Lott in the Dinosaur room and we laid out a compromise. He did not balk but he did want to talk to Gingrich. When he returned a few minutes later with Gingrich, it was clear the Speaker was not a happy camper. He agreed to sign the letter, but he vowed he would work actively with Charlie Rangel and other House Democrats to use some of the education money for poor urban elementary and secondary schools and then he would watch us try to oppose our own Democrats. We said that if there were such an effort, we would look at it. We did not say that our real concern had been vouchers.

We were done. It was past 6:00 on May 15. It had taken nearly two weeks beyond our original Friday, May 2 announcement to reach a level of agreement that would allow the congressional budget resolution to proceed (see table 8-1).

White House press secretary Mike McCurry kept calling, wanting to get the jump on the announcement, but we asked him to wait. We had not yet met with House Democrats. Our internal politics were more important at this point than the public announcement. Mike understood. He was a consummate professional and a vital part of the White House team. As press secretary, he found a way to both befriend and win the respect of a very tough Washington press corps, making him doubly productive for the White House.

Erskine returned to the White House. Jack Lew and I went to brief the Democratic members of the House Budget Committee. Our agreement would

Congress of the United States
Washington, DC 20515

May 15, 1997

The Honorable William J. Clinton
President of the United States
The White House
1600 Pennsylvania Avenue, N.W.
Washington, D.C. 20515

Dear Mr. President:

We would like to take this opportunity to confirm important aspects of the Balanced Budget Agreement. It was agreed that the net tax cut shall be $85 billion through 2002 and not more than $250 billion through 2007. We believe these levels provide enough room for important reforms, including broad-based permanent capital gains tax reductions, significant death tax relief, $500 per child tax credit, and expansion of IRAs.

In the course of drafting the legislation to implement the balanced budget plan, there are some additional areas that we want to be sure the committees of jurisdiction consider. Specifically, it was agreed that the package must include tax relief of roughly $35 billion over five years for post-secondary education, including a deduction and a tax credit. We believe this package should be consistent with the objectives put forward in the HOPE scholarship and tuition tax proposals contained in the Administration's FY 1998 budget to assist middle-class parents.

Additionally, the House and Senate Leadership will seek to include various proposals in the Administration's FY 1998 budget (e.g., the welfare-to-work tax credit, capital gains tax relief for home sales, the Administration's EZ/EC proposals, brownfields legislation, FSC software, and tax incentives designed to spur economic growth in the District of Columbia), as well as various pending congressional tax proposals.

In this context, it should be noted that the tax-writing committees will be required to balance the interests and desires of many parties in crafting tax legislation within the context of the net tax reduction goals which have been adopted, while at the same time protecting the interests of taxpayers generally.

We stand to work with you toward these ends. Thank you very much for your cooperation.

Sincerely,

Newt Gingrich
Speaker

Trent Lott
Senate Majority Leader

PRINTED ON RECYCLED PAPER

be going to the committee the next day—John Kasich was in a hurry. John Spratt had done a good job keeping his colleagues up to speed. It was all business; the time for speeches had passed. I went through the tax letters, and Jack covered the rest of the agreement, provision by provision in a clear and concise way. In an hour they were satisfied and ready to go forward. It would

Table 8-1. *Deficit Reduction in the Congressional Budget Resolution*

Billions of dollars

Deficit reduction	2002, projected	Five-year total
Discretionary		
Defense	-28	-77
Nondefense	-32	-61
Mandatory		
Presidential initiatives	6	31
Medicare	-40	-115
Medicaid	-6	-14
Other mandatory	-19	-40
Net tax reductions	21	85
Total policy changes	-99	-190
Debt service	-7	-14
Total deficit reduction	-106	-204
Resulting surplus	1	

Source: Senate Budget Committee Republican Staff Table, May 15, 1997.

be an all-nighter for the staff to conform the budget resolution to our agreement, but we were ready to go.

Back with the staff of the Republican negotiators, everything was falling into place. I returned to the White House. It was eleven o'clock, just as we had told the president.

THE NEXT DAY, the House Budget Committee reported a congressional budget resolution enacting the bipartisan agreement by a vote of 31 to 7. On Monday, the Senate Budget Committee reported the budget resolution by a vote of 17 to 4.

CHAPTER NINE

The Center
Must Hold

With passage of the budget resolution by both budget committees, the next challenge would be to hold the budget agreement together on the floors of the House and the Senate. In both Houses of Congress, however, powerful interests and players were intent on opening up, recutting, or defeating the bipartisan agreement.

The first major test of the agreement would come on Tuesday, May 20, when the full House took up the budget resolution. But we were already running into trouble. In the House, the Transportation Committee under its powerful chairman Bud Shuster was intent on driving a truck through the agreement.[1] Despite the large chunk of money put aside for transportation as part of the agreement, these highwaymen and their large band of allies wanted to recut the deal. They wanted money, and lots of it.

If the highwaymen prevailed, we would have a disaster on our hands. A victory for Shuster would be a signal for others to come calling for their money. And those who were flat out against the agreement could play political games, piling on to cripple it. I called John Kasich and asked for his assessment. At that point, he said the Republican leadership felt they could defeat the amendment.

Meanwhile, we had other problems in the Senate. Contrary to earlier representations, the committee-reported budget resolution left open the option to combine the tax and spending bills into one. The Republicans confessed that Lott had intervened at the last minute to have the provision inserted. He was fearful that otherwise the Democrats would use the Byrd rule to defeat specific tax provisions, notably the Republican-proposed cuts in the capital gains and estate taxes. Of course, if partisan warfare broke out, the Republicans could kill the president's HOPE scholarship and his other policies. But they did not need the Byrd rule to do that. They were the majority. Lott's problem with the Byrd rule was that it would empower the Democratic minority.

Lott's fears were off base. We were equally desperate to disarm the Byrd rule. The Democrats' best leverage was the president's ability to veto a stand-alone tax bill. But if the Byrd rule weren't waived, the Republicans would not separate the tax bill from the rest of the budget. It would come to the president all tied together, and that package would be much harder to veto. The best solution was to have Daschle and his policy director Larry Stein work from the inside on getting the Byrd rule waived. If it could be done, they would know how.

TUESDAY, MAY 20, 1997

The White House meeting with the bipartisan leadership the morning of Tuesday, May 20, was the first since February 11, when the nation's elected leaders had gathered in the President's Room just off the Senate floor to make a first tentative reach across the aisle. The five task forces that had been conjured up on the fly that day had never materialized. Instead, with the exception of Dick Gephardt, our bipartisan team had been working together for more than three months to achieve a real agreement to balance the budget.

The president thanked all those gathered for their extraordinary efforts. He said that many hurdles still needed to be crossed to bring the agreement to completion and asked everyone to dedicate themselves to the common goal. Then he went through a laundry list of legislative issues on which both sides should work together: ways to address gang violence and youth crime, implementation of the chemical weapons convention, granting most-favored-nation trade status to China, taking a run at campaign finance reform, expanding NATO to include more Eastern European nations.

Gingrich went next, mentioning an op-ed by columnist E. J. Dionne that had raised the possibility that Clinton would veto the tax bill.[2] Gingrich said that if that perception took hold, it would be harder to have two separate bills. And he said the Byrd rule was a still a problem in the Senate.

Lott was excellent, saying that the agreement had been worth all the hard effort. But he warned that we had to be careful not to let it unravel or ask it to carry more weight than it could bear. The budget resolution would soon be on the Senate floor for up to fifty hours of debate and amendment, and Lott was asking Democrats to help in defeating killer amendments. Daschle responded that he felt there would be eighty votes in the Senate for the agreement.

Gephardt said there would be good support in the House for the agreement. Nonetheless, we knew from Gephardt's staff that he would oppose the budget resolution. He would state his concern about the tax cuts being skewed toward the wealthy—a fair criticism. But he would also argue that the agreement was not based on firm numbers and did not do enough to deal with the nation's long-term problems. He had no standing to make that criticism. But in this meeting with the president and the congressional leaders, he kept his intentions to himself.

AT THE HOUSE Democratic caucus later that day, Gephardt was more open, stating his opposition to the agreement. But he said he expected a majority of Democrats to support it. He urged every member to do what she or he thought was right. His remarks were as muted and fair as the administration could have hoped. Following Gephardt, Spratt made an excellent case for the agreement, aided by his command of the details.

In the Senate caucus, Daschle did his normal excellent job of presenting the highlights of the agreement and urging his colleagues to support it. Paul Sarbanes, Tom Harkin, and Paul Wellstone expressed principled worries about the tax bill. The bottom line, however, was that the caucus would vote overwhelmingly for the agreement.

The White House team kept up our outreach throughout the day, with Erskine seeing the Blue Dogs, while the budget team and legislative affairs staff briefed friends and fence-sitters alike. The New Democrats were on board; the members of the Hispanic Caucus were grateful for our efforts on the immigrant provisions but, like the Black Caucus, had heartfelt concerns about what they perceived as the rightward tilt of the agreement.

Kasich was calling. They were in trouble on the Shuster transportation amendment. It added $12 billion for transportation, paying for it with an across-the-board cut in discretionary spending. If the amendment passed, it would undermine the president's initiatives, as well as destroy the delicately crafted compromises reached in the bipartisan negotiations. And Shuster was out to win. He was exerting maximum pressure on Republicans and Democrats alike. He was going beyond twisting arms. He was directly threatening loss of funding for members' transportation projects, including those already announced or under way. It was about as hard a hardball as was ever practiced.

We had a lot of ground to make up. Kasich and the Republican leadership said they would press House Republicans to oppose the Shuster amendment.

We deployed the entire White House legislative affairs office in an effort to rally Democrats against the amendment. Being in the minority, Democrats were already on shaky ground in getting Shuster to fund their projects. This vote could be the death sentence for a legislator's favored transportation project. Then there were other Democrats who favored the chaos that a budget meltdown might produce. This was their opportunity.

Coming up on midnight, the news was not good. The Republican leadership was asking for one hundred Democratic votes against Shuster. Our early guess was that we could supply sixty to seventy, but that was turning out to be optimistic. The Blue Dogs and New Democrats were with us in concept, but their projects were being directly threatened. Virginia's Jim Moran said that Shuster was threatening the new Wilson Bridge over the Potomac if he opposed his amendment. After several hours of all-out effort, we had about thirty Democratic votes.

Even as our team kept working the votes, we started to consider fallback positions. The House might have to rise, a parliamentary maneuver to suspend consideration of the bill that would give both sides more time to mobilize their votes. That would be risky business at best, and our side would be seen as losing momentum on the overall deal. We also discussed returning the bill to the House Rules Committee, which could then write a new rule that would allow the full House to consider alternative amendments that might let members vote for a less damaging provision and against Shuster. But, in truth, that would not work since any new amendment or vote would be viewed completely in the context of Shuster's amendment.

At 1:15 a.m. the Speaker called. They were only doing "fair." He wanted to know how many votes we could provide. A hundred? No way, out of the question was the honest reply. We'd be lucky to get fifty Democrats—even if the Speaker made some sort of public pronouncement that he would do all he could to protect their projects. He told me he was considering putting the bill into suspended animation by having the House rise. It would be an extraordinarily high-profile move and a clear indication that Shuster's amendment was about to carry. And this was a big enough issue and a big enough number that it would be difficult to toss out in the conference between the two houses, where differences between the versions of the budget resolution would be resolved.[3] If that was our last resort, the conference report on the budget resolution itself could well be voted down.

I told the Speaker that the White House was continuing its full-court press to maximize Democratic votes, but fifty would be a big lift from our side. It was clear that the Speaker felt the budget agreement was in peril.

At 1:30 a.m. our team had thirty Democratic votes in hand, about twenty leaning in our direction, and about twenty members we had not yet been able to reach. It was slim pickings, but it looked like we might round up fifty Democratic votes.

But then in an emotional Republican caucus, Gingrich and the rest of the Republican leadership turned large numbers of votes. The argument was simple and compelling. Republicans could stay true to the promise to balance the budget, which was a centerpiece of their successful campaign to gain control of the House, or they could demonstrate that "pork-barrel spending" was more important than principle. There was hope.

All sides kept working until the critical vote. Shortly after 3:00 a.m., the Shuster amendment lost by two votes. The vote had been gaveled down and brought to a close as members were starting to reconsider their brave stance against the powerful chairman of the Transportation Committee. The Republican leadership had gone beyond the extraordinary and won. Through their responsible actions and that of forty-eight Democrats, the agreement had been pulled back from the brink.[4] In the next moment, the House was voting on final passage of the budget resolution, which carried by an overwhelming vote of 333 to 99. The final tally affirmed our strategy of finding and defending the middle. Seventy-seven percent of the House had supported the budget resolution. On the Democratic side, 132 voted for the agreement—nearly two to one in favor. [5]

WEDNESDAY, MAY 21, 1997

The budget resolution had survived the House. Now it was testing time in the Senate. Democratic senator Ted Kennedy of Massachusetts and Republican senator Orrin Hatch of Utah were intent on offering an amendment to raise the cigarette tax by forty-three cents a pack, bringing in $30 billion of revenue to be used for two things: $20 billion to expand children's health coverage, and $10 billion to reduce the deficit. The substance of the amendment lined up perfectly with White House policy preferences, but its passage could undermine the bipartisan agreement. The White House would have to help defeat it.

No other administration in history had fought harder against tobacco and its harmful health effects. The tobacco tax would discourage smoking by making it more expensive. And the proceeds would be put to a marvelous use. The bipartisan budget agreement would provide health coverage to five million children; Kennedy and Hatch were claiming that their proposal would cover another five million kids, putting America within shouting distance of universal health coverage for its children.

When the Kennedy-Hatch proposal had surfaced two months earlier, there was no way it could have been included in our deliberations. Lott was flatly opposed to the tobacco tax. And Kennedy had consistently declined our offer to work together. Now Hatch and Kennedy were lying in wait, ready to throw a bomb that could wreck the bipartisan agreement.

Our health experts had analyzed the Kennedy-Hatch proposal, and they had doubts that it would work as intended. Our own kids' health initiative had stretched the envelope in extending coverage. Beyond the first five million additional children, the cost per child of extending health coverage started to skyrocket. America had neither a universal mandate for health coverage nor the infrastructure to fund it. Providing full coverage of America's children (never mind adults) would require a major restructuring of the U.S. health care system, and that was not on the table.

The other problem came from the nature of the budget resolution. We had protected the president's policies as part of the negotiation. But if the Kennedy-Hatch amendment passed, it would not be binding in its specifics on the Finance Committee. Passage of the amendment would simply instruct the committee to raise $30 billion more of revenue, and spend $20 billion of it. There was no telling what that might mean to the carefully crafted budget agreement. The tax agreement between the congressional leaders and the White House would be superseded, with uncertain effect.

Our first choice was to avoid the fight all together. If Kennedy and Hatch would just stop trying to screw up the budget agreement, the administration would be happy to help them in the future. And with the White House out front, their measure would have a good chance of being enacted. We offered Kennedy and Hatch a "reserve fund" that cleared numerous procedural hurdles for a separate bill in the Senate, in effect disarming the normal points of order against a bill.[6] But they weren't taking. This was their hour, and they were going for it.

We were hurting on the vote count. Daschle was up for reelection in 1998, and he wanted to be squarely behind this initiative on extending health coverage. And, of course, Lautenberg was with Kennedy and Hatch all the way. He was against big tobacco every time. That left us to try to scrape together enough Democratic votes to help the Republicans defeat Kennedy and Hatch.

Lott phoned and said he needed eight Democrats to defeat the amendment, but we felt he was upping the ante to be safe. We had three Democrats from tobacco-growing states who could be counted on to oppose the proposal—Senators Chuck Robb of Virginia, Wendell Ford of Kentucky, and Max Cleland of Georgia. And then there was John Breaux, wanting to do all he could to support the budget agreement. I called Breaux and asked for his help. He would check with members of the Finance Committee.

The Kennedy-Hatch amendment directly endangered the budget agreement. If it passed, the Republicans might take a walk on supporting the budget resolution. If we were lucky, the White House could stay in the background and let the amendment fail. But, of course, that was exactly what Lott was not going to let happen. Saving the agreement meant we would have to stand shoulder-to-shoulder; the White House could not take a pass and leave the lifting to Republicans. Lott was on the Senate floor calling the amendment a deal killer and demanding that the White House come forward in opposition.

At the same time, Kennedy's people were putting out the false claim that the vice president was coming to the Hill to lobby in favor of their amendment. Usually they were more subtle and more substantive. This was a frontal assault intended to put the White House, and particularly the staunch antitobacco vice president, under pressure and in political harm's way. Ron Klain, Gore's chief of staff, was calling. "John," he said, "I have two words for you: no tie." Ron was one of the most capable people in the White House and a staff veteran of the Senate. He knew the vote on the amendment could be awful for the vice president. The worst case would be a tie vote, with the vice president's vote needed to defeat the Kennedy-Hatch amendment. The vice president, who had lost his sister to lung cancer, was the administration's most ardent advocate and leader on the tobacco issue. Voting against the amendment to break a tie vote would force him to go against his core beliefs. I gave Ron the vote count. It looked like we would be all right—I hoped.

After returning to the White House, I met with Erskine and the president. Clinton had already heard from Lott who wanted him out front in opposition. The president had done the right thing, telling Lott that he favored the Kennedy-Hatch amendment but understood that it could unravel the budget agreement. He would oppose Kennedy-Hatch to keep the agreement together. We briefed McCurry, who would deliver the message to the White House press corps.

Lott wasn't wasting any time. He went to the Senate floor and announced the president's opposition to the amendment. It was a smart move to shift opposition from Senate Republicans to the White House. Soon the calls from our Democratic friends and allies were coming in. They all wanted to know the same thing. What the hell were we thinking? Either they were not aware of or they did not care about our obligation to hold together the bipartisan foundation of the agreement. The House Republican leaders had delivered a nearly unbelievable defeat of Shuster's transportation amendment. They had been true to their word, and we were going to be as well. We were out of stealth mode and into the open. The White House staff—the one that had just worked through the night to help defeat Shuster's amendment—was running flat out again.

Senator Breaux was making progress. He had Senator Joe Lieberman of Connecticut leaning in our direction. Frank Raines phoned in offering to help lobby—he took five senators. Then the president called. I asked him to talk to Senators Dan Inouye and Dan Akaka of Hawaii, and Herb Kohl of Wisconsin. These were Democrats who would always listen and try to be helpful.

Then back to the Hill where I found Bill Hoagland. He had good news— the Republican leadership was ready to vote. Lott had pulled back several Republican cosponsors of the Kennedy-Hatch amendment. The White House could call off its troops. In the end, eight Democrats voted against the amendment, and a handful more would have answered the call but were not asked to.[7] The agreement had been pulled back from the abyss a second time in less than twenty-four hours.

FRIDAY, MAY 23, 1997

By midday Friday, the Senate was ready to pass the budget resolution. The tally was 78 to 22. The Senate percentage in favor was nearly identical to that of the House. But the composition was different. In the Senate, 82 percent of the Democrats (thirty-seven out of forty-five) supported the agreement, compared with 64 percent in the House. The difference showed the power of the leadership in both bodies—Gephardt had opposed the agreement, while Daschle had helped push it through.

The few remaining disagreements between the House and Senate versions would be quietly and quickly worked out in conference. With our budgeteer allies controlling the action, we were confident that the conference report on the budget resolution would be passed in both houses after the upcoming congressional recess.[8]

CHAPTER TEN

The Challenge of
Reconciliation

With the outlines of the bipartisan agreement memorialized in a congressional budget resolution, Congress and the Clinton administration now faced two parallel challenges. The first was shepherding the passage of thirteen different appropriations bills in each house. The House and Senate Appropriations Committees would take the pot of money made available for discretionary spending and divide it up among their subcommittees. Each subcommittee would then be responsible for writing a bill that allocated its share of the total among the programs under its jurisdiction.

The second task was the challenge of reconciliation, which dealt with mandatory spending and taxes. As part of this process, two massive pieces of legislation needed to be enacted.[1] The first would reduce spending on entitlements, such as Medicare; the second would cut taxes. The leading parts in this process would be played by the House Ways and Means Committee and the Senate Finance Committee. But other authorizing committees, such as the House Committee on Energy and Commerce, which had jurisdiction over Medicaid, would also participate in reconciliation.

The appropriations and reconciliation processes would proceed largely on separate tracks. But passage of the reconciliation bill was crucial because it would legislate the maximum amounts that the appropriations committees could spend in defense and nondefense programs over the five years of the budget agreement. That would ensure that the savings achieved in discretionary and mandatory spending would be large enough both to fund the tax cuts and to achieve the goal of a balanced budget.

This year the reconciliation process would be particularly difficult. Reconciliation is never easy because it involves hot-button issues like entitlements and taxes, but the efforts to achieve a bipartisan solution that could win the support of all four congressional caucuses made the challenge even greater. While the budget agreement had the blessing of the president and three of the four top congressional leaders, only a small group of individuals had participated in its negotiation. This was a top-down deal agreed to in a short period of time. And while Congress had broadly endorsed the principles on which the agreement rested—a balanced budget, tax cuts, and public investments—the players who would be so critical to the reconciliation process had not yet bought into the specifics of the agreement. Many of them would be more than happy to go off on their own, deciding which spending got gored or whose taxes got cut.

To get the reconciliation measures enacted, it would not be enough to wave the bipartisan agreement and demand an appropriate final product. That is not the way Congress works. The White House and its allies would have to reach out to key players and congressional power centers. We would have to quickly engage the subcommittees, committees, caucuses, and influential members whose actions would determine the fate of the balanced budget agreement.

This was particularly true because "must-pass" pieces of legislation such as this were attractive vehicles for all sorts of passengers, many unwanted. The possibility of hitching a ride on a major piece of legislation that the president and key congressional leaders were intent on enacting was extremely attractive for those with a special ax to grind. A significant part of our work would be to hold off and pry out all those poison pills.

THE WHITE HOUSE approach was to make contact and engage at every level, letting our positions and oppositions be known to key members and staff at the subcommittee, committee, and leadership levels. No one would be surprised by where the White House stood on anything. We were committed to making incremental progress wherever and whenever possible. If an issue could be resolved at a lower level, that would leave less lifting as we moved up the chain of command.

A tremendous amount of activity was going on at the staff level between the White House, OMB, Treasury, and other cabinet agencies on the one hand and Congress on the other. Both sides had an amazing amount of expertise. And since most of the administration's policy experts had Hill experience, they could draw on their relations with Democratic and Republican Hill staff—particularly in the committees and leadership—to identify and solve problems. To facilitate this task, the White House staff deployed to the Hill had wide leeway to make decisions and commit the administration to positions.[2]

THURSDAY, MAY 29, 1997

Treasury was reporting that Ways and Means Republicans had not yet agreed to a tax package to be marked up in committee. But this report could not be trusted; Ken Kies, the chief of staff of the congressional Joint Committee on Taxation had not attended his staff's briefing to Treasury. Kies would know exactly what Ways and Means chairman Archer and Speaker Gingrich were thinking; he was their go-to guy, their taxman. It was time to go to him.

Ken Kies and I had been through some pretty tough spots together. Most significant, we helped put together the CBO-certified budget that allowed the government to reopen on January 6, 1996. At the time, both parties wanted to wave the white flag and disengage from the failed negotiations. But they could not bring themselves to just blow the whistle and walk away. That would have left too many hard questions, the principal one being, "You guys put the country through all this for what?" It had been better to call a tactical retreat, one that opened the government but also seemed to assure the public that there was a road map for breaking the budget impasse. The plan we put together would have been that road map—if politics, personalities, and sheer exhaustion had not overtaken the participants. Ken, Bill Hoagland, Sue Nelson, and I all knew that our bipartisan compromise wasn't real; it was a front to let the nation move on and allow our elected leaders to accept defeat without declaring it.

Now in 1997, Ken started our meeting by asking for forbearance when Archer's opening proposal was made public. There would be elements we would not like. Not only would it reduce the capital gains rate from 28 percent to 20 percent, but it would also index capital gains against inflation and tax only the gains on qualified assets that exceeded the rate of inflation. In a smart and constructive recommendation, Ken urged us to leave a big gap between our capital gains position and the Republican one. They needed to show they had gotten more than the president wanted. If we were too generous up front, it would be harder to bring their guys back to something both sides could accept. The Republican taxman was urging the White House to lie low on capital gains.[3]

ACROSS THE AISLE, Richard Gephardt was rallying House Democrats to devise a tax bill whose benefits would not be tilted so much to the rich. His concern with the tax bill's fairness was completely legitimate; the White House was worried about the same thing.[4] A reduction in the capital gains rate as well as other tax provisions on the Republican wish list—such as an increase in the value of assets exempt from the estate tax—would benefit mainly the well-to-do. In addition, an expansion of IRAs was also more likely to benefit better-off Americans. But the child tax credit, the president's HOPE scholarship, and the higher education tax deduction would largely benefit lower- and middle-income taxpayers. Improving the distribution of the tax bill was one of the reasons the White House was still tweaking the president's tax proposal, for instance by letting low-income college students who received assistance in the form of Pell grants also receive the full benefit of the HOPE scholarship. When all was said and done, however, a broad-based capital gains rate cut dominated the distribution of tax benefits. No amount of juggling could overcome that central fact.

Of course, it was easy to produce a tax bill with a better distribution of benefits simply by limiting the amount of capital gains that could be taxed at the lower rate or by providing the benefit only to those below a certain income level. There were plenty of policy levers to be pulled. The problem was that none of those fixes came close to what would be acceptable to Republicans. But Gephardt's goal, and that of his allies, was not to enact a tax bill but to show a sharp contrast to the Republican one.

BACK WITH ERSKINE, I described the meeting with Ken Kies. We would have to move quickly on Archer's proposal for indexing capital gains. We would attempt to intervene with the Senate Finance Committee to try to keep that provision out of the Senate tax bill. If it were to appear in both the House and Senate bills, it would be harder to pry out in the tax conference.

But the Finance Committee was creating its own uncertainties. The Kennedy-Hatch proposal to increase the tobacco tax to pay for child health care could resurface there. With Republican senators Hatch, Jim Jeffords, and John Chafee in favor, they could join with Finance Committee Democrats to roll Lott and include the provision. Depending on Lott's reaction, we could be in a crisis again.

MONDAY, JUNE 2, 1997

Treasury produced an analysis of the tax proposals in the president's budget, Archer's bill, and the plan we were considering shopping as our negotiating position. The results were sobering, attributable almost entirely to the effects of the capital gains tax cut. The tax bill we were considering as our negotiating position gave 40 percent of the benefit to the top 20 percent of income earners. That was double the amount in the president's original tax proposal, but far less than the 68 percent going to the top quintile under Archer's bill.

TUESDAY, JUNE 3, 1997

Meeting with Ken Kies the next morning, I gave him an overview of the Treasury's distributional analysis. Archer's tax plan was heavily tilted to the wealthy. Ours was a lot better but would still draw heavy fire from Democrats. I told him the president would agree to a lower capital gains rate but would oppose indexing capital gains for inflation. Ken asked again that we not come forward with a specific capital gains proposal. If indexing were put aside, our capital gains proposal would be too close to theirs and that would incite his right-wingers to want more. His suggestion was sensible not only in dealing with Republicans, but also our Democrats.

On education, Ken said the House Ways and Means Committee would treat us better than the Senate Finance Committee. We would get the education tax credit and deduction we were seeking, but he warned we would not get as much as the Republican leaders had promised.

WEDNESDAY, JUNE 4, 1997

The Ways and Means Democrats, including Dick Gephardt, had put together a wonderful tax proposal—as a starting point. It had $31.5 billion for the president's education proposals, far better than what we were getting from the Finance Committee. On almost every one of the president's proposals, they were with us. And on capital gains, they had a creative proposal that set a lifetime limit of $1 million on gains that could be taken at the most preferential tax rate but still lowered the rate from current law for gains above the $1 million limit. It was a reasonable approach, and it had a much better distributional impact than anything else on the table. Here was opportunity knocking. This plan endorsed almost all of the president's policies and had a creatively defensible capital gains plan that also endorsed a broad-based reduction in the capital gains rate. Getting behind their plan would help us navigate the roiling political waters on taxes. We would be united with House Democrats; we could avoid putting forward our plan on capital gains; and we could buy time to produce a comprehensive tax plan designed to get an agreement in the middle.[5]

THURSDAY, JUNE 5, 1997

Meeting again with the White House group of eight, Bob Rubin and I suggested that the administration line up behind the Ways and Means Democrats' tax proposal. It was better on the merits than any other tax plan that had surfaced. It was also a big help on the politics. It increased the likelihood that House Democrats would support a bipartisan compromise, and it might be useful in pushing Senate Democrats away from the bill that was emerging from the Finance Committee. We agreed that I would go to the House Democratic caucus that morning and strongly support the Ways and Means Democratic alternative.

THE HOUSE CAUCUS was supposed to start at 10:00 a.m., but the meeting of House Democratic whips that preceded it was running late—and for the wrong reasons.[6] The liberals were dead set against the alternative tax proposal and had staged a revolt. To the liberals, the proposal was not progressive enough, nor was it sufficiently far from the Republican position. They did not see the tax proposals as we did, as part of a negotiating process to get to an acceptable bill. Those objecting were not particularly interested in getting a bill or any agreement with the Republicans for that matter. They were focused on a message of opposition and on drawing lines in the sand.

Walking into the caucus, I could see that caucus chairman Vic Fazio was upset. The Democrats' Ways and Means package was falling apart. There was no longer a proposal for the White House to support.

At the caucus, Gephardt urged his colleagues to come together around a Democratic tax proposal. But given what had just occurred in the whip meeting, he suggested that they move at a deliberate pace. In his view, the caucus should not worry about producing a proposal in time for Archer's markup of the tax bill. Archer, he argued, was rushing things and "taking a garden hose, cramming it down Democrats' throats, and turning it on full blast." Democrats should take their time—as much as was needed—to agree to a tax proposal. He was signaling two things we didn't need: a slowdown and a recrafting of the proposal that the White House considered a nearly ideal negotiating position.

Fazio announced that each speaker would have two minutes. That provoked a diatribe from liberal George Miller of California who demanded more time so each member could be fully heard. Fazio shot back at Miller, saying that a lot of members had stopped coming because certain members kept hogging the mike. That further provoked Miller, and the meeting had to be gaveled to order.

The liberals did their thing. The common procedural ploy is to demand caucus assent before going forward. Since consensus is rarely reached, it is a way to delay or stop the suggested course of action. Many Democrats were content to howl against the Republican tax and spending proposals and let it go at that.

But some of the moderates fought back. Tim Roemer directly challenged his colleagues, asking if anyone seriously believed that the president and congressional Democrats would have health coverage for five million additional children, or would have corrected the egregious provisions of the welfare bill, or would have a major new initiative in education if they had not engaged the Republicans in a negotiation. And just as we had secured these wins, Roemer said, we would do better by engaging the Republicans on taxes. He urged his colleagues to be part of the White House strategy of engagement.

FOLLOWING THE CAUCUS, Erskine, Bob Rubin, and I were scheduled to meet with Senator Lott. But before the meeting, I received a call from Dave Hoppe, Lott's chief of staff. Lott did not want Bob at the meeting.

The Republican leaders did not like Bob Rubin. The reasons were not completely clear, nor were they a total mystery. Bob and the Republicans had gotten into it during the budget battle of 1995 when Treasury creatively drew on government trust funds to keep the government afloat, thereby delaying the moment of confrontation the Republicans sought over the Contract with America budget. But most of their coolness toward Bob was a professional compliment. They recognized him to be an informed, strong, and effective negotiator, and an individual who had the complete trust of the president. But that was not the only reason for their coolness. They would wonder how a guy as rich as Bob Rubin could be opposed to a capital gains tax cut. My guess was that they did not understand just how rich Bob was. Finally, a lot of it was a matter of style, a disconnect between a taciturn Wall Street financier and gregarious southerners who tended to wear their emotions on their sleeves.

Lott's demand put us in a difficult position. Erskine and I would steadfastly refuse to exclude Bob from any meeting that had anything to do with taxes, and at this point taxes were topic number one. But the Republican leaders would perform their own kind of silent protest with Bob in the room. They would refuse to be open or, at times, to even discuss tax matters. And that's what happened at this meeting. When we raised the budget, Lott would only say that "the broad categories were in good shape." And on taxes, all he would offer was that "most of the issues could be worked out in conference." Not very helpful support for the hand-to-hand engagements we were conducting in the caucuses, subcommittees, full committees, and with individual legislators.

THE SENATE FINANCE Committee had jurisdiction over the key policies that would either make or break the reconciliation bills—taxes, health, and welfare. Fortunately for us, the current chair, Senator Bill Roth, was a gentleman through and through. Along with his very capable staff director, Lindy Paull, he always listened politely to our often long list of concerns.

On this day Bob and I were pressing Roth on two major issues: the indexing of capital gains and the potential for large and increasing revenue losses in the outyears beyond the five-year budget agreement. Knowing that Archer would include the indexation of capital gains in the Ways and Means bill, we wanted to try to keep indexation out of the Senate bill, thereby making it easier to remove in conference. And on the outyear revenue hemorrhage, we were going to the source of the problem—Roth and his beloved IRAs. Most troubling were the back-loaded IRAs.[7] Through this savings vehicle, a taxpayer could take out his entire nest egg, including all accumulated earnings, tax free in the future. Backloading was a huge revenue loser in the long run.

After hearing our concerns, Roth told us that he was trying "to develop a bill that a majority of both caucuses as well as the president of the United States could support." We would see.

THAT EVENING, KEN KIES called with an update on Archer's tax package. Archer and his supporters were proposing several changes that undermined the president's proposed tax cuts. They wanted to offset the $500 child credit with the child care deduction—if a family took the child care deduction, it would not get as big a break on the child credit. This provision, which was advocated by the stay-at-home Christian Coalition was a slap at low-income working parents who needed two incomes just to make ends meet.

On the HOPE scholarship, Archer was proposing a 50 percent tax credit for up to $3,000 in tuition payments. Fairly generous on the total, but relative to our 100 percent credit for up to $2,000, this proposal penalized those going to less expensive schools such as community colleges.

They also had a back-loaded IRA, and on capital gains, they had indexed against inflation as we feared. But their rate structure for the capital gains tax was 20 percent for taxpayers whose incomes were large enough to put them over the 15 percent rate on income tax, and 10 percent for those paying a top rate of 15 percent. Those rates were not bad, particularly if we could get rid of the inflation indexing. Archer and his allies had also cut the corporate capital gains rate. But on the estate tax, they had shown some restraint, raising the unified credit in stages over a long horizon.[8]

MONDAY, JUNE 9, 1997

The emergency supplemental appropriations bill funding disaster relief in the Midwest and Pentagon operations arrived on the president's desk with Senator John McCain's "no shutdown" provision included. We had tried multiple times to pry it out, to no avail. The president wasted no time vetoing it and pointed the blame at the Republicans. Lott and Gingrich had tired of the congressional intramurals on this one, and to their credit once again came down on the side of supporting the bipartisan budget agreement. They threw out the offending provision and quickly sent the president a clean emergency supplemental bill, which he immediately signed.[9]

THEN IT WAS back to finalizing the details in our agreement. Medicaid was still a major headache. We had used a portion of the CBO windfall to drop the per capita cap on federal payments to the states. Now we were looking for $17 billion of five-year savings that would come almost exclusively from disproportionate share hospital (DSH) payments—federal funding directed toward hospitals that served a disproportionate share of low-income and needy patients. Although funding would be reduced under our proposal, it would also be redirected to the hospitals that really needed it. But opposition was mounting. The governors had not even said thank you for dropping the plan for the per capita cap. Now they were gearing up to beat back our other Medicaid savings. Representative Tom Bliley of Virginia, who chaired the House Commerce Committee, wanted our help. He thought he could get about $12 billion in DSH savings. That would leave him about $5 billion short. To make up the difference, he proposed to jettison our plans for expanded Medicaid coverage for residents of the District of Columbia and Puerto Rico,[10] as well as the subsidies needed to offset the impact of the Medicare home health premium on poor seniors. Democrats on the committee were not being particularly helpful. Bliley asked for our help to bring several on board, including John Dingell and Bart Stupak of Michigan, Bart Gordon of Tennessee, and Tom Sawyer of Ohio.

If Medicaid was in trouble, another of our budget savings was in even worse shape— our proposal to auction off portions of the electromagnetic spectrum. The powerful broadcasters who wanted to pay little or nothing for this resource had been busy undermining this part of the agreement. In this case, Bliley's problems were not partisan: he was facing industry-funded opposition on both sides of the aisle.

TUESDAY, JUNE 10, 1997

After the previous week's caucus confrontation over capital gains, Ways and Means Democrats had responded to their liberal brethren by lowering the lifetime cap on capital gains exclusions. But they were still accepting an across-the-board reduction in the capital gains rate. Running the distribution table on their plan, we saw that it conveyed 30 percent of the benefit to the top quintile of income earners, far better than Archer's emerging plan which gave 68 percent of the benefit to this group. And on all other counts, their proposal was nearly ideal. They were funding the HOPE scholarship and had wisely loaded up the total education money well above $35 billion—a good negotiating position. The door was still open for the White House to get behind the House Democratic plan, allowing Democrats to hold together politically while setting the stage for a later compromise with Republicans.

DASCHLE HAD ASKED us to consult with Senate Finance Committee Democrats before going public with our plan. We were short on time to prepare the president for the meeting at the White House, but I was able to make the key point. Their education package provided $35 billion for education but contained a number of initiatives that reflected their priorities, rather than the president's. In particular, their plan provided only $21 billion for the HOPE scholarship program, less than Archer's.

The president began by asking Democrats to stick together and be faithful to the agreement. He criticized Archer's plan as "not being faithful to the agreement, particularly on education." He also criticized Archer's child credit as being slanted against working and low-income parents. Archer had put in not only an offset of the credit against the child care deduction but also an offset against the earned income tax credit, another hit on the working poor.

The president said $35 billon was needed for his education initiatives, and that funding for any other education priorities Democrats supported should be in addition to that $35 billion. He said he had campaigned and been elected on these proposals; it was essential, he argued, for Democrats to have a strong opening position on education.

Unfortunately, Daschle was stuck on the Senate floor, so our key ally was not there to respond. Instead Senator Moynihan led off. He commented that the committee had no problem with the emphasis on education but did not come even close to saying he would help us. It was clear from his words, and from the Democrats' proposal, that they had accepted the Republican argument that $35 billion was the most that could be spent on education.

It was a short-sighted strategy. By buying favor with Roth, they were tightening the size of the box for education. They should have been joining us in increasing the size of the education box, thereby increasing the odds that the White House would be able to protect their priorities once the tax bill reached the leadership level. Senator Jay Rockefeller of West Virginia got it and strongly supported the president's position. Then various members spoke in favor of particular policies, provoking the president to implore again that all of these good policies be added to, rather than substituted for, his proposals.

The meeting was about to break when the vice president stepped in. The president had been insistent but not tough. The vice president took a harder line, saying he was extremely disappointed that Finance Committee Democrats would dismiss the president's policies out of hand. He said it would look bad for Democrats to split with the president on his key priority of education, pointing out that the president and he had sounded these themes a thousand times on the campaign trail. It would be a political slap for Democrats to desert their president.

Moynihan reacted angrily: Senate Democrats were not "rebelling." He became flustered and bolted. The president had been given his audience. The Finance Committee Democrats were returning to the Senate—and to their underfunding of the president's flagship education initiative.

WEDNESDAY, JUNE 11, 1997

Numerous rough spots were cropping up as the spending reconciliation bill moved through the House committees. Erskine and I needed to get in sync with Speaker Gingrich. In our meeting it quickly became clear that the bonds forged during the negotiation of the bipartisan agreement were still strong. We were all intent on finishing the job.

The leaders' involvement in this process was indispensable, not only to help push the committees in the direction of the bipartisan agreement but also to follow behind and fix what the committees were unwilling or unable to get right. In the House the Speaker could use the Rules Committee to propel changes to the bill.[11] In the Senate the majority leader could put together a manager's amendment as the bill came to the floor.[12] But it was at the end of the process, when the separate House and Senate bills went to conference, that the power of the leaders was greatest. The conference report that was presented to the House and Senate required an up-or-down vote with no amendments. The conference, then, was our last chance at crafting a bipartisan bill that no one could pick apart.

On the electromagnetic spectrum auction, Bliley's committee was likely to come up about $10 billion short of what we needed, and that unbalanced our balanced budget. Given the intense lobbying effort of the broadcasters, the committee would not be able to get these savings itself. This issue would have to be fixed at the leadership level.

On legal immigrants, we had a principled disagreement with Clay Shaw, chairman of the Human Resources Subcommittee of the Ways and Means Committee. Both Shaw and the White House were trying to deal with the difficult issue of legal immigrants. The White House had chosen to cover disabled legal immigrants who were in the United States before the passage of the 1996 welfare bill, both those who were currently disabled as well as those who might become so. To pay for that, we were willing to drop from the rolls immigrants who were elderly but not disabled. Shaw had taken another route. He wanted no part of taking people off the rolls. He would cover all immigrants currently on rolls—elderly and disabled—but no more. Given Shaw's views, we tried to convince Gingrich that covering the current and future disabled as well as current elderly enrollees was the right course.

On Medicaid, the Commerce Committee was having trouble getting sufficient DSH savings, and to make up ground was knocking out our initiatives to expand coverage for the District of Columbia and Puerto Rico. But Gingrich rightly pointed out Democrats on the committee were not helping at all. John Dingell, a powerful Democrat from Detroit, was playing the outsider—possibly because he was angry with the administration's new clean air regulations that had the auto industry stirred up.

THURSDAY, JUNE 12, 1997

Since it was clear Senator Moynihan was not going to help us out, Bob Rubin and I decided to intensify our efforts with Roth. After all, we might as well deal directly with the true power in the committee. At the same time, we would continue to lobby individual Democratic senators to support a larger number for education. Finally, we would ask Daschle to use meetings of the Democratic caucus to push Finance Committee Democrats back. We would try to litigate the tax bill in caucus by forcing Finance Democrats to defend their actions in front of their colleagues.

LATER THAT EVENING Treasury received Roth's tax bill proposal, which would be the starting point for the Finance Committee deliberations. On capital gains, it reduced the top rate to 20 percent but, unlike Archer's bill, did not call for indexing capital gains for inflation.[13] The absence of indexing was great news and a major win. On the estate tax, the Roth plan raised the amount excluded from taxation to $1 million. As expected, the proposal allocated only $21 billion for the president's education program, and the remaining $14 billion had been doled out among numerous education policies that the Finance Committee members wanted. Finally, Roth had gone hog wild on IRAs, expanding existing ones and adding new ones.

FRIDAY, JUNE 13, 1997

The next day, Bob and I complimented Roth on several parts of his bill. Not only had his bill excluded the indexing of capital gains, but he had also forgone any reduction in the corporate capital gains rate. And he did not offset the child tax credit against the dependent child care credit. In many regards, his plan was superior to the Archer bill.

But on education, it was a long way from what Clinton could accept. Bob told Roth that the education package presented an "exceedingly serious problem" for the president. In addition, we had serious problems with his numerous IRA and savings plans. Although we didn't say it, he was in danger of reverting to the Bill Roth of 1981, whose tax bill had contributed mightily to nearly two decades of fiscal headaches. And here he was at the helm of the Finance Committee, proposing several key provisions whose outyear costs could be enormous.

MONDAY, JUNE 16, 1997

Nearly all the political energy was directed toward the tax bills. The Republicans were worried about a stare-down with the White House that might lead to a veto of the tax bill. Balancing the budget was an important part of their program, but in the hearts and minds of many Republicans, it was the tax cut that really counted. Appearing on the national Sunday morning TV talk shows, Senator Lott had let his worries about the tax bill come out publicly, openly expressing his anger at the president.

I went to Lott's office first thing Monday morning for a reality check. He was upset about any number of things. But his real problem was that he wanted to know what all the talk about vetoing the tax bill was. I told him I had no idea since everyone from the president on down was assiduously refraining from uttering the veto word. We had all been extremely disciplined in our language. We would say that we had serious problems with certain provisions and were at pains to express those concerns to whoever would listen. But we also said we expected those problems to be worked out and the president to sign a tax bill both parties would support. Lott's claim was simply off base. He was listening to the wrong people.

On the substance of the tax bills, I told the Republican leader that Roth's proposal was a marked improvement over Archer's bill. There were just a few items that needed to be fixed. First and foremost were the president's education policies. The Finance Committee had gone off on its own—ironically, on a bipartisan basis—and the leaders and the White House would have to repair the damage. In addition, Roth had stuck way too many IRAs and savings vehicles in the bill. Lott laughed and said, "We can get a few of those out." But he did not want to fix the bill on the floor; it would cause less controversy if it was fixed in conference or later where the leaders had maximum control. As we went along, he was reverting to the Lott we knew we could deal with—the leader who knew how to do business.

THE PRESIDENT'S POLLSTER, Mark Penn, was making the rounds inside the White House, arguing that the president should put out his own tax bill. All the press reports were focused on the Republican tax bills moving through committees, and the president was lagging the Republicans by fifteen points in being identified with a tax cut. If there was going to be a tax cut, Mark wanted the president to get the credit for it. He wanted the president to have his own plan and quickly.

No one disputed the political facts, but the issue was timing. We had intentionally delayed our own proposal in order to form a unified front with House Democrats. In addition, Daschle had asked us to forgo launching our own plan until the Democratic caucus could at least make a pass at a unified proposal for the Senate floor. We were caught between two competing objectives—to unite with congressional Democrats on their plans and to put the president out front with his own.

Gene Sperling suggested the correct strategy. We would support the Democratic alternatives on both floors, standing side-by-side with our congressional brethren. But as soon as those plans went down to defeat, we would come out with our own proposal. Our tax plan would be largely consistent with the Democratic plans but would lean toward the Republicans in order to get to the final compromise. Equally important, it would identify the president as the person with the solution to the budget impasse. Penn was happy.

TUESDAY, JUNE 17, 1997

Treasury had produced the distribution tables for the Roth plan. To our surprise, it was nearly as bad as the Archer plan. Nearly two-thirds of the benefit of the tax cut went to the top 20 percent of taxpayers. And the top 1 percent received a greater benefit than the bottom 60 percent of taxpayers. That was the kind of fact that took a minute to sink in.

The distribution was driven both by capital gains tax cuts and all the IRA provisions Roth had put in. Since low-income taxpayers already had access to a front-loaded IRA funded with pretax dollars, the major new benefits would accrue to those who could contribute to the back-loaded IRA using after-tax dollars. As well, income tests had been eliminated for some of the new IRAs, giving the wealthy another opportunity to reduce their taxes.

MEETING WITH THE Senate Democratic caucus, Bob Rubin began by saying that the president wanted to sign a tax bill, but it had to be a good tax bill. He said that the $35 billion for the president's education proposals was "a symbol of the agreement." The Roth bill was an improvement over Archer's. But despite its good aspects, it had significant problems. He noted that under the Roth proposal the top 1 percent of taxpayers got more benefit than the bottom 60 percent. Several senators asked him to repeat the statement—the distribution of benefits was so out of proportion that it astonished. The package's impact on low-income taxpayers was also disappointing. The Roth bill offset the child credit against the EITC, denying the full benefit to the working poor. And it offset the Pell grant against the HOPE scholarship. Finally, all those IRAs were likely to explode in the outyears, planting a time bomb in the budget.

Moynihan arrived late. He was protective of his committee, saying they were doing what they could to improve the Roth bill. Then he began to attack the White House. Democrats had raised taxes in 1993 and taken all the political heat. Why was the White House even considering tax cuts at this point? And he criticized the president for proposing a child credit that was not fully available to those with low incomes, even though he knew we had pushed for just such a credit in the negotiations. The next complaint was that Democratic senators should have been able to consult directly with the president on the tax bill—until he was reminded that was what had occurred the previous week at the White House.

WEDNESDAY, JUNE 18, 1997

In both houses, several committees had failed to live up to their instructions in the budget resolution.[14] Provisions not addressed by the bipartisan agreement that were anathema to Democrats had been added, particularly in the House. We were confident we could repair the damage in areas explicitly covered by the bipartisan budget agreement, but these newly added poison pills posed a significant challenge. If they were not removed or altered, we would lose a large number of Democratic votes.

Our goal was to supply up to 130 Democrats in support of the spending reconciliation bill in the House. If we were to get anywhere near that number, the Speaker would have to use the Rules Committee to correct several of the major problems. Meeting with Gingrich's chief of staff Arne Christenson, I went through the list. On legal immigrants, the Republicans had protected the elderly rather than the disabled who entered the country before 1996. On Medicaid they had failed to make the needed investments for Puerto Rico and the District of Columbia, and had failed to shield the poor from increased home health Medicare premiums. The Agriculture Committee had come up short on funding for government-financed jobs for those receiving food stamps, and the Commerce Committee was short on savings from auctioning portions of the electromagnetic spectrum. The budget did not even balance in 2002. Arne got the message. But he wanted some of the needed fixes to wait until conference. He said that the Speaker would ultimately help the District of Columbia on Medicaid, but given some Republicans' dislike of the District, it would be better to do it quietly.

Beyond this list, there were two new problems threatening Democratic support for the bill. Both were of prime concern to a key Democratic constituency—organized labor. Traditionally, labor and Democrats had been joined at the hip—on policy, politics, and campaigns. And despite the unions' decline over the years, organized labor remained an important source of money and support for Democratic candidates.

The first issue in dispute was the treatment of people on workfare, a program in which welfare recipients must work a certain number of hours to be eligible for governmental assistance. The work requirement was not the problem; the question was how demanding it should be. Under existing law, workers had to work enough to earn the value of their cash and food stamp assistance— up to a maximum twenty hours a week, rising to thirty hours over time. Now the Republicans were trying to add the value of Medicaid and subsidized housing to the sum that needed to be worked off before workfare workers could receive cash compensation. Part of the motivation was financial. In states like Mississippi with less generous benefits, the value of cash and food stamps could be worked off in fewer than twenty hours. That meant the state had to pay these workers a cash wage. By including the value of Medicaid and housing in the workfare requirement, those states could avoid a budgetary hit.

The other labor issue was more contentious and concerned the rights and protections of workfare workers. Democrats believed that they should receive many of the protections accorded regular employees, such as health and safety in the workplace, protection against discrimination, and so on. The Republicans took a much narrower view, arguing that these workfare participants were not full-fledged members of the workforce and should not receive the range of worker protections available to true employees.

As was the case with all labor issues, the politics were polarized. The full contingent of proponents and opponents was weighing in. I urged Arne to have the provisions removed from the bill. The balanced budget agreement was not the place to slug it out on these labor issues.

MEANWHILE, WE HAD absorbed a loss in the Senate. The Finance Committee had marked up portions of its bill the previous night, and Lott and the Republicans—with the help of Democratic senators John Breaux, Bob Graham of Florida, and Richard Bryan of Nevada—had defeated the Chafee-Rockefeller proposal on child health care that we had supported. The bipartisan Chafee-Rockefeller plan would have reserved the major portion of the funding for the initiative to be paid through Medicaid and left the rest to be distributed as grants to the states.[15] Instead, the committee had given the states wide leeway to design their own programs in this area. The proponents of this approach touted it as a level playing field, but it wasn't. Since Medicaid required that recipients be given a more robust range of health benefits, cost-conscious states would opt out of using Medicaid for child health coverage. Under the committee plan, there were two major problems: kids might receive a limited package of health benefits, and the states would have yet another way to channel federal funds for their own purposes.

The loss on the Chafee-Rockefeller amendment was a defeat, pure and simple. The president had publicly endorsed the amendment, and he had been beaten in a bipartisan manner. Governors across the country had prevailed on their senators to give them more control. But in relating all this to Erskine, I found that he was actually relieved by the loss. We had been winning so decisively on our key issues, he said, that our ability to work with Republicans could be hurt. He liked them to have something in their win column. And in any case, we would have the chance to revisit the issue in the quiet of our leadership negotiations.

LATER THAT AFTERNOON, the Speaker and Kasich called. They had good news and bad news. They would fix the immigrant provisions and the protection for poor Medicare seniors. But they could not get the labor provisions out of the bill.

This was bad. The issue of benefits for immigrants would be fixed at some point; it was an explicit part of the agreement. But the labor provisions were not. They were pure poison pills—potential deal busters. Labor and some of its strongest allies in the White House were already geared up for a showdown that could drive the president to veto the bill.

I suggested to the Speaker that he take the offending provisions out of the spending reconciliation bill and put them in the Labor Committee's appropriations bill.[16] In fact, he could put them in all thirteen appropriations bills if he wished. But this bill was too important for the country. Surprisingly, Gingrich had not considered this alternative. He said he would talk to Bob Livingston, chairman of the House Appropriations Committee.

THURSDAY, JUNE 19, 1997

Over in the Senate, the Finance Committee kept throwing unexpected bombs our way. In the late hours the previous night, the committee had abandoned the Part B Medicare premium for home health visits, substituting an income-tested deductible.[17] It was a ridiculous policy—it would only hit the sick-wealthy, was impossible to administer, and would do next to nothing to curb utilization. The committee had also initiated a phased-in increase in the Medicare eligibility age from the current sixty-five years to sixty-seven years. From one perspective, that was good policy. Given the financial outlook for Medicare, the increase in the eligibility age would be needed at some point. But the Finance Committee had initiated the policy in a vacuum. There was no policy to assist those who would have no health coverage as a result of the transition. People between ages sixty and sixty-five already had trouble finding affordable health insurance. This provision would just add two years to the problem. But we did not expect this provision to survive. A sixty-vote Byrd rule point of order could be lodged against the provision, and the powerful elderly interest groups would mobilize. Finally, the Finance Committee had adopted an income-related premium for all of Medicare Part B. We had been down that road before with the catastrophic health bill and had been run over by the senior groups. The Finance Committee had taken a bold step; we would see if it could be made workable—and survive.

THAT EVENING, KASICH called with another of his "good news, bad news" reports. He had Clay Shaw in the room with him. He began with the good news. They had gotten the labor provisions out of the bill. What a relief! Kasich said that Gingrich had gone through unmitigated hell for an hour and a half to turn his anti-labor guys around.

The bad news was that they were not going to fix the immigrant provisions. It would have to wait until conference. The reason was that Vice President Gore had done a press conference with some immigrant groups earlier in the day and had called the House policies "un-American." He had blasted away, getting deeply under the skin of Representative Clay Shaw, who was now so upset that he refused to fix the provision.

LATE THAT NIGHT the vice president called. He had learned that he was being fingered for blowing up the immigrant fix. He began by saying that his remarks had been cleared with my people. In fact, they had not been. I told him we would win on immigrants at some point, I just couldn't say when.

To clear up any misunderstanding, I quickly called Spratt and then Representative Xavier Becerra, the leader of the Hispanic Caucus. They both understood that the White House was with them on the immigrant provisions, and we would fix the House bill. Then I called an exhausted John Kasich around 11:00 p.m. He would not engage Shaw on the immigrants again. I would have to take it up with the Speaker; Kasich was tapped out with Shaw. But he urged me not to ask the Speaker to force the immigrant provision now: "Newt was on the edge with his caucus." Given what they had done on the labor provisions, forcing the immigrant issue now would be a bridge too far.

After I hung up the phone with Kasich, Erskine and Gene called with another bombshell: the Finance Committee had just voted to increase the tobacco tax by 20 cents a pack and use the resulting $18 billion four ways: kids' health ($8 billion), a partial restoration of the child credit for EITC recipients, a reduction in corporate tax rates, and airline ticket tax relief.[18] Ted Kennedy was upset that Hatch had gone ahead in Finance Committee and used the money for things other than kids' health.

I apprised them of our House problem on immigrants and that the fight could break into the open in the House Budget Committee markup of the spending reconciliation bill. First thing in the morning, I would talk to the Speaker and then draft a letter from the president that tried to thread the needle and keep the process going.

CHAPTER ELEVEN

House on Fire

The politics were much more polarized in the House than in the Senate where leaders Lott and Daschle were actively backing the agreement. And the all-important Senate Finance Committee was working in a bipartisan manner—even if ignoring many of the policy preferences of the president. In the House, the Republican committee chairs had largely written the reconciliation bill without the involvement or support of Democrats. Those bills deviated from the bipartisan agreement in numerous ways, including the insertion of many poison pills. The White House found itself in an extraordinarily difficult position in the House: trying to fix those bills, rally Democratic support to keep the process moving, and overcome the opposition of Democratic leader Gephardt.

FRIDAY, JUNE 20, 1997

Fridays were getting to be frantic and frightening; that's when crises seemed to come along. On this Friday, we were again staring down the barrel at one.

I was back at the White House by 6:30 a.m. after an almost sleepless night. I needed a presidential letter on immigrants that would meet two, not completely compatible, objectives. It had to reassure Democrats that the president would insist on restoring Medicaid and SSI benefits to disabled legal immigrants who had entered the country before enactment of the 1996 welfare reform bill. That was part of the bipartisan agreement, and for Democrats, it was a line in the sand. I settled on wording that would clearly be taken as a veto threat without using the veto word. At the same time, the presidential letter had to acknowledge the Republican desire to maintain the current coverage of elderly immigrants, indicating our openness to covering both disabled and elderly immigrants if the budgetary resources could be found.

When Gingrich called at 9:00 a.m., I asked if he could fix the immigrant provision in the Rules Committee. He said he couldn't. We agreed not to try a floor amendment; that would just fan the flames on both sides. I asked the Speaker for a hard commitment to fix the provision in conference—a pledge that we could quietly use to bring key Democrats around. But he would say only that it would be a key issue in conference and that he expected it to be worked out. I told him I needed to send the letter threatening a veto to the Hill and read it to him. He said, "Perfect, go ahead and send it."

THEN BACK TO the Senate. Senator Lott had previously opposed the Kennedy-Hatch tobacco provision that had just raced through the Finance Committee. What was going on? Lott's chief of staff Dave Hoppe explained that the vote count in the Finance Committee had simply become overwhelming. Sixteen of the nineteen committee members who were working to put together the package that night were in favor of the increased tobacco tax. Lott had agreed to get out of the way if the tax hike did not go above 20 cents a pack. At least we were potentially looking at another $8 billion for kids' health care, which, on top of the $16 billion already agreed to as part of the bipartisan agreement, could bring the grand total to $24 billion.

I relayed Hoppe's explanation to Erskine and Gene. There might be something else going on; we would know soon enough. But we should quickly get the White House position in public circulation: the tobacco tax should be directed toward health and children.

LATER THAT DAY, Frank Raines, Jack Lew, and I went to the Hill to meet with the House Budget Committee leaders. Although each legislative committee is responsible for the specific provisions of the reconciliation bill under its jurisdiction, the budget committees in both houses are charged with the function of packaging together all the provisions reported by other committees and voting, without amendment, on whether to send the bundled package to the entire body for consideration.

Spratt and Kasich were both pleased with the presidential letter on the immigrant provisions. Spratt excused himself to run it past Dick Gephardt and Xavier Becerra. He was back in ten minutes with good news; it had done the trick. We had a green light on the issue.

As he had the night before, Kasich stated that the controversial labor provisions had been dropped from the bill. Spratt had been careful to identify language that was objectionable to labor, including the definitions of what would be counted as the benefits to be worked off by workfare workers, as well as the limitations on the rights and protections for these workers. Based on Kasich's remarks, we thought the necessary changes had been made and we had gotten past this most politically charged issue.

SPRATT DELIVERED THE same message to House Budget Committee Democrats, when they gathered to prepare for the committee meeting to report the spending reconciliation bill to the floor. One of John Spratt's strengths was his straightforward manner. No spin, just the facts. He did an excellent job of walking through the list of outstanding issues, separating those in conflict with the agreement from those that were highly objectionable but not covered by the agreement. After his run-through, Spratt said he was satisfied with the progress that had been made on bringing the bill into compliance with the agreement and would support reporting it out of committee. The key validator in the House was on our side.

But Ben Cardin of Maryland questioned whether Democrats could increase their leverage by opposing the committee bill in unison. Wouldn't the Republicans have to make more concessions to win Democratic votes as it moved toward the floor? I strongly disagreed, stating that our best strategy was to continue what we had been doing, supplying Democratic votes to move the process along. If we abandoned that approach, the Republicans would have to pass the bill on a party-line basis. But to do that, they would need to satisfy their right wing—the very members behind all these provisions we hated. All the stuff that we and the Republican leaders were trying to get out of the bill would come back in if Republicans had to carry the bill by themselves. Supplying Democratic votes was crucial both to improve the bill and ultimately to get a bill Democrats could support.

Spratt spoke next, making the same argument. He said that if we walked away, all the bad stuff would come back in. That carried the day, and I thought we were home free. I wrote in my notebook, "Ds OK" and put a check beside it.

LESS THAN AN hour after we broke with the House Budget Committee Democrats, Kasich called. There was a big problem; he could not deliver on the labor provisions. This was the opposite of what Spratt had just told his committee members, an assurance that had been central to their support of the bill.

Frank, Jack, and I marched from the Democratic offices to Kasich's budget committee office. It was crowded with budget and legislative committee staffers. They were all wound up, and Kasich clearly was in a jam. He honestly believed he had resolved the issue. But he had not understood enough of the details to realize that people had been talking past each other. The Republicans had not resolved their labor issues and we were in trouble again.

For nearly half an hour, the conversations went back and forth. Finally, we adjourned to a private room with Spratt and Kasich and told Kasich we had just garnered Democratic votes to support the bill in committee based on his previous assurances. All Kasich could do was pledge to try to work it out by Tuesday when the bill went to the Rules Committee. If we could invent a solution by then, it could be inserted in the bill, clearing the way for passage.

After conferring with the policy experts, we came up with two possibilities. One was to start from a base of full worker protections and then preclude certain ones for workfare workers—such as family and medical leave, unemployment insurance, and the earned income tax credit. The other approach would be to apply the definitions and protections of the 1988 Welfare Reform Act.[1] It was not clear what the policies and politics of that approach would yield. We would have to work it out with both sides.

KASICH WAS CALLING, wanting to meet again. When I got to his office, Kasich was with a bunch of Republican members. Jim Talent of Missouri had been designated to carry the ball for the conservatives on the labor provisions. Mike Parker of Mississippi and Dave Hobson of Ohio, allies of the Speaker, were there to add balance.

Kasich asked me to talk to Gingrich, who was on the speakerphone. Gingrich went through some of the alternatives, suggesting that the best approach might be to go with the 1988 law. But his main message was that no matter what the issue, he wanted to work it out. He was committed to finding a solution. It was exactly the right statement and tone for his assembled colleagues—and for the White House.

After the Speaker signed off, the bipartisan budgeteers, augmented by experts on labor issues, assembled back at Kasich's office. The staffs on both sides thought we could work out a deal around the 1988 law. We agreed verbally to the main outlines of a compromise and asked the staff to write it up. Then we would run the traps on both sides. We thought we had threaded the needle again.

Half an hour later I got a page from Martha Foley. The labor fix had fallen apart. Worse still, Kasich was proceeding to the committee vote on the spending reconciliation bill, and Spratt was going to vote against reporting it from committee. After failing to track down Spratt, I reached his staff director, Tom Kahn, and pleaded for Spratt's support. In the end, Democrats Spratt, David Minge of Minnesota, and Jim Davis of Florida voted to report, while Ben Cardin and Ken Bentsen of Texas voted present. The five other Democrats in attendance voted no. Under the circumstances, we were lucky to do that well. Spratt and other Democrats were willing to put aside their misgivings at this point and look down the road, trusting we could fix the problem.

We were all disappointed and drained. But there was no time to waste. The Rules Committee would meet on Tuesday—just four days away. We had until then to come up with a solution that could be plugged into the bill, hopefully preventing a major loss of Democratic votes. I called Jack Lew and asked him to assemble a team to figure it out. We would use Ken Apfel of OMB, Tracy Thornton from my Legislative Affairs office, and Bruce Reed's Domestic Policy Council.

MONDAY, JUNE 23, 1997

Over the weekend the White House policy experts coalesced around a solution that would exclude workfare workers from certain government programs—unemployment insurance, the Social Security wage tax, family and medical leave, and the earned income tax credit. But we would draw the line on excluding these workers from coverage under the basic workplace safety and health standards, as well as the antidiscrimination laws. Even if a compromise could be found around this model, there was the difficult issue of litigating grievances and enforcing the protections. The Republicans were dead set against granting a right of private action in which a workfare worker could initiate a complaint to be adjudicated all the way up to the secretary of labor and ultimately the courts. They wanted all of the appeals to stop at the state level.

IN THE HOUSE, word of the breakdown on the labor provisions had energized the left wing of the Democratic caucus and renewed their hopes of defeating the reconciliation bill. Janet Murguia, my deputy in charge of relations with the House of Representatives, attended the House Democratic whip meeting and made the case for continuing to improve the bills by providing Democratic support. She must have given a strong performance, for shortly after the whip meeting my phone lit up. It was Gephardt's staff calling to complain.

We each knew what the other would say; Gephardt's people were not going to change our minds, and we were not going to change theirs. It was a fundamental difference of political strategy. Given this, the charge was usually reduced to, but amplified over the phone as, failing to consult. Of course, that is exactly what Janet had done, telling the Democratic whip organization exactly what we believed and what we wanted done. But that is not what consultation meant to them. It meant tell us first so we can stop you.

Our message to Democrats had been the same since the beginning. But something very important had changed. On the budget resolution, which was crafted at a high level of generality, Gephardt had given his caucus the freedom to vote as they wished, and 132 Democrats had voted in support of the budget resolution. Now we were at the stage of reconciliation, and all the objectionable policies and poison pills that had come out of Republican-dominated committees were laid bare for all to see. Although the Republican leaders truly wanted the agreement to work, they were limited in the amount of control or capital they were willing to spend at this stage. There would be less political turbulence on their side if they fixed the contentious issues in conference. But those unresolved problems opened the door for Democrats to take a walk. In skirting their own problems, the Republicans were creating bigger ones for our side.

THE GEPHARDT STAFF calls would be followed by one from Gephardt to Erskine. We needed to coordinate our response. Gephardt's key argument would be that the president would be best served by Democrats demonstrating that they could organize a veto-sustaining bloc on the spending reconciliation bill in the House. This brute political fact would gain the attention of the Republicans and convince them that they had better give the president what he wanted or face a veto that would be sustained courtesy of Richard Gephardt and colleagues. After all, that's what congressional Democrats and the White House had agreed to do to Archer's tax bill. We were beating up on that measure at every opportunity, offering a Democratic alternative and urging Democrats not to support Archer's version. We were demonstrating a veto-sustaining majority on the tax bill. Why not the same strategy on the spending bill?

This argument was off-base. Archer had gone off on his own on the tax side, but we had negotiated all the major elements of the spending bill with the Republicans and codified them in a detailed written agreement. The bipartisan negotiators had a road map, and they were working together to stay on course.

It was also crucial not to let the fringes of either party capture the spending bill. The bill had to be one that majorities of both parties could support.

If Democrats walked at this point, the Republican far right would get the upper hand, making it more difficult to reach a final agreement. And if, at the end of the day, the Republicans went back on the agreement, a presidential veto would undoubtedly be sustained. But at this stage, that was the last thing we needed to demonstrate.

Of course, Erskine and I knew that these arguments would have no impact on Gephardt. We were practicing our talking points for members in the middle—the ones who would be open to listening.

FOR AN UPDATE on the state of play in the House, I called John Spratt, who reported that the Democratic leadership was whipping votes against the bill. He estimated that unless the labor and a few other provisions were fixed, the White House would lose about half of the Democrats who had supported it on the budget resolution. To shore up our base, we scheduled meetings with the Blue Dogs and New Democrats. It was time to ask our compatriots for their support to push the balanced budget forward.

Spratt also revealed that the leadership was putting pressure on him to slow down the negotiations. We needed Spratt at an afternoon meeting with Republicans that was intended to resolve the labor issues. But Gephardt had asked him to "keep his powder dry" until a Democratic leadership meeting that evening. It was clearly a stall to weaken the chance for compromise. Monday was slipping away, and we were coming up on our last day.

THAT AFTERNOON A bipartisan group of House members and staff assembled to try to work out the labor provisions. Before the meeting, I spoke to David Hobson, the number two Republican on the House Budget Committee and a stabilizing influence on Kasich and the rest of the committee Republicans. The key participants at the meeting were to be Spratt and Cardin on the Democratic side and Talent and Shaw for the Republicans. Hobson would be the facilitator, the guy everyone knew was trying to guide us toward a solution. Whatever that group agreed to would be the compromise to be inserted by the Rules Committee.

It was a strange meeting. The key decisionmakers on the Republican side were there, but Gephardt had stepped in to prevent Spratt and Cardin from attending. Instead, we had recruited Debra Colton and Broderick Johnson, two House Democratic staff members who were expert in the subject matter but who did not have the authority to reach an agreement. Without the House Democratic principals in the room, there was no hope of closure. Monday had gotten away from us.

TUESDAY, JUNE 24, 1997

We had one day to fix all we could in the House spending reconciliation bill. Erskine and I went to the Hill to meet the Speaker, Armey, and Kasich. The toughest outstanding issues were in the labor area. We agreed to rekindle the group that would try to reach a compromise—Spratt, Cardin, Shaw, Talent, and Hobson.

It was clear that without the labor and other fixes to the spending bill, support from Democrats would be weak—limited to the moderates. Gingrich had his own problems. Before taking up a bill, the House must pass the rule that sets the conditions under which the bill will be considered, such as amendments eligible for consideration, time limits, and the like. But Republican Joe Barton of Texas and others were threatening to oppose the rule when it came up for consideration on the House floor if the Speaker's plan did not allow a vote on their budget enforcement mechanism. If they took eleven or more Republican votes with them and Democrats stayed away, the rule could fail. Gingrich said that if Democrats could supply twenty votes, they would be all right on the rule. But the Democratic Blue Dogs were indicating that their support for the rule might depend on a vote on their particular budget enforcement mechanism as well.

We told Gingrich that we could get up to 100 Democratic votes for the spending bill if we could work out the provisions on the labor issues and food stamps, as well as a provision extending SSI benefits to disabled children who were about to lose them under the tighter standards of the 1996 welfare law. Without those fixes, the number of Democratic votes would be much lower. At this point, everyone was caught in a tough situation. All the high-profile issues cut at least two ways. If the leaders tried to impose their will, the losing side would take a walk. The only way to maintain a precarious balance was to try to let the sides work it out—as we were attempting to do on the labor provisions. If they could not resolve the differences it was better not to escalate and overrule one side or the other at this stage. By appealing to members to move the process forward, we would try to slide by in the House without elevating the conflict and then trust that the leaders and the White House could fix it in the end.

I CALLED DEMOCRATIC caucus chair Vic Fazio requesting permission for the senior White House team to appear at the House Democratic caucus. He said he would seek Gephardt's assent. He advised us to have Bob Rubin go hard against the tax bill to soften them up for the sure-to-be-heated discussion of the spending bill.

We obtained a copy of the House Democratic leadership's letter used by the Democratic whips urging members to vote against the spending bill. It was quite slanted, not fully open about some of the improvements that had been made to the bill. It cited every particular deviation from the agreement, using the detailed lists of issues we had drawn up to improve the bill. The Democratic leadership was in full battle mode to deny us votes. It would be a rough caucus, but we could not win by backing down.

Gephardt and his allies had the advantage. They had been at it for several days, working hard to turn votes against the bill. Not only did they have the means to reach out to every member, but they also had a ready-made cadre of loyalists to carry their side of the argument in caucus.

HAVING LET THE whip letter and organization do much of his work for him, Gephardt could afford to be balanced in caucus. He did a wonderfully fair job of describing the conflicting approaches to the bill. He wanted a veto-sustaining majority, and we wanted Democrats to support the bill. He acknowledged that improvements had been made in the bill, but he believed it was still far out of compliance with the budget agreement. And the best way to get it back into sync was a credible veto threat, backed up by a veto-sustaining majority in the House.

Erskine responded with a strategic overview, trying to shift emphasis from specific problems to the overall game plan. He was supposed to go slowly and methodically, laying out the several stages of negotiations and building support for our claim that the bill would be easier to fix in conference if Democrats were part of the team supplying votes. But Erskine was too eager to let Bob Rubin have the podium and did an uncharacteristically weak job of getting the message out.

Bob's discussion of the tax bills was largely ignored. The House Democrats had already pocketed our opposition to Archer's bill. They wanted to beat us up on the spending bill. Around forty members spoke. The liberals in opposition had divided up all the shortcomings in the bill, taking them straight from the whip letter. The designated batters knew how to hit the discrepancies between the bill and our bipartisan agreement, as well as the poison pills inserted by those on the right.

Spratt delivered his normal fair rendition of the state of play and was followed by Marty Sabo of Minnesota, the former ranking member on the Budget Committee. But unlike in the previous caucus when he had come to the defense of the agreement, this time Sabo was only defending Spratt. He offered a passionate defense of Spratt's performance—an evaluation endorsed by everyone in the room—and said that Spratt should be free to vote as he wished. But his bottom line was that the goal of the caucus should be 145 votes against the bill—enough to demonstrate a veto-sustaining majority. It was not at all what we wanted to hear from this influential member.

The speakers continued. Most opposed the bill, but several moderates spoke in support. It was clear that the White House was at a tremendous disadvantage. The bill was still ugly at this point, and the House Democratic leadership was mobilized against us. Not only that, but if we were able to repair the damage later as we were promising, members would still have a chance to vote for the final product. They could follow their leadership now and vote against the bill, then reverse course on the conference report if we made good on our promises. Of course, getting to that stage depended on passing the bill now. But to many House Democrats that was our problem, not theirs.

I called the Republican leaders and told them we would be lucky to get between sixty and eighty Democratic votes on the bill. The White House legislative affairs team, under Janet Murguia and Susan Brophy, was lobbying nearly all of the 132 House Democrats who had supported the budget resolution. Those members were in a tough position, and so were we.

WEDNESDAY, JUNE 25, 1997

Gingrich's chief of staff, Arne Christenson, called in the afternoon. The Republican leadership had won the support of Joe Barton and his colleagues by giving them a vote on their enforcement mechanism. They would support the rule.[2] The Republicans now had enough votes to carry it without Democratic support. Arne asked us to shift our lobbying efforts to the bill itself. When the full House voted on the rule, only six Democrats voted in favor of it. The Blue Dogs felt burned at missing their chance on their enforcement mechanism and would not support the rule.

THAT NIGHT THE House spending reconciliation bill passed with 219 Republican and 51 Democratic votes. One hundred and fifty-four Democrats voted against passage.[3] Our inability to repair the labor and other controversial provisions—aided and abetted by the Democratic leadership—had set the stage for Gephardt to deliver the veto-sustaining majority we didn't want. And Gingrich and Armey had pulled their troops together with sufficient strength to pass the bill even with meager Democratic support. It was an impressive display by the leadership on both sides.

I phoned Kasich after the vote and congratulated him. He asked, "What happened to the Democratic votes?" There were two answers. First, it was those damn labor provisions. In the Senate the spending reconciliation bill had passed easily, by a vote of 73 to 27, largely because it was not burdened by those nasty labor provisions. Second, for House Democrats the path of least resistance was to stay with their leadership now but then vote for the final product if the White House managed to improve the bill. Kasich repeated my points about the labor provisions to the people in the room with him. He was still helping, already working the issue for the next stage.

CHAPTER TWELVE

Tax Tribulations

Once the House had passed its version of the spending reconciliation bill, we turned our attention back to the tax bill, which the full Senate was expected to vote on by the end of the week. In what was becoming a surreal experience, the Senate Finance Committee Democrats had bonded fully with their Republican colleagues on the committee, generalizing the pledge to stick together on the tobacco tax amendment into an oath of fealty on the entire committee-reported bill. They had temporarily, we hoped, shifted their allegiance away from the views of the Democratic president, the Democratic caucus, and the principles of good tax policy to support a committee creation whose capital gains, estate tax, and IRA provisions combined to give the top 1 percent of income earners as much benefit as the bottom 60 percent.

Despite this, the Finance Committee bill was superior to the one Archer had passed out of the House Ways and Means Committee. Erskine Bowles, Bob Rubin, and I wanted to focus chairman Bill Roth on the handful of issues that would transform the Senate bill into one the president could sign. The biggest problem was the shortfall in the HOPE scholarship and the higher education deduction. We also needed to further alter the $500 per child credit so that more of the working poor could take advantage of the benefit. And then there were all those IRAs with their exploding outyear revenue losses.

THURSDAY, JUNE 26, 1997

Meeting with Roth, Bob and I were surprised, but should not have been, to find Moynihan in attendance. It was fine with us; they both needed to hear the same things. Bob went through our list of problems with the bill, pointing to the inconsistencies with the bipartisan agreement. Roth responded that they had worked hard to produce this bill and believed it was consistent with the agreement. Moynihan recited the standard line: the bipartisan agreement had not been specific on many matters, and the committee had worked out a good bipartisan compromise.

Looking ahead to the conference on the tax bill, we urged Roth and Moynihan to include Treasury and the White House in all staff discussions. It would help clear the underbrush and we could work together to get a bill the president would sign. But they turned a cold shoulder. The Finance Committee liked doing things on its own. It was clear that the tax bill would ultimately have to be taken from the committee and resolved at the leadership level.

AFTER THE TURBULENCE of the last few days in the House, Erskine and I wanted to make sure the lines of communication stayed open with Gephardt. Even if he was not going to support the reconciliation spending bill, he needed to understand that we were determined to fix the offending provisions in that bill. If the legislation could be brought into compliance with the bipartisan agreement, he would be forced to let members go their own way.

We shared our list of problems and how we hoped to deal with them. If it came to it, we said, we would use the Byrd rule in the Senate to force the controversial labor provisions out of the conference agreement.[1] On immigrants we were in good shape since the Senate committee version of the spending bill had provisions that dealt with both the disabled and elderly. But on health care, we had a problem: Representative Henry Hyde of Illinois had attached an amendment to our kids' health initiative, stipulating that these funds could not be used for abortion services. The attempt to have the Hyde amendment dropped in the Senate got only thirty-five votes. It would be tough to get out, and we really did not want a fight over federal funding for teen abortions.

OUR NEXT STOP was Representative Archer's office: Bob and I needed to deliver the message that Archer needed to change a lot about his tax bill before the president would agree to sign it. What we found was a very happy chairman. His tax bill had just passed the House by a vote of 253 to 179, with twenty-seven Democrats supporting the bill.[2]

Archer asked us what we thought of his bill, and we had to laugh. He had not read the administration's extensive and detailed letter threatening veto—his chief of staff had read it, but Archer had chosen to ignore it. Rather than rerun the list of particulars, we appealed for full cooperation between his committee and the administration as the legislation moved toward conference. He quickly agreed to have his staff work with experts from the Treasury and White House throughout the process, a refreshing difference from what we had just heard from Senators Roth and Moynihan.

FRIDAY, JUNE 27, 1997

It had been a big week for Senate leader Trent Lott. Both the spending and tax bills had passed with large bipartisan majorities and relatively little bickering—a very different story from what had happened in the House. The Senate tax bill was passed on June 27, 1997, by a vote of 80 to 18, with Republicans supporting it 51 to 4, and Democrats, 29 to 14.[3] Not only was Lott instrumental in driving the bipartisan process, but he was able to deliver his troops. With both leaders Lott and Daschle supporting the effort, the Senate was in great shape—setting aside our troubles with the tax bill.

Of crucial importance was the appointment of conferees for the spending and tax bills. Fortunately, we and Lott were thinking along the same lines; we would control the conferences to as large a degree as possible. If our allies could resolve issues in conference, that would leave less for the leaders to hammer out in the final push.

The normal practice is to divide the conference on the reconciliation bill (or in this case, bills) into subconferences, with each dedicated to a particular subject matter, such as taxes, Medicare, Medicaid, and welfare. Each subconference would be largely responsible for working out the differences between the House and Senate versions on its particular provisions. This could get cumbersome, and Lott wisely wanted to hold the number of conferees to a minimum—two Republican and one Democratic senator for each subconference.

For a conference agreement on a bill to be returned to the House and the Senate for a vote, a majority of all the conferees must support the conference report. Even if unhappy or gridlocked subconferees opposed reporting the bill, they could be overruled if a majority of conferees agreed to report. Lott and Daschle agreed to appoint as conferees trusted Senate allies in sufficient numbers to ensure a majority vote for reporting the conference report. Gingrich would do the same in the House, ensuring sufficient Republican conferees to override any opposition from Democratic conferees. We would make sure our bipartisan group had the last say.

On the tax bill we told Lott that the Roth bill was only a few steps removed from being a signable one. We needed our education dollars and program; we needed to throttle back the IRAs to contain the outyear revenue loss. And we needed to make sure the working poor who got the earned income tax credit also got the benefit of the child credit. We spooked him a little, alluding to all the cops and teachers in Mississippi who got the EITC but who would not get the full benefit of the $500 per child credit under the Republican tax bill.

Then he returned to the tobacco tax. Lott said he hated taxes, hated the tobacco tax, and hated spending more than the $16 billion in the agreement on kid's health. But he had almost gotten run over by a "tidal wave" on the tobacco tax and had decided to "ride the crest." He said he had crafted the late-night compromise in the Finance Committee to contain the damage.

Monday, June 30, 1997

Now that the committee-reported tax bills had passed both Houses, it was time to launch the president's own tax proposal. We had three goals: to emphasize the provisions that we needed to win, to establish a negotiating position leading to a bipartisan compromise, and to put the president in front of the public on tax cuts.

The president's June 30 tax proposal was an amalgam of previous Democratic plans.[4] It was a positioning move pure and simple, and we knew the Republicans would not be particularly happy with it. We upped the ante on education to $45 billion—$35 billion on the HOPE package and another $10 billion on all those education incentives that the Finance Committee and others loved. On children's health care, we asked not only for the $16 billion in the bipartisan agreement, but also for the additional $8 billion that the new tobacco revenues were intended to fund. We threw most of Roth's IRAs out the window to staunch the outyear revenue losses. And we insisted that the working poor get the full benefit of the $500 child tax credit. Finally, we had taken Ken Kies's advice on our capital gains proposal and proposed an exclusion from taxation of 30 percent of capital gains rather than the 50 percent that the Republicans favored. True to expectations, Archer and Roth were not at all pleased with the latest tax entry proffered by the White House.

Tuesday, July 8, 1997

As we gathered to review the major issues on both the spending and tax bills, Tom Daschle was in a good mood, the result of a favorable article about him in the *New Yorker*. We were together on all the key elements, but Daschle was hoping conference negotiators could hold the capital gains exclusion to 40 percent, midway between the Republican and the president's position. We told him that would be difficult. The capital gains provision was our leverage on everything else in the tax bill because it was the number one, two, and three priority for Republicans. Not only was a lower capital gains rate a central element of the supply-side faith, but it was also a way to reward their upper-income constituency. President George H. W. Bush had made a capital gains tax cut his most important tax initiative, but his efforts had been substantially defeated by a Democratic Congress. Now we needed the Republicans to yield on six or seven key issues, and although we would bargain hard on all of them, we knew we would ultimately trade capital gains to get the Democratic wins.

Daschle asked about the role the president would play in the closing stages. The question was completely legitimate, but hit us as strange. Inside the White House we had settled into a division of labor and never puzzled over the working arrangements to which we had become accustomed. The first fact was that the president was totally engaged. He understood and authorized every major position we took. He was the boss.

In answer to Daschle, we said the president would continue to engage at the leadership level, keeping the lines of communication open, maintaining the tone and trust that were so critical for success. When needed, he would do what he had been doing so effectively for all these months—meeting with members of both parties, urging them on toward this bipartisan accomplishment. For Democrats, he was the indispensable validator and voice who promoted the agreement as part of a broad-based political strategy to move beyond taxes and budgets and into the party's core strengths in education, health, environment, and other areas.

But the president would not negotiate for several reasons. At one level, it was the nature of the office. Both Presidents Reagan and Bush stayed out of direct budget negotiations, playing the role of overseer instead. Their staffs had done the day-to-day lifting, leaving the chief executives free to take the broader view. The scope of the federal budget is enormous and the issues are complex. It is difficult for a president to be immersed in the nitty-gritty while also attending to the many other responsibilities of the office.

But that was not the issue for Bill Clinton. He knew the federal budget as well as anyone. He was a brilliant public policy president who grasped both the power and limitations of governmental action. But he would not negotiate the agreement. It was better to have the ultimate decisionmaker above the fray, one step removed from all the bumps and bruises that are part of the day-to-day engagements among strong-willed partisans. When things got rough or a change of direction was required, it was always good to be able to "take it back to the president"—giving everyone time to assimilate, think anew, and calm down.

In 1995 President Clinton had become directly involved in negotiations with the congressional leaders. For many reasons, those negotiations failed, leaving hard feelings all the way around. Erskine and I had been granted a fresh start and had built a bond of trust with the Republican leaders. He and I and the president agreed that it was better for Clinton to stick to his part and let us play ours.

Wednesday, July 9, 1997

That afternoon Erskine and I met with Gingrich and Armey. At this point, we needed more from them than they needed from us. Part of it was the length of our wish list, but part was also a result of the Republicans controlling the congressional committees. In moving their bills, they had deviated from the balanced budget agreement in significant respects while adding a goodly number of poison pills. Part of our "must have" list was to undo problems they had created.

Before convening the conferences, Gingrich and Lott wanted to get House and Senate Republicans on the same sheet. They would be ready to negotiate with us next week. It was a smart move. Both needed to fully understand how far they could move their guys before using the power of the leadership to close the deal. And even at the leadership level, Gingrich wisely wanted to keep his key players—Kasich, Archer, Thomas, and Bliley—in the loop.

We highlighted the principal areas of disagreement that would have to be resolved. On the spending bill, the most important were the labor provisions. If they emerged intact from conference, they would be subject to a Byrd rule point of order in the Senate, and we had the votes to pry them out. But they needed to come out right away, or the negotiating atmosphere would be poisoned. Gingrich was open to adding them to an appropriations bill. We didn't care as long as they were no longer part of reconciliation.[5] We also needed a structure on allocating funding under the children's health care initiative that really worked. We would not go along with giving a blank check to the governors.

Erskine went through our big items regarding the Roth tax bill. Education was a must. Second, we needed to make sure that low-income workers on the EITC received the full benefit of the child credit. Next we needed the tax incentives for cleaning up the environment, as well as the president's welfare-to-work proposals. Then there was the problem of outyear revenue losses triggered by the expansion of IRAs—Gingrich jokingly invited us to negotiate that with Bill Roth. Finally, we said the Republican estate tax provisions were too rich. Gingrich took it all well, but we were unsure if we were all using the same frame of reference—the Senate bill, rather than the House bill. So we circled back, hitting the unacceptable provisions in Archer's bill, including the indexing of capital gains and the cut in corporate capital gains taxes.

In addition, the Republican tax-writers had inserted a provision granting relief from the Alternative Minimum Tax (AMT) to small corporations. It was a smart move in a couple of ways. Not only would it help with an important constituency, but the proposal was taken directly from a previous Clinton budget proposal. Our negotiating position was that given the improved state of the economy, the corporate AMT provision was now unnecessary. In reality, our current opposition was rooted in the need to get something in return.[6]

We asked Gingrich for his list of must-wins. He had four: the $500 child credit, a reduction in the estate tax, some expansion of IRAs, and a capital gains rate reduction. He said Republicans could give up indexing of capital gains if they got the 20 percent rate for high-income taxpayers and a 10 percent rate at the low end. It was all doable if those provisions were not too rich and they met our must-have list.

THURSDAY, JULY 10, 1997

Ken Kies, chief of staff on the Joint Committee on Taxation, was the key to solving the tax bill. Archer was busy digging in and had little experience at compromise. He had been in the minority for many years, where he was marginalized and rolled by the majority Democrats. It had been Republicans alone that passed the Contract with America tax bill. And Archer was prepared to go it alone this time too; Bob Rubin was getting nowhere with him.

It was time to engage the Republican tax man. Meeting privately, Kies and I focused on the major elements of the tax bill. A new problem was staring us in the face—the promised five-year tax cut of $85 billion was down to somewhere around $60 billion. The major source of the problem was the Senate Finance Committee's decision to increase the tobacco tax. Only a portion of those increased taxes had been used to lower other taxes. Much of the $18 billion had been designated to pay for increased spending on the children's health initiative and on providing the benefit of the child credit to low-income workers who received the EITC.[7]

Ken and I focused on how the conference might play out. The staffs were wading through the second-level issues on a bipartisan basis. That process would be complete in a few days and then the crunch would come. Ken suggested that Archer and Roth make an offer on taxes that would go about 80 percent of the way to a solution. They would expect us to reject the offer, setting the stage for the next round. I told Ken I was uncomfortable with this approach. We needed to know the end game before they made their move. I urged that we figure out a solution near the final compromise with everything fitting within the balanced budget agreement, which had called for $85 billion in tax cuts over five years and $250 billion over ten years.

FRIDAY, JULY 11, 1997

On Wednesday Bob Rubin had led a discussion of the tax bill with the House Democratic caucus. Erskine Bowles, Gene Sperling, Jack Lew, Chris Jennings, and I went up to the Hill on Friday to further discuss the controversial spending bill.[8]

Erskine said the president wanted to sign both the spending and tax bills but that both bills would first have to meet his requirements. The members of the caucus actually clapped. Erskine repeated the requirements on the tax bill that Bob had been through two days before. They got all worked up again, not on the substance, but on our show of resolve and the conflict that such resolve might bring.

When Erskine finished, I went through the controversial provisions in the spending bill. I said that we expected to engage the Republicans next week after they got their act together. We would bring the spending bill into alignment with the agreement. We were down to a few issues—immigrants, SSI kids,[9] protections for low-income seniors subject to the new premium on Part B Medicare services, and food stamps. We expected to win on all of them.

The tougher list included the issues that were not covered by the agreement but that caused major heartburn for Democrats: the labor provisions, the Hyde abortion restriction, and the formula for finding our needed savings in Medicaid. Before taking questions, I addressed the Medicare issues. We did not support raising the eligibility age for Medicare to sixty-seven. We did not support co-payments on home health, but we were open on the income-related premium for Part B of Medicare, if it could be done properly. Gephardt had just concluded a press conference opposing the income-related premium. It was important to put our marker down.

LATER THAT DAY, Erskine and I followed up with Gephardt. His first request was that the Democratic conferees to the tax and spending bills meet with the president. We did not respond to him, but a meeting was not something we were about to do. Many of the Democratic conferees were the most senior and liberal Democrats in the House, and we saw no point inviting disruption in the stretch drive. Then he asked that the House Democratic freshmen meet with the president. That was something we might do.

I asked the Democratic leader how he saw the caucus voting if we delivered on bringing the reconciliation bill into alignment with the bipartisan agreement? Then it came—what we had been half-expecting given his national aspirations. He said he would oppose the tax bill but might vote for the spending bill if it turned out as advertised. Gephardt was an extremely decent human being who had led the Democratic Party and nation in many constructive and positive directions. But he had given us a red ass for six months and now he was telling us he might jump on the bandwagon. That was more than fine with us. With his support, the vote in favor of the spending bill would be overwhelming. At the end of the day, we were all on the same team and wanted Democrats both to do the right thing and to get the political credit.

We told him that our internal polling showed a twenty-five-point swing in public opinion against a member who did not support the bipartisan balanced budget agreement. He knew it was true.

SUNDAY, JULY 13, 1997

Ken Kies was calling. Archer and Bob Rubin had met on Friday, and it had not gone well. Ken said Archer was pessimistic, feeling that there was no way to get to a signable bill as long as Rubin was part of the equation. I let it go, but our opinion was the opposite. We could not get a bill without Rubin. He had simply conveyed the list of requirements we needed to get a signable bill—the same list that had been shared with the Republican leadership and Ken. Ken wanted to meet but was afraid of our being seen together by the committee staffs, even on a Sunday. We agreed to meet at his home that evening.

AT HIS McLEAN home, Ken and I were intent on solving several of the remaining tax problems—and we had a big one coming down the pike: the child credit and its interaction with the earned income tax credit (EITC). The White House mission was to allow as many of the working poor with children as possible to get the full $500 per child tax credit. After all, they needed the help the most. But the House Republican proposal only allowed the child credit to be taken against the taxpayer's income tax liability net of the EITC. Many low-income workers already had their income taxes fully offset by the EITC, and under the Republican provision there would be no remaining income tax liability against which the $500 child credit could be applied.

In the president's February budget, we had proposed allowing the taxpayer to take the child credit first against income tax liability and then apply the EITC to whatever income tax liability remained. The child credit would reduce the income tax liability, leaving less to be offset by the EITC. Our approach would not only reduce the worker's income tax liability, but in many cases it would completely extinguish it, leading to a larger EITC payment from the Treasury. Under this proposal known as "regular stacking," low-income workers would clearly be better off.[10]

The president's June 30 tax proposal had actually upped the ante even further. That proposal would allow the child credit to be taken against both the workers' income tax liability and the 7.65 percent tax on workers' pay that helps fund the Social Security system. By expanding the base of tax liabilities against which the child credit could be taken, the proposal went a long way to ensuring that all of the working poor could get the full benefit of the child credit, particularly those with several children and several $500 tax credits to take.

Ken was trying to find a compromise that was both affordable and would meet Republican political tolerances. He offered to apply the child credit against half the income tax liability and then apply the EITC. This was movement, but he remained completely unresponsive to our new proposal.

We continued through the list of issues, making some headway on the outyear explosion in the IRAs but not nearly enough. Finally, as we were nearing the end of the evening, Ken told me the good news. He had fit in $33 billion on the president's education proposals, including the HOPE scholarship. The Republican tax writer had us home free on the president's signature education initiatives. But the child credit and the outyear explosion still needed work. We would keep at it. Tomorrow was Monday.

Monday, July 14, 1997

OMB had done some back-of-the-envelope calculations of the emerging deficit outlook. The budget agreement would result in $200 billion of budget savings over the first five years— and $900 billion over ten years. Along with the improving economic and revenue projections, it now was likely that the budget in 2002 would be in substantial surplus—the first surplus the federal government had recorded since 1969. This was excellent news, something we had been quietly hoping for. If the projection proved to be accurate, we would have set the foundation to tackle the enormous fiscal problems that the retirement of the baby boomers would bring. With responsible leaders—and bipartisanship—the long-term problems of Medicare and Social Security could be addressed.

Our current worry, however, was directed to the present and what the improving budgetary situation would mean to our negotiations. The president wanted to take credit for the improving situation. After all, the Democrats-alone deficit reduction package of 1993 had been passed at a significant political cost, and he was eager for vindication. The massive deficits he had inherited would be cured during the two terms of his presidency. It was a remarkable accomplishment, achieved through a virtuous cycle of economic growth and fiscal responsibility. He and many others deserved credit.

But this was no time for a premature victory lap. After all, that good news depended on actually enacting the balanced budget bill. If we predicted a sizable surplus in 2002, the budget conferees might stop doing their work. We had almost died of good news with the CBO surprise. This death from good news would be self-inflicted. Moreover, the new OMB numbers also showed that the deficit could actually rise over the next couple of years. Just imagine the public's reaction to the announcement that the deal had collapsed because of an event we expected to happen several years in the future while actual deficits were still on the rise. Our team had been through too much to risk the deal. We would sit on the good news until we finished our work.[11]

KEN KIES WAS calling under an assumed name, an artifice we resorted to when searching each other out in settings where our cooperation was best kept quiet. Dick Morris, President Clinton's lead political advisor during the 1996 election, often used this subterfuge. Currently Dick was going under the name "Champ." It was not a particularly effective choice. Whenever one of the assistants yelled out "Champ on one," it just made everyone think something weird was going on.[12] In 1996 Dick had titled himself the prime minister. When he was trying to reach Senator Lott, a message would come in that the prime minister was on the phone for the Republican leader. When this happened in front of members of Congress, it was pretty hilarious. Which prime minister would be calling the Senate leader? It had to be very, very important. If only they had known it was the Democratic president's chief political advisor.

Speaking with Ken, I highlighted a very difficult issue we needed to finesse to make more of the child credit available to the working poor without sending his right wing over the top. The normal custom was for legislation to be scored for its direct effect on revenues or spending. The new $500 per child tax credit would directly result in less taxes being collected and was scored as a tax cut. Tax cuts were something Republicans had no problem with, and the child credit would even help take the net tax cut up to the agreed-upon $85 billion. But like many policies it would also have indirect effects. In this case, our policy of letting taxpayers take the child credit before the EITC would result in the government writing larger EITC checks to many low-income workers. That spending was viewed by many Republicans as a kind of welfare to which they were opposed. To submerge the issue politically, I told Ken of the sleight of hand we had devised with the help of Republican and Democratic budget committee allies. The greater EITC spending would be counted as a secondary effect. That meant that it would not be explicitly counted as part of the budget bill but would be appropriately included as part of the overall budget to be balanced.[13] In this politically charged atmosphere, those of us who knew better would need to calm the waters, not stir them. Ken said he would think about it.

WEDNESDAY, JULY 16, 1997

We had been running ahead with Gingrich and Ken, working hard to solve the tax bill. Lott had gotten out of the loop somewhat, being focused on the appropriations bills and keeping the trains running in the Senate. He was just starting to refocus on the spending and tax bills. We needed to get him on the same page with us.

Fortunately, Lott was ready to "kick the conference into gear." The Republicans would resolve their internal differences and be ready to negotiate the final agreement by Sunday or Monday, he said. We thought this was optimistic, but it was always good to push the schedule.

Like other Republicans, Lott was fixated on the $85 billion net tax cut. It was completely understandable; it was part of the very agreement we had been holding over their heads to get our education and other priorities. In fact, we were relieved that Lott was not trying to reach the $85 billion net tax cut by throwing the increase in the tobacco tax overboard. Instead, he took a completely different tack on tobacco, proposing that whatever revenues were raised from the increased tobacco tax would be counted against the overall tobacco settlement that the tobacco industry was negotiating with the states' attorney generals. We let it go, not wanting to engage on an issue that could upset the very large antitobacco crowd. We simply told him we had heard the proposal before and knew it was being shopped. In fact, it was John Spratt who had floated it. The tobacco members and lobbyists had been making the rounds.

THE CONFERENCE ON the tax bill was in the Capitol meeting room of the Senate Finance Committee. At this first meeting of House and Senate conferees were Senators Roth and Moynihan, Representatives Archer and Rangel, and their key staff aides. Bob Rubin, Larry Summers, Linda Robertson (Rubin's legislative assistant), and I represented the White House. Don Nickles, a member of the Senate Finance committee, attended as Lott's representative.

Archer began by listing the key issues that needed to be resolved—capital gains, IRAs, the child tax credit, education, estate tax, and the alternative minimum tax. He started with the issue that should have been saved for last—capital gains. The atmosphere quickly started to go south. Bob rightly asked that we move away from capital gains, saying that we all knew it would be one of the last issues. The Republicans acceded, but then Archer started in on the $85 billion net tax number.

He was pointing right at the written agreement, asking point blank if we intended to honor the agreement and commit to a deal that had an $85 billion net tax cut. It was a weird moment. At one level, we felt we had found a way to deliver the $85 billion net tax number, one that was fully consistent with the agreement and the win-win list we had discussed with the Speaker and Senator Lott. But we sure weren't going to describe our quiet scoring agreements to this group. It would open up a whole raft of issues, including questions about the EITC. Given the uncertainty, we decided to waffle. And the best way to waffle was simply to describe in detail how we had come to this situation.

We hemmed and hawed. Bob, Larry, and I played off one another, filling in the story line everyone already knew. We admitted that the president had certainly agreed to a net tax cut of $85 billion. But the Finance Committee had come up with a tobacco tax and had spent a good portion of it on children's health care. So that's what took us from the net $85 billion tax cut to a lower number. So, in effect, we were in agreement with the $85 billion tax cut, but there was this other "box" that had not been of our making—although we saw the merit of the Finance Committee actions. We were all put in this position by the action of the tax-writing committees. That's where we were.

Our response set Archer off. He waved the tax letter from the Republican leaders in front of us. The letter said there would be an $85 billion tax cut. He said we had insisted on our $35 billion of education credits, and we must commit to their tax cut. Bob suggested that it was an issue between the House and Senate, maybe they should talk to each other.

Unfortunately, the quite knowledgeable Senator Nickles was in the room. As a member of the Finance Committee, he had been a party to the late-night tobacco amendment that not only put more money into children's health care, but also made the child credit more fully available to EITC recipients. Don Nickles fully understood the EITC and hated it. He believed that it was rife with fraud and abuse and wanted to reform it out of existence. He started to home in on the program. Weren't EITC payments scored as spending? And wasn't that also a factor in pushing the net tax cut down? Ken was asked about the scoring, and he cleverly left an opening. He said that on tax bills, changes to the EITC had been scored as changes to revenues by the Joint Committee on Taxation—even though the committee includes a footnote saying that CBO traditionally scored the EITC payment as spending. Nickles would not let go. So it was spending in CBO's view? Ken had to answer yes. But he remained silent on the crucial distinctions between direct and secondary effects and our ability to bury the induced spending in the upcoming August baseline. It was a perfectly truthful but incomplete answer, given to save our budget scoring maneuver. It was definitely time to move on.

The meeting got better after that, maybe because we had already been arguing so much, maybe because we were all tired and the room was getting hotter. On our $35 billion of education tax incentives, Roth was forthcoming, saying "We hear you on that."

On the IRAs it was the same old story. We wanted them curbed and Roth had a nearly religious zeal for them. This one was headed to the leadership level. On the estate tax, we were down to a numbers debate. We all agreed to increase the unified credit. The questions were the size of the increase and its projected effect on the budget in the outyears. On the urban agenda, the remaining problem was the president's brownfields cleanup incentives. Brownfields cleanup was part of the leadership tax letter, but Republicans Bliley and Michael Oxley of Ohio wanted that provision taken out of this bill and used as one of the engines to help pass their hoped-for Superfund cleanup bill. Last on the Republican tax writers' list was the corporate AMT. They smartly hauled out a previous Clinton budget proposal that would have exempted small companies from the AMT and said that we all wanted the same thing.

THURSDAY, JULY 17, 1997

Kasich was becoming the designated worrier. He was being tremendously helpful on the spending side but could not restrain himself from constantly bending our ear on taxes. He said that we were asking too much for education. And the tobacco tax was a big problem, both in terms of getting the votes to pass it and in its impact on the $85 billion net tax cut. On this issue, he was representing Archer and the right wing of his caucus.

I reminded him that we had wanted to work with Archer from the beginning, but he had refused, telling us to veto a bad tax bill. Nonetheless, we could work out the tax bill; the Speaker was on the same page with us. But Kasich and Domenici needed to keep helping on the spending bill. We had to keep whittling the list.

THURSDAY EVENING ERSKINE and I met with the Speaker and Majority Leader Dick Armey. To our great relief, Newt Gingrich was still the Speaker despite a vigorous attempt by disgruntled House conservatives to unseat him.[14] The opposition had gathered and conspired but was unable to pull off the coup as it became clear that Gingrich still had the support of his caucus. Although Armey had been open about his displeasure with the Speaker's leadership, when push came to shove, he supported the Speaker. As a result, both he and Newt were still alive—and still our allies in the quest to pass a balanced budget agreement.

Erskine told the Speaker that we wanted to help him. Our interests were aligned as we both wanted our balanced budget agreement to work. And without Gingrich, it would be exceedingly difficult to manage the bills to passage. From Gingrich's viewpoint, the successful culmination of the agreement was crucial for his political future. He needed to get the balanced budget that was at the core of the Republican Party's Contract with America. And if he could deliver a capital gains rate reduction, that would be the icing on the cake.

Armey's involvement was also critical. He would raise red flags from the viewpoint of conservatives and also help on process. Gingrich was the driving force on the agreement, but Armey made an important contribution. As was his custom, Armey was seated at the far end of the table. He liked to smoke and courteously kept the fumes out of range. He would sit at his end of the table, smoking and eating peanuts, fully engaged in the discussion.

Newt began with the tobacco tax, reiterating that a dozen of his guys hated it. They would have to vote against the tax bill. But we needed the money and the Senate had put it in, so it had to stay. Also, he really didn't like the fact that the net tax cut was well below $85 billion. That was an official line in the sand, and we all had to deliver. Being Gingrich, he took a political approach to the problem, drawing two boxes. In the first were all the things that had been agreed to as part of the bipartisan deliberations. The second box contained the tobacco tax and the child care it was paying for. He said that was the Democratic win and that the Democrats needed to place something else inside the second box, something the Republicans wanted, such as a cut in the corporate capital gains tax or corporate AMT relief. It would take the net tax cut up toward $85 billion while pleasing a core constituency.

The House Republican leaders really did not object to raising money through the tobacco tax and using those resources to pay for other things. The money made the tent bigger, accommodating more of the ingredients needed for an agreement, including Republican priorities. They were getting a bargain in raising a sin tax to be counted against the net tax calculation; using an $18 billion tobacco tax increase to reach a net tax cut of $85 billion meant other taxes could be reduced.

Armey said that Archer was the key validator in their caucus. To win him over, we would need to offer a corporate tax cut with the potential to spur economic growth. At different times, both Gingrich and Armey mentioned the corporate AMT, a proposal the president had proposed in 1993. It was the one that Ken Kies and I were planning to include in the final deal.

FRIDAY, JULY 18, 1997

The next meeting of the congressional–White House tax conference would be that evening.[15] Ken called early in the morning to say that the Republicans intended to make an offer on the six big pieces—education, capital gains, AMT, child credit, IRAs, and estate tax. He said we wouldn't like it but it was part of the process. We should lower our expectations.

That is what we had always expected out of the tax conference. It would be too slow and unproductive to be the vehicle for the final agreement on taxes. Nonetheless, the tax bill was coming together. The outlines of the tax bill had been agreed upon at the leadership level, and now Ken had fit both the president's education initiatives and an improved version of the child credit into the final agreement, getting us close on two of the White House's major priorities. But there were still major problems, including provisions related to IRAs, the estate tax, and the capital gains tax that could trigger massive outyear revenue losses.

AT THE TAX CONFERENCE, Roth began by saying that the Republican proposal was a good-faith offer and he hoped that it would advance the conference. With both sides knowing what to expect and having lowered our expectations, the mood was quite good—different from the first testy meeting. After going through the Republican document, the conferees broke so the two sides could caucus. Since the Republican proposal was a nonstarter, we needed to shift to a different subject—the outyear revenue losses. We decided not to respond to the proposal until the conference reconvened the following night. We were treading water while waiting to move to the leadership level.

SATURDAY, JULY 19, 1997

Meanwhile Ken Kies had been fitting more of the pieces together. He was preparing a serious offer from the Republican leaders that would get us 80 percent of the way toward an agreement and leave room to close in a mutually supportive way. On the HOPE scholarship, they would offer $28 billion but leave room to settle at $33 billion. They would come about half the way on stacking but would finally accept regular stacking of the child credit, allowing taxpayers to take the child credit before applying the EITC to their remaining income tax liabilities. They would put in indexing for capital gains, and when we wanted it removed, Archer would want the corporate AMT provision.

THE TAX CONFERENCE reconvened late Saturday evening. Bob Rubin began by pointing out that Democrats were the ones who had made the meaningful concessions, moving beyond a capital gains break for homeowners to a broad-based one covering a range of financial assets. Roth countered by claiming Republicans had made a concession by reducing the ten-year cost of their original IRA proposal. In fact, they had just shifted the entire program deeper into the outyears without changing anything. Archer again voiced the argument that they could not do anything in conference beyond the scope of the House and Senate bills, even though this position was at odds with the tax letter signed by his leaders. We were going round and round, repeating the same speeches we had all heard before. It was not productive.

Then Archer shifted tactics by asking Rubin if we were authorized to reach a final agreement in this room. Bob was somewhat taken aback. He said that all of the White House positions were developed through a process of analysis and consensus involving a team of key participants, including the president. He said we would entertain any proposal but would have to take it back to the White House before final agreement.

Archer jumped on this. He demanded to know how we could ever get anywhere if the White House team was not authorized to reach agreement in the room? It was a clever ploy and turned reality on its head. The real problem was that their bills were far out of compliance with their own leaders' tax letter commitments, and the Republican conferees were too dug in to move toward a common solution. This group could have taken nearly forever and never found its way to the bottom line. But Archer was smart to deflect attention from the structural and substantive problems of this negotiation and focus on our supposed lack of authority. In fact, we had all the authority in the world if it was the right deal.

At this point, there was a quick decision to clear the room of staff—some forty to fifty people. The conference would be left to the legislators and our negotiating team. The civil mood was restored, but Roth was still pressing. He wanted to know when the White House would be making a proposal to respond to his. Roth, more than anyone, was under the mistaken impression that the deal could be made inside this room. It was a natural and understandable desire. That was the way the tax-writing committees were used to doing business, and forging an agreement among the conferees in the room gave him the best chance of protecting the IRAs he cared so passionately about. But nearly everyone else understood that the negotiation would have to be kicked upstairs, in large measure because of the nature of the agreement. The tax and spending bills were linked. The final agreement would have to be acceptable across all the provisions, and it was only the leaders who had the comprehensive view and the authority to make the trades that would make the totality of both bills acceptable.

Rather than respond to Roth's request, we shifted the discussion to the outyear explosion. Treasury had prepared an analysis of the ten-year revenue trends—particularly at the end of the ten-year window. The conclusion was unmistakable. In ten years, the Republican proposals on estate tax, IRAs, the alternative minimum tax, and capital gains would capture a huge share of the tax cut, even under the estimates of the Joint Committee on Taxation. Symmetrically, the education and child care provisions were shrinking rapidly as a proportion of the total. Unlike the first five years in which the education and child credit provisions dominated the total tax cut, by the end of ten years the Republican proposals were large and growing rapidly. The outyear explosion, beyond the ten-year, $250 billion constraint, was obvious. The trajectory of the current Republican proposals in the first ten-year window clearly showed a trend toward large revenue losses.

SUNDAY, JULY 20, 1997

The president had called on Saturday with an invitation to play golf at the Robert Trent Jones course in Virginia the next morning. President Clinton is a wonderful golfing partner. He roots for everyone and truly loves the game. On a beautiful Sunday morning, we were partners against Max Chapman, one of Erskine's good friends, and Mike Berman, another successful Wall Street financier. We were playing a penny-ante Nassau—a few bucks a side.

Max was a scratch golfer and was playing even better that day. I shot an 82, while the president's score, while always hard to calculate, was somewhere around 89ish. The bottom line was that, thanks to Max, they beat us decisively. The president was the official scorekeeper, and I'm not sure how many strokes they were supposed to be giving us, but I was absolutely and ontologically certain that we lost the bet. After a few minutes of going over a scorecard littered with his indecipherable scratch, the president announced that they each owed us a few bucks.

It was an amazing moment to see the look on our opponents' faces—first surprise, then wonder, a quick mental calculation, and then the reasoned conclusion that a Wall Street multimillionaire should fork over three bucks rather than question the scorekeeping ability of the president of the United States. They were more than pleased to do it; it was a small investment for the laughs we shared. Mike Berman told me later that the scorecard was one of his prized possessions. Later, I received a photo from the president. We were both in the golf cart, him working away on the score and me looking over his shoulder. The inscription: "What shall we use—CBO or OMB?"

MEETING ON SUNDAY evening with the tax writers, Bob Rubin pushed for the group to "get to where the deal might lie." He asked the Republicans if they could go back and put together a proposal that would be forward-leaning. Senator Nickles was extremely helpful. He said these meetings had been constructive and had identified and narrowed a number of issues. But time was getting short. He said the reconciliation bills needed to be enacted before the August recess, and that meant conferees needed to reach an agreement by the end of the week if we were to pass both bills the following week.

I suggested that we needed to confer with the leaders to discern our ability to come together on a compromise. We should go back to our respective leaders and report on our progress to date and agree on how to proceed. Everyone but Roth got it. He wanted to meet in the morning—keep working until we were done. The fact was that we were done.

Finally Archer weighed in. He said that this had been a difficult process because of the budget agreement. The understandings among the leaders and the White House had changed the regular order. He suggested that we reconnoiter and see where we were. He knew the tax bill had to be kicked upstairs if we were to succeed.

As we adjourned, there was a sigh of relief. Almost everyone understood that this process had run its course. We had spent several evenings but had finally succeeded in turning out the lights in the Finance Committee room. That was hopeful.

CHAPTER THIRTEEN

Into the Hands
of the Leaders

Having succeeded in kicking the tax bill upstairs to the leadership level, the two sides needed to finalize the structure of the negotiations—who would be in the room and who would not. Gingrich, Armey, Lott, Erskine, and I were definitely in. Beyond that, it got problematic. Lott realized that Roth's presence would be a problem. He was a single-issue man. Everyone understood we would have to give him something on the IRAs, but it would be easier to figure out that something and the rest of the tax bill without him in the room.

As for Archer, his bill was much worse than Roth's, but his participation was much less problematic. He was close to Gingrich, Armey, and Ken Kies, and his interests were aligned with theirs. Given the aborted coup against the Speaker, his approval of the final deal would be crucial for House Republican support. But to his great credit, he understood that others were more capable of getting to the bipartisan compromise. He wisely trusted his leaders to get to yes.

I was pressing to have Senator Daschle participate based on the fact that he was a signatory to the May 16 budget agreement. That distinction would allow us to keep Gephardt out while increasing our strength inside the room. The Republican leaders knew that and were anxious to keep Daschle out. But from the Republican viewpoint, the major problem on our side continued to be Bob Rubin's participation. Erskine and I were demanding that he be in the room. We simply refused to reach an agreement on taxes without his participation.

TUESDAY, JULY 22, 1997

The next day the budget team met with the president in the Cabinet Room. The White House had no message event that day, and we wanted to get the president into the news on the reconciliation bills—both the spending bill and the tax measure. So the meeting began as a media event for the White House press corps. The president made a brief statement, saying that he wanted an agreement but it had to be fair and include his education initiatives. He also emphasized that the tax cuts could not explode in the outyears. Then he took a few questions.

After the press had left, Bob started in on the tax issues. He wanted to get the president's approval on our negotiating positions. On education, we knew we would win on the HOPE scholarship. We could pare the funding back a little and make way for the other education programs popular among Democrats and Republicans alike.

On the child credit, we had moved beyond regular stacking in the president's June 30 tax proposal. Even though our original regular-stacking proposal allowed taxpayers to take the child credit before calculating the EITC, it still left low-income families with several children unable to take full advantage of the child credit. For these families, the dependent exemptions for their children already eliminated or reduced their income tax liability to very small amounts. These families effectively had little or no income tax liability to be taken against the child credit. (For an explanation of the various proposals on stacking, see box 13.1.)

The House Democratic tax writers had spotted the problem and come up with a possible solution. The idea was to increase the taxes that could be taken against the child credit by including the employee share of the FICA payroll tax. With the FICA tax rate near 7 percent, a worker earning $20,000 of wage income faced a FICA tax liability of approximately $1,400. Combining that FICA tax liability with the worker's income tax liability would create a significant sum to be offset with several $500 child credits.

From a political perspective, both Democrats and Republicans disliked the FICA tax. From the Democratic viewpoint, it was a regressive tax that fell on working men and women. From the Republican viewpoint, it was an antiemployer levy, making it more expensive for employers to hire workers. Given this, we felt we could make the political case for letting the child credit be taken against both the income and the FICA taxes.

But in a moment of extreme political stupidity or smarts, depending on your perspective, House Democrats had dubbed this creative proposal

Box 13-1. *Child Credit and EITC Stacking Proposals*

Assumptions for numerical examples:

Income tax (before EITC)	$1,200
EITC amount	$1,000
Employee FICA tax	$2,050
Child credit	$500 per child

House Bill (child credit stacked after EITC)
Income tax (before EITC) – EITC = Maximum allowable child credit
$1,200 – $1,000 = $200

Because the EITC reduces income taxes to an amount smaller than the full child credit the taxpayer can only take advantage of $200 of the child credit (no matter how many children).

Regular Stacking (child credit stacked before EITC)
Income tax (before EITC) = Maximum child credit
$1,200 = $1,200

Regular stacking allows the child credit to be taken against income tax before applying the EITC. A taxpayer with two children would take advantage of the full child credit for both children—equal to $1,000. A taxpayer with three children with $1,500 of potential child credits could take advantage of those up to the $1,200 of income taxes due. Taking advantage of the child credit reduces the amount of income tax liabilities remaining to be offset against the taxpayer's given EITC amount. As a result, the refundable portion of the EITC amount rises.

President's June 30, 1997, Proposal (full stacking)
Income tax (before EITC) + Employee Share of FICA – EITC = Maximum Child Credit
$1,200 + $2,050 – $1,000 = $2,250

Under the president's June 30 proposal, a taxpayer with three children could take advantage of the full $1,500 of child credits since the credits could be netted both against income tax and the employee share of FICA.

The president's proposal can also be transcribed to show that the child credit plus the EITC can never exceed the sum of the taxpayer's income and FICA tax liability. Put equivalently, EITC payments cannot rise because of the child credit.

Income Tax (before EITC) + Employee Share of FICA $ EITC + Child Credit

"refundability." That word had become an inflammatory term to Republicans. In the context of the existing EITC, it meant that if a taxpayer's income tax liabilities were less than the EITC amount, the taxpayer received the difference as a payment from the government. Republicans were happy to cut taxes, even for low-income workers. But they sure hated writing that check. To them, the term *refundable* signified all that was wrong with the EITC: a program that went beyond reducing taxes to making what many Republicans considered welfare payments.

The White House team decided to try to sell the new concept to Republicans by calling it something other than refundability. We would call it super-stacking, or kid-stacking, or whatever the Republicans needed to call it in order to agree to it. And to immunize the proposal from the charge that it would lead to larger "welfare" checks being written, we added the stipulation that the taxpayers' combined FICA and income tax liabilities had to be greater than the amount they received from both the child credit and the EITC. The importance of this restriction is that it meant that no matter how many children a family had and no matter how many $500 tax credits it received, its EITC check would not *increase* as a result of allowing the child credit to be taken against both income and FICA tax liabilities. The working poor could take greater advantage of the child credit, even as we immunized ourselves from the charge of increasing welfare.

On capital gains, we would insist on no indexing and on dropping the corporate capital gains rate reduction. And, at the end of the day, we would agree to the 20-10 rate structure that was the Republicans' top priority—20 percent for those in the highest income tax bracket and 10 percent for others. On the estate tax, Bob Rubin recommended not going beyond a unified credit of $800,000—and he did not want to index that amount for inflation. On the IRAs, we had a solution that dealt with the outyear explosion; all we needed to do now was persuade Roth to agree. We would give three IRA choices, but place a limit on the total contribution and a limit on their availability based on income, setting this limit at between $80,000 and $100,000. We would also agree to a prepaid tuition plan not subject to the overall limit. Senator Nickles had rightly pointed out that families with more kids needed more investment opportunities to save for college.

Having spent so much time with the Republican negotiators, Erskine and I knew that movement on the corporate AMT would break the remaining logjams on the tax bill. Archer would have to give up on indexing of capital gains, give us our education proposal, and would be more open to our child credit-EITC proposal. To do all that, Gingrich and Archer needed something to sell to their caucus, and the exclusion of small corporations from the AMT was the least harmful option. Not only had the president proposed it during his first term, but the cost was fairly small. Bob had opposed the proposal in this round, thinking it unnecessary in light of the strong economy, but Erskine had been quietly working on Bob to bring him around to the need for this provision. As the meeting came to an end, Erskine's quiet diplomacy with

Bob was rewarded as Bob told the president that we could go with a limited corporate AMT proposal.

DOMENICI AND KASICH called early in the afternoon, asking for an urgent meeting with Erskine and me. We jumped at the opportunity. The Republicans had just spent the last several days reaching agreement among themselves. This would be our chance to see where they stood.

Domenici started right in. The refundability proposal on the child credit was a nonstarter in the Republican caucus. He said we had to give it up. They would give us regular stacking—taking the income tax liability against the child credit before applying the EITC. But they would not agree to include the FICA tax in the liability that could be offset by the child credit. I had quietly been pushing this proposal with Ken Kies for several days, warming him up by suggesting that it be phased in the second five years. Now the word was out that we wanted it up front, and Kasich and Domenici were out to short-circuit our move. On the surface, our proposal smelled like a massive expansion of EITC. And that was something the Republicans hated.

Kasich put on his most pained expression. He said that if we forced them down this road "it could cost Newt his Speakership." It was a smart ploy. Weakened by the attempted coup, Gingrich was trying to navigate very carefully within his own caucus and did not have his normal freedom to roam. And Democrats were energized by the thought of his possible downfall. The partisan warriors in the House had been promoting the refundability provision not only because it was good policy but because it gave the Republicans such heartburn. No other remaining issue carried as much political weight as the EITC. If the conflict became elevated enough, it could bring the deal down and the Speaker along with it. Maybe it was not an oversight that House Democrats had called the provision refundability.

Although the Speaker clearly had been weakened, we still felt there was room to accommodate the new provision. We had been careful to craft the provision as a tax cut, not an expansion of the EITC. And we had absolutely no interest in seeing the Speaker fall. The road ran both ways. The loss of the deal could doom the Speaker, but Gingrich's downfall would likely kill the balanced budget agreement. We were not interested in putting him in harm's way. We were interested in finding a way to an agreement.

KEN KIES WAS calling and it was time to come clean. I asked if he was wearing his seatbelt. I had been pushing past regular stacking of the child credit, but only in the outyears where we could bury everything. Now I told him we needed the refundability provision in the first five years. He yelled an incredulous "You have got to be kidding me!" He said he couldn't do it. I let him vent.

As he calmed down, I told him that our guys were fixated on this—not only the White House but the Democrats in the House and Senate whose votes were needed to support the agreement. And, I said, the White House political people believed the refundability provision was a winner. Boiled down to its essence, why shouldn't working people who are poor—and who pay taxes—get the child credit like everybody else? Ken was silent; at least he was listening.

WEDNESDAY, JULY 23, 1997

The next day Erskine and I met with Gingrich, Lott, and Armey to talk schedule and strategy. We all resolved to finish both bills by the August recess, which began at the end of the following week. If we did not finish, we would lose momentum, and, more important, the new, optimistic deficit projections would be staring us in the face when we returned.

Gingrich said that neither side could ask the other to carry something that was impossible. We could not have agreed more. Our goal was to balance the budget by allowing both sides to have the wins they needed to carry the bills. We told him we were not interested in imposing losses; we wanted an agreement in the middle.

Then he came at us. Refundability for the child credit was a nonstarter in his caucus. He simply could not carry it. Erskine drew back, smartly avoiding confrontation. No need to raise the stakes; we needed to work it through. Erskine said that we had obviously identified a "raw nerve" but the issue was of importance to the White House. Gingrich said he could not take the provision to the tax conference or to his caucus; it would cause both to break down. He said that if we insisted on our position he would have to speak to the president himself and determine if a budget agreement was possible—or if we would have to give up on our bipartisan efforts. He said that refundability was a line that could not be crossed in the Republican caucus.

It was a grave moment, and all of us were silent for a few moments, thinking about where to go next. There was not a shred of animosity, only the awareness of a conflict that perhaps could not be resolved. Through events beyond our control or making, or perhaps through insufficient foresight, we might have arrived at a true dead end.

I broke the silence, asking if I could restate our proposal without the nametags and labels. We could agree to a new name if we could agree to the policy—but I wanted to make sure they understood our proposal. I said this was a tax cut, not an expansion of the EITC.

I told the group that a person could not get the child credit unless there was a net tax liability to take the credit against. And that net tax liability was the sum of the income taxes and FICA taxes. In plain English, you needed to owe taxes to get the child credit. It was not a check from the government, but a tax cut.

Gingrich broke out into a broad smile—a smile of relief. He said he was fine with the proposal. What he had meant previously was that he could not sell his caucus on a broader concept of tax liability against which the child credit could be taken if it led to bigger checks being written under the EITC. He said his caucus would understand that FICA was a real tax and should be included in a legitimate notion of tax liability. A tax was a tax was a tax. What he couldn't sell to his caucus was the notion that our child credit proposal would lead to an expansion of EITC expenditures—more "welfare" in their parlance. To his caucus, the child credit wasn't about welfare, it was about cutting taxes.

There are times when labels mislead. This was one of those times, but we had worked past the label to agree to a policy that could work for both parties. Many more of the working poor would be able to take advantage of the child credit. I took out a sheet of paper and tore off two thin pieces and twice wrote out the operational concept that ensured that our proposal could only be construed as a tax cut.[1] I attached one to my notebook and handed one to Gingrich. I knew he would give it to Ken, who would have to give his assent and make the proposal fit within our budget and tax boxes. After this breakthrough, we started to move quickly. Republicans would drop the labor provisions in exchange for a moratorium on regulations related to workfare workers.[2] On Medicare, the White House was done pretending about the viability of any of the three Finance Committee provisions. They would not be part of our $115 billion of Medicare savings.[3]

TEN MINUTES AFTER the meeting broke, Ken found me. He had a panicked look. He came right up to me, breaking from our normal discretion. He had the piece of paper I had handed to Gingrich. Ken said that the Speaker had been mistaken, that he had not fully understood what he was agreeing to. The Republican caucus would not accept what Gingrich had agreed to less than half an hour ago.

Ken and I returned immediately to the Speaker's office. Gingrich was in the Dinosaur room, and we asked him to come to his private office. Ken started in. They could not accept the White House proposal to offset the child credit against FICA taxes. He said that Archer would never accept it. Income taxes were the only legitimate basis to offset the child credit. They could do regular stacking, but that was it.

I started in with the political argument. Everyone knew that FICA was a large tax—a large antibusiness tax from the Republican viewpoint. The proposal simply said that to get the child credit, a taxpayer had to have a tax liability. It was truly a net against taxes—not a payment, not welfare. It was plain as day. I asked him to step back and see it as the average person and legislator would—the child credit allowed a taxpayer to reduce his taxes. Taxes were taxes were taxes, whether on income or wages. This was not welfare.

Gingrich was focused and believing. He told Ken that if he could work out the technicalities, then he could sell it to the caucus. That was music and what Ken needed to hear. We needed Kies on our side, not only to make it all work but, just as important, to help persuade Archer to go along.

After the Speaker left, the old Ken came to the fore. He was looking for something to trade. He started in, "If, and that's a big if—if we did this, there would be a price, a big price." He started running his laundry list of Republican priorities on the edge of the envelope. I did nothing to discourage him, saying only that I understood. I just needed him to help the Speaker sell the concept to Republicans.

AT 8:30 THAT evening Gingrich called. The tone of his voice—the very first sound—was all I needed to hear. He had done it. Archer and his members were on board.

Our proposal was a tax cut, and they were for it. Not only that, but our proposal would increase the size of the tax cut to be counted toward the net $85 billion that was part of the agreement. It was Gingrich and Ken at their best, carrying the political argument, but also being versatile enough to adjust the boxes to accommodate our new agreement. It was nice to be dealing with professionals.

To cement the agreement, the Republicans had adopted a new nomenclature. For a good while now, we all had agreed to stack the child credit in front of the EITC – allowing it to be netted against income taxes first. At that time, Democrats had called it regular stacking, and Republicans had called it full stacking. And now Republicans had accepted that both income and FICA tax liabilities could be netted against the child credit. Although they had accepted the new policy, they could not use the radioactive term refundability. So they called it the same term as before—full stacking. It was a smart choice. In terms of perception, Republicans were saying that they were where they always had been—willing to reduce taxes, but not spend a penny for refundability. The policy was a tax cut, and they were for it.

In exchange for agreeing to our proposal, Newt wanted the corporate AMT and a $1.2 million unified credit on the estate tax. I told him $1.2 million on the estate tax was impossible, but $1 million was doable. And after fitting in our child credit proposal, it looked like the net tax cut would rise to $92 billion. I said that the president and Erskine would agree to the AMT and $1 million estate tax—as well as lifting the net tax cut to $92 billion. After all, we were the ones breaking the limit in order to help working men and women. It was a great feeling.

THURSDAY, JULY 24, 1997

We were still going round and round on the structure for the leadership tax meetings. The Republicans did not want Bob Rubin in the room, and if he was included, Archer would need to participate. But then the Republicans would be hard-pressed to keep Roth out. If Roth were in, Lott would lose some of the freedom to move that made him such an effective leader. And if Archer and Roth were both in the room, our side would want to balance with Daschle and might end up having to invite Rangel and Moynihan. But those were effectively the participants in the Finance Committee meetings we had suffered through for several evenings earlier in the process. We knew that would not work. The Republicans proposed a premeeting and then a full meeting—the real meeting and the show meeting. But we refused to exclude Bob from any of the meetings.

I walked down to Erskine's office, finding Bob and Rahm Emanuel with Erskine. We were stuck between a too-big meeting and no meeting. And the day was starting to get away from us. Then it hit me. We would revert to "shuttle diplomacy," splitting the groups in the House and Senate. We would have a separate meeting on the House side with Erskine, Bob, and me on our side, and Gingrich, Armey, Archer, and Ken on their side. After that, we would shuttle over to the Senate for a meeting with Lott, Roth, Daschle, and anyone else they wanted to include. It would get us off the dime. Lott and Gingrich would coordinate on their side, and we would sit in both meetings. From these meetings, a consensus would be engineered, setting the stage for the leaders and the White House to reach the final agreement. I called the Republicans and they accepted immediately. We would meet in the Speaker's Dinosaur office in an hour.

AS WE WERE ARRIVING, there was confusion in Gingrich's office. The Republican tax writers, including Roth, had assembled. We stayed in the hallway leading to the Speaker's balcony, while Roth and company were told that they would attend a later meeting on the Senate side. As they marched out we marched in, teasing each other in feigned confusion and vowing to meet later. As the press followed us around the rest of the day, the operative word became "reconnoiter." The White House was on the Hill to reconnoiter the various positions. We would start with the House Republicans, then go to the Senate, and then return to the House to see the Democratic leaders—a meeting that was hastily arranged. It looked natural to the press, simply seeking information and a consensus. If only they had known: hard feelings and entrenched positions were forcing us to devise an elaborate kabuki at one level, even as we were driving toward a final agreement at another.

The mood in the Speaker's office was good. We had averted a collision on the child credit, and Gingrich was practicing his lines for selling the deal to his caucus. He would go to full stacking but not beyond. But now, he was using the term in a more expansive way to include the FICA tax liability. Even if a low-wage worker took full advantage of the child credit, the government would not be writing more or larger checks based on our broader concept of tax liability. That is what his Republicans needed to hear. Gingrich put it succinctly: "We wouldn't be sending these people a check."

For our part, we were willing to live with this assurance that gave the other side their needed political cover. The provision had been thoroughly scrubbed by the White House policy people and the Treasury. They had determined that this was the best way to expand the benefit; we believed we could simultaneously improve the financial position of the working poor while securing Republican political support.

After Gingrich spoke, Armey chimed in. He did not like the EITC one bit, but he would support this provision. Giving people a check—welfare—was one thing. But letting them pay less tax was another. I could only imagine the meeting in which the Republicans came on board with the proposal, and the job Gingrich and Ken must have done.

We turned to the estate tax, and Archer and Ken went through their proposal. They would phase in the $1.2 million increase in the unified credit over ten years. And after ten years, the credit would be indexed to inflation. They would reduce their proposed unified credit for small business and farmers to $1.2 million, down from $1.5 million, but the full credit would begin immediately.

Bob explained that the White House had a problem with the indexing and the level of the unified credit. It was not a philosophical issue but rather a matter of affordability and the outyear revenue losses. Because of demographic patterns, a wave of estates was expected over the next few years, he said, and raising the credit would lose a lot of revenue. That was exactly the point, the Republicans shot back. Without an increase in the credit, a large number of Americans would be unfairly subjected to the "death tax."

Bob said we were currently willing to go with a $600,000 unified credit but could see our way clear to $800,000 if indexing were dropped. We were $400,000 apart, and $1 million was the split. I made a check in my notebook.

Archer was pushing corporate AMT relief, knowing that his proposal was the same as ours from a few years earlier. It was fun to watch Bob Rubin dance on this one. He acknowledged that Democrats had once supported this provision, but economic circumstances were different now. Back in the day, corporate productivity had been lagging, the cost of capital was higher, and the economy was weaker. Thanks to the 1993 deficit reduction package, the cost of capital was now low and corporate profits were good. The proposal was not needed now. In his matter-of-fact recounting, Bob managed to slip in a glowing reference to the 1993 Democrats-alone deficit reduction package, to the annoyance of the proud Republican tax cutters in the room. But they should have been thrilled with Democrats' action in 1993. That Democrats-alone budget package with its large tax increase had been a major political factor in Republicans gaining control of Congress. And it had put the current Congress and administration in a position not only to balance the budget, but to cut taxes in the bargain.

Gingrich abruptly shifted gears. He wanted to know if the White House could go along with putting the tobacco tax increase in the spending bill. We saw no downside. By shifting the tobacco tax increase to the budget bill, his tobacco guys could vote for the tax bill and against the spending bill. We had a number of members in the same position. They were from marginal districts where tax cuts were important. It worked for our side, too.

Then Archer revived an issue that we thought had been settled long ago. He offered to let us completely write the $35 billion of education tax incentives if they could write the estate, IRA, and capital gains provisions. This one was right out of right field. We all smiled and went on, ignoring his suggestion.

On the urban agenda, they offered to enact the brownfields tax incentives for hazardous waste cleanup for a three-year period. And we would work out the Medicaid and other provisions for the District of Columbia in a mutually agreeable way. The Republicans were also willing to make several smaller concessions, such as going along with increased funding for enterprise zones.[4] And they would agree to remove several of the smaller poison pills, such as provisions and restrictions on lobbying by labor.

We agreed to take these ideas to the group on the Senate side and then do our missionary work with House Democrats. We would be back.

AFTER THE MEETING with the House leaders, Gene Sperling tracked me down. He dropped a bomb—not a little one, but one that could kill the entire agreement. The policy folks in the administration had been wrong. The child credit proposal that Republicans had just agreed to created a big problem. As much as I liked Gene, it was all I could do to contain my anger.

We had just lived through two harrowing days in which political creativity and a lot of goodwill had saved the agreement from a fatal rupture over the EITC. Now Gene was saying that our hard-won compromise needed to be reopened. The policy people had found that under the administration's construction, a significant number of the working poor would not get the full benefit of the child tax credit.

We had stumbled into a potentially deal-breaking situation, driven by the incongruities between a very complex EITC program and the need to create the political cover to sell our child credit proposal to the Republicans. To win their support, we had agreed that the sum of the child credit plus the EITC would always be less than the sum of income and FICA taxes due. Under this condition, the proposal could only be construed as a tax cut. But it turned out that there were a significant number of low-income working families for whom the EITC was already greater than the combined income tax and FICA liability. Under the constraint we had used to sell our proposal to Gingrich and his caucus, these workers would not get the benefit of the child credit.

THE SHUTTLING TAX diplomats convened in Lott's office—with Daschle and Roth joining the crowd. Erskine and Bob started through the major tax issues. I paid little attention to the back and forth as I tried to figure out a way to deal with the child credit bomb that had just been hurled into the mix.

There seemed to be no way to square the circle within our concept of full stacking. If we removed the constraint in order to help these people, it would undermine the political argument that had carried the day with the Republicans. Not only would workers' taxes be offset but they would also get larger EITC checks. That was a nonstarter with the Republicans.[5]

We had to try to find an alternative. I realized that one solution would be to split the baby and have two policies—depending on the number of children. Families with three or more children were better off with full stacking. For them, the standard deduction against income tax wiped out almost all of their income tax liability, and using FICA tax liabilities against the child credit was crucial for these families to receive the benefit of the child credit. But taxpayers with fewer children would be better off with regular stacking as long as they were not subject to the jerry-rigged political constraint we had cooked up to ensure that EITC checks would not increase as a result of our broader concept of tax liability.[6]

I ran the hybrid idea past Gene and he agreed that it worked. The hard part would be getting the Republicans to agree. Ken would understand the many sides of this hybrid proposal very quickly. We would need his help, but he would have very little freedom to maneuver. The Republican leaders had gone way out on a limb on full stacking, and we would be asking them for something else again. Not a good way to do business. We knew this could be trouble.

All this time, Erskine and Bob had been carrying the discussion on taxes. As expected, they and Roth were locked up on IRAs. Erskine and Bob continued to make the case for both an overall contribution limit as well as income limits on those who could contribute. They might as well have been talking to a wall. Roth kept coming back to the supposed $10 billion cutback he had made in his proposal—even though he had only shifted the program further into the future. He had not even begun to address our concerns. Lott was careful to side with Roth throughout all of this. He needed to be a friend and ally of Roth if he were to get Roth's blessing for the compromise at the end. As the discussion was ending, Lott said, "Remember, we ain't got shit without the chairman."

I GOT A MESSAGE that the Speaker wanted to see me in his offices. It was a lovely summer evening and Gingrich, Armey, Archer, Ken Kies, and Arne Christenson were assembled on the Speaker's balcony overlooking the National Mall. In our phone conversation the previous evening, Gingrich had made it clear that he would need something in exchange for accepting full stacking. Now he wanted to play it out in front of Archer, thereby demonstrating his resolve to the Ways and Means Committee chair.

Gingrich began with indexing on capital gains. But he knew we could not give him that. Then he asked for an extremely generous estate tax provision. He said we owed it to them. I tried not to respond directly, knowing that we would be asking for more. And as part of that, we might have to give them something really big if we still had a deal. I tried to joke away their pressure, saying that the Christian Coalition would be happy with their win on the child credit. That hit a raw nerve with Archer. He felt that the Christian Coalition had gotten its due and more. Archer said bluntly, "What do we get?" I said I would take it back to the president.

LATER THAT EVENING in a meeting with Gephardt, Rangel, and Spratt, our White House team gave a full report on the day's meetings. We said we were moving toward an agreement but were not there yet. Gephardt asked if Gingrich was ready to deal. It was a very strange question to those of us who had been dealing with Gingrich for months. It illustrated the gulf between Democrats and Republicans in the House and the absence of communication.

AFTER THE DAY's shuttle diplomacy, the White House team decided to convene the full group of bipartisan leaders and tax writers in the Speaker's offices. The participants wanted to talk about education, and they had us outnumbered. Senators Daschle and Moynihan joined the Republicans in trying to reduce the size of the president's HOPE package in order to make more room for their education priorities. That gave Ken the opportunity to put forward a variation of the education proposal he and I had discussed as their next move. He offered $28 billion for the HOPE scholarship. That left $7 billion to spend on other initiatives within the $35 billion allotted for of education programs. Our congressional Democrats liked it. We didn't.

I WAS ABLE to connect with the president at 11:00 p.m. I told him about our problem on the child credit. We had an alternative, but it was complicated and could blow up the whole negotiation. We had dubbed the hybrid *superstacking*, and I told him I thought we could get it in the second five years but might not be able to get it started in the first five years, where it would be sitting naked for all to see. And even if the Republicans agreed, they would want the corporate ATM and probably more. The president got it. He wanted to press for the start of superstacking in the first five years.

Taxes and Death

The major pieces of the budget agreement were falling into place—with one glaring exception. Unknown to the Republican negotiators, the White House was about to reopen the agreement on the child credit and the EITC. No other issue was as controversial or had as much potential to blow up the bipartisan negotiations.

FRIDAY, JULY 25, 1997

The next morning the president gathered the budget group in the Oval Office. He repeated what he had told me hours before; we should stretch the envelope on the child tax credit and put forward our superstacking hybrid proposal. The president said that the cop with four kids should get the benefit of the child credit; that benefit should start right away but in no case later than three years. He wanted it in effect while he was still president.

In return, the president said we should accept $1 million unified credit on the estate tax: "It's their issue." I could almost hear Lott saying those words to the president.

On the HOPE scholarship, Erskine recommended that we accept $31 billion. That would leave enough to take care of a host of other education provisions important to Democrats and Republicans alike.[1]

On the IRAs, we would need limits on those who could take advantage of the tax break. In our view, the program should begin to phase out at $80,000 of income, with those above $110,000 ineligible to contribute to these tax-preferred savings vehicles. All we needed was for the Republican leaders and

Senator Roth to agree. On capital gains the rates would be 20-10 but without indexing if everything else fell into place. And the president was willing to give them a limited corporate AMT provision to close the deal. We also had to have our urban agenda, especially brownfields and enterprise zones.

But we could not let the spending bill be forgotten, and we could not close on the tax bill until all the spending issues were resolved. Numerous poison pills still needed to come out of the spending measure. As part of that, we would have to find a way to deal with those nasty labor provisions. And we had to make sure we got the immigrant provisions right. On children's health care, the president established his bottom line at $22 billion.

Frank Raines ran through a number of smaller issues on the spending side. The president wanted to blunt the impact of Medicaid cuts to hospitals that took care of a disproportionate share of low-income patients, particularly in Louisiana—John Breaux had been weighing in. And the president wanted to make sure that the welfare-to-work grants did not get diverted into governors' hands; a good portion had to go directly to cities. We also had to work something out on the Hyde abortion language. Raines, who had been so valuable on the spending bill, emphasized that we needed to see the language on all these provisions. We could not declare victory based only on conceptual agreements.

WE HAD MADE substantial progress on taxes with the Republican negotiators on Thursday and had agreed to turn next to the spending bill. Even as the leaders were primarily focused on the tax bill, the spending issues continued to be worked. Congressional budgeteers and staffs, White House policy advisors, and OMB staffers would monitor and interject themselves into each of the spending subconferences, urging the conferees to enact the bipartisan agreement while keeping poison pills and other extraneous provisions out. Although many spending issues had been resolved, those that remained were the tough ones that needed to be elevated to the leadership level. Back at the Capitol, Erskine, Frank, Gene, and I convened with Lott, Gingrich, Domenici, Kasich, Bill Hoagland, and Rick May, Kasich's chief of staff.

We began to go through the list of issues. The first, on restoring lost benefits to legal immigrants, was resolved quickly. The bipartisan agreement had locked in benefits for the disabled. And Clay Shaw had rightly raised the issue of benefits for elderly immigrants. After checking with Hoagland on the cost, the Republicans did the right thing and agreed to confer benefits on both groups. Much of the damage done to legal immigrants in the 1996 welfare reform law had now been repaired. In truth, helping both the elderly and the disabled was not an outcome we had foreseen or had brought about through some brilliant strategy. We had been fortunate that the Republican leaders were willing to help unwind an injustice.

We also reached a quick agreement to maintain Medicaid eligibility for disabled children whose families were coming off the welfare rolls under the tougher requirements of the 1996 welfare reform law. We agreed to pay the $100 million cost out of the money we were setting aside for child health care.

The next issue was a big one: the structure of the welfare-to-work grants to provide jobs, training, and assistance for people making the transition from welfare to work. The negotiators had already agreed to spend $3 billion on the grants, but the structure was still in the air. The House Ways and Means Committee had been good to us. They had divvied up the money between formula grants and ones that could be openly competed for by government and other entities. In addition, the bulk of the money was guaranteed to go to localities rather than being given to governors to channel as they liked. The Senate bill was much worse on all counts. To our surprise, Republicans made a quick concession in our favor, agreeing to let the Department of Labor administer the program. That meant the administration could guarantee that the dollars would flow to localities. The Republicans also gave a 75-25 split between formula and competitive grants.

Then the meeting took up the issue that had become the bane of my existence: the labor provisions regarding workfare recipients. Gingrich said they would drop the provisions if we would place a moratorium on any new regulations in the area. We were happy not to issue new regulations for a while, having already put in place the key ones. But it was a good guess that the moratorium they had in mind would be retroactive. We had been intentionally talking past each other on this one, and once again we passed up the opportunity to clarify the difference. We, and perhaps the Republicans as well, were hoping the other side would cede when it came to the final crunch.

Down the list we went, restating the merits and demerits, as we had for months. The number of issues remaining to be resolved was dropping, but some issues were still truly in disagreement. One example was the required health benefits to be offered as part of the children's health care program. As the meeting ended, we made a short list of the remaining items: the labor provisions, states' roles in administering federal social service programs, several Medicare provisions, protection of low-income seniors subjected to the Part B premium, and the size of a medical savings account demonstration project.[2] As always, abortion was part of the mix. We would have to resolve the Hyde prohibition on abortion services within the new children's health care initiative. The negotiators on both sides redeployed their policy troops, asking them to redouble their efforts to find solutions in the middle.

THAT AFTERNOON, A small group assembled in Lott's office to discuss taxes—Erskine, Bob, and I on our side; Gingrich, Lott, and Ken Kies on theirs.

The White House had hoped to put off the child credit issue until the end. If we could get everything else tied up, it might be easier to win Republican assent to our revamped hybrid proposal. But Lott wanted to force the issue now. He congratulated us in a mocking way, saying that he had sworn to himself that he would not go forward with the negotiation until the child credit issue was resolved. But here we were near the end and the child credit was still hanging out there. Now he was insisting that we start with the tough one or there would be no point continuing.

Gingrich chimed in then, saying he would go to full stacking but not beyond. They could support the child credit being taken against both the income tax and the employee's share of FICA. Lott followed, expressing much the same sentiment. Knowing we needed to reopen the child credit issue and introduce our hybrid approach, I tried to recast the issue. I said that we had made substantial progress on the child credit and had addressed much of the problem. They had given us what we needed to take care of the families with lots of kids. I then tried to slide in the new element of the proposal, representing it as a clarification. For people with three or more kids we would use full stacking as Lott and Gingrich were offering. But for families with two or fewer kids, we would go back to regular stacking and let them apply the child credit only against their income tax liability. Stated this way, the proposal sounded narrower than the tax rule that included the employee share of FICA. But, of course, it wasn't. The accepted concept of regular stacking did not include the constraint on increased EITC spending we had invented to sell full stacking.

To my relief, Ken let it pass without objection. He was the only one who would fully understand all the nuances and the perils it posed for the agreement. We moved on. I thought the child credit had been finessed one last time.

Next came IRAs. We stated the need to contain the outyear revenue losses. Bob put forward the overall limit on contributions and suggested that those with incomes above $110,000 be ineligible. The Republican leaders weren't the problem, it came down to what they would need to sell the agreement to Roth.

On the estate tax, the Republicans insisted on a unified credit of $1.2 million for farmers and small business, starting right away. And for everybody else, the credit would rise to $1.2 million over ten years. The higher limit for farmers and small businesses was fine with us, but we pushed back on the higher limit for other taxpayers.

Then to education. We could settle. We would go to $31 billion on the HOPE scholarship. With that amount, we could afford to give eligible low-income families the annual $1,500 tax credit for the first two years after high school, as well as a 20 percent credit up to $10,000 for subsequent years.[3] Ken called his tax estimators who said this plan would work with a small adjustment that we readily accepted. That agreement on the HOPE scholarship package freed up the necessary resources for all the other education benefits both sides wanted.

On the urban agenda, Lott and Gingrich agreed to business tax credits for the District of Columbia and would agree to whatever else Frank Raines could work out with the Ways and Means Committee on the urban agenda. They would also agree to three years of tax incentives to clean up brownfields in return for a letter saying the White House would push for Superfund legislation later in the year. On empowerment zones and enterprise communities, they felt we were spending too much but would give us wide leeway to allocate the money. The Republicans were being generous.

Then Gingrich started in on a general fishing expedition. They needed us to reciprocate. And they also needed to go above the $85 billion tax cut to fit in the child credit. We said we understood and agreed. Erskine said they would get 20-10 on capital gains, a "good" estate provision, something on corporate AMT, and more than $85 billion for the net tax cut. It was what they wanted to hear. Erskine continued. Our win list would be education, the child credit, and the full $24 billion on children's health care. Bowles called this the path to "win-win."

The $24 billion on kids' health threw them back. Gingrich was upset at this major spending demand, saying that to get that amount we would have to "give something big or lower our appetite." He started to pull back, bemoaning our plays on the child credit. He said that their win list was not big enough to compensate for the child credit we wanted. Our machinations on that were big baggage for them, even if only symbolically.

Erskine came back strongly. Did they or didn't they want a deal? We wanted an agreement, but they had to accommodate us on what was important. Things got calmer. They wanted a deal.

7:50 P.M., AND THE Speaker was calling. He told me he was a little surprised at our insistence on some of the provisions—our "rigidities," he called them. He thought we could work everything out, but we would have to be flexible.

The abortion restriction on the children's health money had to satisfy their caucus. He said we each had our constituencies and had to recognize that fact of political life.

Then he laid out the deal he thought would work for both sides. On the estate tax, they would need a $1.2 million unified credit for farmers and small business. I said we could do it, knowing it was a Daschle proposal. And he wanted $1.2 million on the unified credit for everybody else. I told him we could only do $1 million, and he said that would be fine.

He said they would need 20-10 on capital gains and the corporate AMT. On the tax cut, he still thought the magic number would be around $92 billion net. I told him we were fine with all of that. And on kids health, they could do a big number of "around $20 billion." I said that we needed somewhere close to $24 billion. We agreed that we would work everything else out. Once again, Gingrich and I thought we were just about there.

THE BUDGET TEAM met with the president at 9:30 p.m. in the library of the residence, updating him and getting our marching orders for the next day. Erskine had kept the president fully apprised on the tax negotiations throughout the day. This meeting was really for the troops—to make their report and get the president's approval.

Bob summarized the day's tax negotiations. He wanted the president to be tough, so he shaded the report in a pessimistic direction. He reported that Gingrich thought this period could be compared with the one in which President Woodrow Wilson and Senator Henry Cabot Lodge had reigned, and that Lodge had gotten the better of Wilson. Almost on cue, the president went off. He feigned anger. He wanted to "kick their ass." Rahm, Erskine, and I smiled at each other. It was show time; he was going to let his troops see the tough President Clinton. He said he would take the Republicans on. If they wanted to fight over kids health, then we'd have at it. Who did they think would come out on top, Wilson or Cabot Lodge?

Erskine, who must have ordered up the president's performance, played his part. He was "pessimistic." Maybe we had tried for a bridge too far. These were easy words to act that night, knowing how close we were. Bob jumped in to amplify the difficulties we faced. We had to hang tough. We should not give up on the corporate AMT, a policy everyone including Bob had agreed was necessary to close the deal. Having put on so many displays of kabuki for others, we were now staging one for ourselves.

Finally Rahm Emanuel cut in, bringing us back to reality. We should trade the corporate AMT for child credit stacking. That would be the last trade.

AT 10:45 P.M. I called the president to convey the ongoing conversations with Gingrich. He was fine with everything in the Speaker's offer but the kids' health initiative. He still wanted all $24 billion. I told him that if we could slide by on the child credit, we could close tomorrow. I suggested that he either vest Erskine with the power to close or tell Erskine that he wanted to be called for the final trade. He said he wanted to be the guy.

GINGRICH CALLED AGAIN at 11:30 p.m. I reported my conversation with the president and the need for the full $24 billion on kids' health. Gingrich said he would do it but not before he made Bob Rubin miserable for a while. The Speaker said he would act recalcitrant but finally give in, convincing Bob that he had driven a hard bargain. He clearly thought we were there. His mind was already reaching beyond the present and looking ahead. He said he was very happy with how this bipartisan effort had turned out and wanted an ongoing relation with the president. He asked me to think how we could make Washington work better in a bipartisan way.

NEAR MIDNIGHT, I made a last call to Erskine, reporting on the agreement with the Speaker. He would meet us on kids' health. And the Republicans had agreed to fund an initiative on childhood diabetes research that Erskine had been quietly promoting, driven by family circumstances and the chance to do something significant to beat the disease. It was a nice finish to a long day.

SATURDAY, JULY 26, 1997

Early the next morning, I rang up Trent Lott at home and started through the entire deal I had reached with Gingrich. He had spoken to the Speaker but was not fully up to speed on specifics of the tax offers. I went through the list. He was fine with all of it, including my statement that he would have to get Roth to be reasonable on the IRA compromise. What Lott really wanted to know was where we were on a relatively minor provision—a tax incentive to promote production of ethanol, an additive to gasoline that was made primarily from corn. Daschle and Senator Charles Grassley, a Republican, were pressuring him to extend the tax incentive. Both were from big corn-producing states—South Dakota and Iowa, respectively—but Archer was dead set against the tax break. It was the Farm Belt against the Texas oil patch. I told him we favored the Senate provision that extended the incentive, but it was not at the top of our list. But I would offer a compromise—support for an eighteen-month extension—and together we would try to move Archer.

I started through the spending side and he listened for a few minutes. Then he said, "John, to tell the truth, Patricia got me out of the shower for this call and I've been standing here naked for about ten minutes and it isn't a pretty sight. I've got to get off." I glanced at the clock. I had been negotiating with the naked Senate majority leader for about fifteen minutes.

I called the Speaker and in a fully dressed conversation relayed the discussion with Lott. We agreed we were ready to close today.

MEETING IN LOTT'S office at 1:30 p.m., Gingrich wanted to settle a local issue first—how much the federal government would pay states to administer the nation's key safety net programs. Governor George W. Bush of Texas wanted more money to administer the federal government's programs in his state. It was quite a brazen move but still only $30 million. I said yes, but. . . . I had been waiting for an opportunity like this to come along. It turned out we had a problem with New Hampshire and the disproportionate share hospital Medicaid hit it was about to take. We needed to reduce the cutback; Vice President Gore wanted to be sure that he was in no way associated with a large, administration-backed reduction in DSH payments in the state that held the first presidential primary. If the Republicans had picked up on his political predicament, they might have said no just for that reason. Ron Klain, Gore's chief of staff, had the good sense to frame the issue as a concession to New Hampshire's Democratic governor. If they needed to help one of their governors, we needed to help one of ours. Gingrich agreed, and I breathed a sigh of relief. Texas got theirs, but so did New Hampshire and the vice president.

Then the group turned to the major remaining tax pieces, trying for agreement. Ken addressed the basic capital gains proposal, suggesting an eighteen-month holding period to qualify for the 20 percent rate. This fit well with Democrats' preferences, a longer holding period to reward "patient" capital.

We were running out of time on IRAs. Roth had agreed to income limits on those making contributions. But he was at the astronomical level of $279,000 as the cutoff point. That was not even close to what we could accept. We repeated our basic offer. Lott would have to exert himself.

As I looked at Ken's number sheet, I noticed the absence of the EITC spending effects that would be a part of our hybrid child credit stacking proposal. I quietly asked Ken what policy was beneath his numbers.[4] He said it was the one we had agreed to—full stacking. A family could take the child credit against a net tax liability that included both the income tax and the employee share of FICA. But in no case would the combination of EITC and the child credit exceed that expanded notion of tax liability. That was the rule we had agreed to all right, but only for families with three or more kids. Our hybrid proposal was to allow regular stacking for people with two or fewer children

I looked at Ken. We had each done what was in our self-interest and the moment of truth was at hand. Rather than argue it out with me the day before when the alternative was presented, Ken had simply gone back and run the numbers his way, perhaps hoping that the White House team wouldn't notice or wouldn't fight for it. But now the difference was real and apparent—at least to the two of us.

I asked that we take a break. Erksine, Bob, and I went to Lott's private office. I explained the problem. The Republicans had stayed with full stacking across the board and had refused the regular stacking we needed for families with fewer children. They had killed our Rube Goldberg hybrid concoction. Having walked their caucus across a great divide and expanded the concept of tax liability, they were unwilling to broach our bastardized hybrid alternative, one that could expose the fact that regular stacking gave rise to more EITC spending—welfare to them. But the full-stacking approach they were offering meant that many poor working families would not get the benefit of the child credit. We had to go back and insist on our bastard.

When we returned, the mood had turned tense and somber. Ken must have explained to Gingrich and Lott what I had just told Erskine and Bob. I tried to take the discussion back to the technical level, asking Ken what was the difference in cost between what they were putting on the table and our hybrid proposal. He said that the difference was $2.5 billion, the size of the outlays that would be triggered by the regular-stacking component of our proposal. Given the number of families involved, that sounded very low, but I didn't question the number. Perhaps, I thought, Ken was intentionally low-balling the cost and leaving a small enough gap to bridge the divide.

The relatively low cost was the good news. As Ken said, the bad news was that all of the $2.5 billion was clearly on the outlay side of the budget. Forget that in the prior acceptance of regular stacking, the Republicans had agreed to this increase in EITC spending and had also agreed to bury the outlays in the new baseline. That was a political universe ago. The White House had come back for more, expanding the concept of tax liability to include the employee share of FICA. And the Republican leaders had agreed to do the right thing, winning their caucuses to a new concept of tax liability that manifestly helped the working poor. But our latest proposal made plain the expansion in EITC spending that the regular-stacking portion of our hybrid would induce. Fully revealed, our bastard undermined the political basis by which the Republican leaders had sold full stacking to their caucus.

Sitting directly across from Gingrich, I could see that a wave of understanding was sweeping over him. He finally understood how far we had been trying to reach. He had carried his caucus an amazing distance into accepting a wholly new and expanded concept of tax liability to help the working poor. Now the realization was hitting him that we were not just asking for the new tax concept, we were also asking him to accept a hybrid proposal that would result in more EITC spending.

The Speaker had initially slumped as he grasped the political meaning of these last few moments. We had all entered the day thinking that this was the day, the day when six months of hard effort would culminate in a bipartisan balanced budget agreement. And now it was not only slipping away, we were on a collision course that meant failure. The difference wasn't about money; money was irrelevant at this point. It went to the heart of a deep philosophical disagreement between the parties.

In seconds Gingrich had absorbed the body blow and was now gathering his strength. Disappointment was turning to anger, and anger to confrontation. Gingrich was a fighter: strong and tough. He began softly, but every word gathered emphasis. "I cannot carry this in my caucus. If it means the loss of the bill, then so be it. My caucus will never agree to an expansion of welfare. I cannot and will not carry it!" His anger was still growing. He was raising his voice, nearly shouting. "I cannot and will not take this proposal to my caucus! As far as I'm concerned, we are finished!" He got up and walked out of the room.

THE REST OF us, including Senator Lott, sat in silence, looking at each other. For several moments, not a word was spoken as we all tried to absorb the new reality. I sat staring at the number written in my notebook—$2.5 billion. The multitrillion dollar agreement to balance the budget was dead. A lousy $2.5 billion, but a political distance beyond calculation.

We had arrived at a great political divide. The Republican Party that had tried to cut $40 billion from the EITC program in the 1995 reconciliation bill was now being told by a Democratic White House that it had to increase the program. Gingrich had stretched the limits of political tolerance in his caucus and had no more to give. Knowing the caucus, I knew he wasn't bluffing. He could not carry this, but we could not back down. We were dead in the water.

Erskine and Bob went to a corner, where they began talking quietly. I asked Ken to walk me through the numbers again. How much additional did our hybrid proposal cost over ten years? $6 billion. Again, cheap, next to nothing in this world where hundreds of billions of dollars were in play. We knew how to deal with those numbers, how to change the boxes, bury the outlays, move money around. We could have done ten times that amount in the outyears if money were the issue. But, of course, it wasn't. This was a real impasse, a real meltdown.

I walked over to Lott and began talking to him quietly. The EITC was not such a big issue in the Senate, although guys like Nickles would go ballistic when they heard the White House proposal. Perhaps Lott could help us steer past the roadblock. I told him we needed this provision, and we knew that we would have to pay for it. These were spending outlays, so we would pay for them. The $2.5 billion was a small number, but we would have to give up something that mattered to them. I walked Lott through my list of "pay-fors" that I kept on hand. I told him we would put real money on the table to get past this. Knowing that the president would ultimately settle for $22 billion on children's health care, I suggested we trim that number. He asked if we could knock off $4 billion? And how about more out of domestic discretionary spending? Lott was reengaging again, looking for a way to move forward, even if the Speaker had bolted.

We talked for several more minutes, and then Erskine came over. Lott started to put forward the approach he and I had discussed. He suggested that Gingrich might come along if the children's health number could be lowered. Lott was probing, trying to help find a way to get going again. He asked Erskine if we would go below $24 billion on the kids' health program.

Erskine shocked us both. "No," he said, shaking his head vigorously. Lott tried again, but Erskine was even more abrupt. "No, we have to have all $24 billion!" Years of experience had taught the very capable Trent Lott to keep his composure. But Erskine was overbearing, immovable, and strangely out of character. Lott said that he was just trying to help, but if we did not want to work this out, then so be it. He was moving away and joining the Speaker's camp.

We broke for a few minutes and I confronted Erskine. What was he doing? We were on the absolute edge and needed to step back. The agreement was in peril if we didn't show flexibility. We had won everything we needed. Yes, the president wanted $24 billion; we all did. But in a pinch—and we were in crisis—the president would settle for $22 billion or even less.

To his great credit, as angry as he was, Lott returned to the room. He said that we would all be failures if the negotiations ended this way. He suggested we put aside this deal-breaking issue and try to agree to other things. It was a critical moment and a crucially important gesture. We had come as close as could be imagined to cutting the one thin thread holding the agreement together—Trent Lott's goodwill and sense of responsibility. In an act of statesmanship, Lott had put the general interest above his own injured feelings.

We started through the tax offer, trying to lock down agreement on the size of the net tax cut, the capital gains tax provisions, the estate tax, the AMT, and IRAs. The Republican Senate and the White House were back to dealing again, even though the agreement had been derailed. The negotiations were broken down—temporarily we hoped—but really broken down. All of us were performing a ritual, somehow believing our actions could breathe life back into the agreement. We kept going, hoping that we would find a way out of the political abyss into which we had stumbled.

We signed off on a complete education policy and agreed on the details of the provision exempting small corporations from the AMT. Ken and Bob went off into another room to try to work out a compromise on the IRA expansion. Whatever they could agree on would fly with the rest of us, and then we would sell it to Roth.

Late in the day, Gingrich returned. He was back to deliver the message one more time. The president could be under no illusions, he said. "I will not and cannot agree to the White House proposal. No way. Never!"

The Speaker's interjection was calm but intense, and there were no misunderstandings about anything. We were honest with each other, all gravely concerned that our agreement had become sidetracked on a very bumpy EITC road. If we couldn't solve this, we couldn't solve anything. If we couldn't overcome this major political hurdle, we were done. It was time to return to the White House.

BOB RUBIN'S OLDER son was in the hospital, having gone into convulsions as a result of a boxing match. Bob had been on the phone many times over the last two days to his wife and then his son. Working through those two critical days was an amazing and selfless feat. Bob had been incredibly effective in our negotiations, happy to play the role of the tough-minded expert. By taking one end of the argument, he had given Erskine and me the chance to meet the Republican leaders in the middle. But now it was time to return to his family, and Bob was flying to New York.

Back at Erskine's office, four of us sat around the table—Erskine, Gene, Rahm, and me. It was a quiet Saturday evening at the White House, and almost no one else was around. We were just four tired friends, nearly immobilized by defeat. We sat for half an hour, despairing and quietly searching.

Gene began mapping a message war that would force the Republicans to capitulate on the child credit issue. But that was too risky. A real blowup at this point, given all the expectations, would be over the top. The battle on the merits would be overwhelmed by the conflict itself.

As usual, Rahm was looking at the politics from every side, trying to figure how Congress would split if we admitted defeat and how we would pick up the pieces. Erskine was the sounding board. He had the pulse of the president and his tolerances. He would know the right answer if it could be conjured up.

I was focused on the immediate problem. The particular line in the sand on the child credit was drawn across the word welfare. The Republicans would not support a child credit that entailed more spending in the EITC program. But what if we could pay for our hybrid stacking proposal by coming up with other cuts in the EITC? Gingrich could claim victory on holding the line on the EITC, and the administration would win a major expansion of the child credit to working families.

I called Ken and explained my solution. We would pay for our $2.5 billion hybrid through other savings in the EITC program. There would be no net increase in EITC spending—no increase in "welfare."

Ken got it right away. The excitement in his voice told me he thought it would work. He grabbed the concept and immediately started coming back on the particulars. He had a ready-made policy proposal worth over $5 billion of EITC savings. I suggested we look for ways to cut down waste, fraud, and abuse, the very argument the Republicans never tired of making. Ken said Gingrich would want those and more, but we agreed we could work it out. And, yes, he had low-balled the estimate on our child care proposal in an effort to keep it in play. Now he was trying to make up for it.

Elated, I explained the idea to Erskine and the others—and Ken's acceptance. This plan could bring us back from the dead. Everyone understood it and was on board. Rahm jumped up and started his uh-huh routine—loud and with full pelvic grind for emphasis. We were like kids, happy beyond description and not even trying to contain our glee. Rahm blurted out, "Who's getting laid tonight?" Erskine, Rahm, and I shot up our hands. Gene, the unmarried one, hesitated, and then followed suit. We laughed until the tears flowed. Uh-huh, uh-huh, uh-huh.

Minutes later, Erskine's assistant Jason walked in with four books, two for Erskine and two for me. They were from the Speaker. One was his book *To Renew America*, the other his book *1945*, a fictional WWII thriller. They contained exceptional inscriptions speaking to our professionalism and service to the President. Not thirty seconds later, Gingrich was on the line. He had talked to Ken and rushed the books to us—hand-delivered to the White House. It was his way of agreeing to the solution and expressing his gratitude. We had been from taxes to death to resurrection.

CHAPTER FIFTEEN

The Triumph of Responsibility

The president was on the West Coast headed to Las Vegas to meet with the nation's governors. Erskine had updated him by phone on our near-death experience and the solution. The president wanted to make sure his administration got credit for the agreement. First and foremost, we were on the verge of balancing the budget and finally filling that trillion dollar hole that had been created so many years ago. But the agreement also looked to the future, investing in education, health care, and the environment. We would mobilize the many facets of the White House media machine to get out this message. And with the EITC issue near resolution, the president still wanted the full $24 billion on children's health care. In addition, to silence the critics within the party, we would need to get the worst of the poison pills out. There were still at least a dozen issues that needed to be resolved.

SUNDAY, JULY 27, 1997

I called Trent Lott at 10:00 a.m. to go over the remaining issues and schedule a meeting for later in the day. Lott was emphatic in his refusal to meet. He had spent the entire day Saturday in negotiations and had been offended by Erskine's behavior. He said he was going to spend the day with his wife. If there was something to talk about, it could wait until Monday.

I tried to move beyond yesterday's emotionally draining events, telling him that Erskine would talk to him about the confrontation. I just wanted to update him on the president and Erskine's conversation. I started by saying the president felt the Republicans had secured major victories on taxes. That was not something Lott was interested in hearing at that point. Then I reviewed the remaining problems, most of which originated in the House. Finally, I told him the president wanted the full $24 billion on kids' health. Lott reacted immediately, not about the money but about the requirements he supposed we wanted to place on states dictating the health services they would have to offer. Senator Lott said he would oppose strict guidelines; states needed maximum flexibility.

I told him we were trying to find a workable solution in the middle. We had grandfathered Florida, New York, and Pennsylvania's health plans as acceptable. And if other states already had good kids' health plans, then we would approve them as well. In addition, Chris Jennings was working on a compromise that would adopt part of the Republican "actuarial" approach by giving states room to vary spending on a particular benefit requirement by up to 25 percent. Lott was listening.

Finally, Lott and I agreed that Ken Kies, Gene Sperling, and people at Treasury would work through the day to come up with the EITC pay-fors needed to settle the child tax credit issue. Erskine and I were headed out to play golf with our sons. Lott was relieved to hear that.

NEXT I CALLED Gingrich, who was in a good mood, buoyed by the hope that we were nearing a successful conclusion. He said he thought Ken and Gene could come up with $5 billion of savings in EITC. I reminded him that our provision cost only $2.5 billion, but of course we were willing to do as much as possible to cut waste, fraud, and abuse. He let it go by saying, "O.K., $4 billion." More important, he hit the real bottom line—whatever Ken, Gene, and Treasury agreed to would do just fine.

On the labor provisions, I asked that they be removed as a personal favor. He said he would but would put a much tougher version on an appropriations bill. He agreed to postpone, but not give up, the fight. That was more than fine with me.

Another remaining contentious issue was a provision inserted by Senator Paul Coverdell of Georgia allowing the use of IRAs for secondary private school education—the provision was too close to vouchers for Democrats. In exchange for removing it, the Speaker wanted the president to personally request it be tossed. I offered that the president would also send a letter threatening veto, if necessary. Gingrich said he wanted the letter in order to clearly identify Democrats as the culprits. It was good politics for his side.

Finally, we agreed to talk to our technical people, describe the agreements, and ask them to work together through the afternoon on putting the agreements into draft legislation. We would meet at 6:00 p.m. to try to finish. And he would talk to Lott about attending.

GOLF AT RIVER Bend Country Club was hot but a welcome break in the best possible way—with Erskine's son Bill and my son Ryan. After the seventh hole, the vice president called, and we retreated to the golf hut to go through his list. He had about a dozen issues he was tracking and we expected to win on just about all of them—the child credit, brownfields, mental health benefits for children (a big issue with Gore's wife, Tipper), protecting DSH payments for New Hampshire, and more. But I warned him that this was all tentative; we weren't yet final.

As we began playing again, Erskine's pager came up with a news story that the budget talks were intensifying at that very moment. We laughed; the twenty-four-hour news cycle had to be fed.

THE BUDGET TEAM reassembled at the White House at 6:00 p.m. Treasury had come up with EITC enforcement initiatives that could produce substantial savings based on ensuring that only the custodial parent got the benefit of the EITC. But Ken was pushing in a different direction. He wanted to change the structure of the ETIC program by phasing out payments more rapidly as income levels rose. And he wanted to include several additional sources of income in calculating eligibility for the EITC program.

Ken and Gene had been at it all day and still were not close to a solution. And the news from the staff meetings on the Hill was even worse. Everyone was worn out and frustrated at having to work another Sunday. The conceptual agreements we had reached with the Republican leaders were not being translated into legislative language. The staff had not been empowered to move off their positions and had been given too little guidance to move forward.

I spoke to Arne Christenson several times over the next hour and a half, but it was clear that progress had stalled. Around 7:30 p.m., we decided to pull the plug and bring our troops back from the Hill. A meeting that night with Lott and Gingrich would be counterproductive.

MONDAY, JULY 28, 1997

The congressional calendar was closing in. If we could quickly reach agreement, we would be able to draft and file the bills and pass them in time for the August recess. But if we failed, the long August recess that was currently our ally would turn against us. If it became apparent that we could not move the bills by the end of the week, those who opposed the agreement would gain the upper hand.

CALLING LOTT EARLY, I joked about our attempt to pull him into a Sunday meeting. It had been a waste of time: he had been right all along. It just took the rest of us most of the day to figure it out.

Getting down to business, I said that although there were a dozen issues outstanding, only three were truly make or break now that Gingrich had agreed to drop the labor provisions. First was the use of EITC savings to self-finance our hybrid stacking plan for the child tax credit. Next was IRAs. I would try to get Bob Rubin to go another round with Roth, but at the end of the day we'd have to hold hands and not let Roth's potential intransigence stand in the way of an agreement. Last was the children's health benefit package.

That got Lott going again. He said he would not agree to any plan that forced states to provide twenty-nine specific benefits for kids. He insisted that the states would have to have more flexibility. All I could do was agree and tell him he had not been given the facts. There were only four benefits that were in question and on each of those we were willing to let the states alter the resources committed by as much as 25 percent. I could feel his resistance fading. We agreed to meet that afternoon.

BOB RUBIN AND Ken Kies had done well working together through the AMT, capital gains, and other tax issues on Saturday, and we would try that again in an attempt to break through on the remaining tax pieces—the EITC pay-fors and IRAs. The prestige for Ken of reaching agreement with the Treasury secretary might help.

Bob phoned in at 12:30 p.m. after his meeting with Ken. They were taking our EITC "custodial parent" and other compliance proposals under consideration; at least they thoroughly understood them. And Bob was potentially open to including other sources of income in the calculation of the EITC payment. We could agree to include nontaxable distributions from IRAs and other pensions, as well as tax-exempt interest. The money was small—$500 million or so over ten years—but politically significant.

The IRA issue was still unresolved. In addition, we still had to deal with the ranking Democrat on the Ways and Means Committee, Charles Rangel. We had agreed to give him something but had not yet agreed on what.

BRUCE REED OF the White House Domestic Policy Council was calling about the labor provisions. In demanding that they be dropped, we were also dropping some language that was actually better than existing law.[1] He was trying to see if we could keep what we liked while dropping the rest. At this point that would be Mission Impossible.

Then he offered a brilliant idea on the child credit and the EITC. Why didn't we offer to exclude workfare recipients from the EITC? We had been willing to do this in discussions of welfare, why didn't we take advantage of it to solve our child credit problem? It would be an EITC budget saving the Republicans would love.

It was a great idea. There was only one technical glitch, but it could be overcome with a little cooperation from the budget committees. The problem was that Treasury had not officially ruled whether workfare recipients were entitled to EITC, and thus our prohibiting it in law would not score as a budgetary savings. But that obscured the reality and the Republicans would understand. Bob Rubin could rule today that they were eligible and then the prohibition would score. But rather than go through all that, we would have the budget committees focus on the substance and give us credit for the savings.

Bruce's idea was a potential dealmaker, but it was important to run the traps on the Republican side and not spring it on them at the leaders' negotiation meeting. I called Hoagland and relayed the idea. He grasped the scoring issue before I had finished. He would be helpful.

FOR ONCE, EVERYONE was on time. Lott started in with some of his problems. On ethanol, Archer was intransigent, so Lott suggested we "disarm" by dropping the onerous restrictions on the program in the House bill as well as the extension in the Senate bill. After a complicated dance, we were back to current law. Lott insisted on a sentence saying that the tobacco tax proceeds would count against the tobacco settlement. The nasty labor provisions that had nearly derailed the balanced budget bill in the House would come out, and we pledged good faith efforts to work out our differences before the provisions reared their ugly head on the appropriations bills.

Then the meeting took up the benefits covered under the kids' health program. We had been working this issue from all angles, with Chris Jennings doing most of the lifting. We went round and round for fifteen minutes with health experts from both sides. Domenici stepped in, walking through the elements in his careful way, clarifying the extra degrees of flexibility worked out as part of the proffered compromise. Finally, he said he was willing to accept the compromise but he would defer to Lott. It was a well-timed and decisive move by Pete Domenici. After a moment of thought, Lott approved. We were done, we thought.

But by sheer bad luck, the president was with the nation's governors in Las Vegas. They were lobbying him hard on this provision, taking his mumbling as agreement with their particular positions. These supposed understandings were quickly finding their way back to the Capitol in all their distorted finery. I was soon called out of the room to talk with the two governors who had been deputized to make their case. They wanted more flexibility—total flexibility on the benefit package would be just fine. Give us the money, and trust us to do the right thing, they said.

Fortunately one of the governors was my first boss in the Senate, Lawton Chiles of Florida. And even more fortunately, we had just issued a waiver for Florida's program; it met our requirements as it was. The Speaker joined me on the phone and was tremendously helpful in explaining the multiple levels of flexibility we had built in. In contrast, Kasich could not resist getting on the phone and jumping in on the side of governors. He was thinking ahead to 2000 and a possible presidential bid. Gingrich and I listened to the governors and said we would convey their position. But we did not offer to change anything. Finally, we were really done with this one.

Next came the child tax credit and the EITC. Bob walked through our compliance proposals. Then Ken went through the Republican list of structural changes that would save $5 billion in the EITC program—lower the income thresholds, disallow EITC for children over eighteen living at home, and adopt broader definitions of income to be used in calculating the EITC amount. Bob responded by going over in detail various additions to income at issue, and then agreed to include them. The concession was well timed and buoyed the discussion.

Then I started to explain Bruce Reed's idea—denying the EITC to workfare recipients. I said it would save billions over the long term. That was the reality, and we should not get hung up on the budget scoring. As the leaders talked it through, we began to win the day. Gingrich saw that the politics would work for his caucus. Hoagland was given the assignment to estimate the savings the budget committees would score.

Then to IRAs. Roth had been asked to Lott's office and was waiting in an adjoining room while we deliberated the offer to take to him. Ken suggested a phaseout of eligibility at $180,000 in income, his logic being that this amount was our suggested threshold indexed for 3 percent inflation for eighteen years. That was a strange justification. Rubin came back with thresholds of $120,000 to $130,000, softening the blow by offering to add $500 to the annual amount that could be put in the education IRA. As Bob and Ken were going back and forth, I left the room to see what Hoagland was coming up with on our EITC savings.

As I walked through Lott's office, I saw Senator Roth, sitting erect and immobile, alone and silent. I said hello, but his reply was barely audible. He knew his prized IRAs were on the table. The moment of truth was at hand and it was almost too much for him; the self-imposed pressure had left him almost frozen. He was awaiting the fate of his cherished children.

I found that Hoagland had slightly misunderstood Bruce Reed's proposal. I explained what we needed, and he did a quick back-of-the-envelope calculation. He came up with a number we could not quite believe because it was so large. But he was right. We were home free on this toughest of issues. In the end, we agreed to a hodgepodge of compliance initiatives, the broader concepts of income that Bob had offered, and Bruce Reed's idea that had saved the day.

When I returned to the room, the Republican leaders were engaged in shuttle diplomacy between Roth and our negotiating team. Finally, Bob agreed to income limits of $150,000 to $160,000. Treasury had run the numbers in advance. Altogether, our modifications—reductions in the number of IRAs available to taxpayers, more stringent contribution limits, and lower income thresholds for eligibility—had cut the outyear revenue loss in half relative to what the Finance Committee had approved.

It was after 6:00 p.m. and the last budget-related issues were seemingly settled. We spent the next fifteen minutes litigating the last member items, including a rollover provision that allowed a 50 percent exclusion on the capital gains from the sale of small business stock, thereby encouraging investment in small enterprises. Daschle had asked for the provision, and both Lott and I were eager to accommodate him.

With the final agreement in sight, we turned to other pieces of legislation that might be attached to our bill. Knowing that the balanced budget agreement would pass by large margins, it offered an attractive vehicle for carrying other legislation that both sides agreed to. At the top of our list was the president's Caribbean Basin Free Trade Initiative. The trade agreement had strong Republican support, but Finance Committee chairman Roth wanted to attach a needed reauthorization of funding for Amtrak as the price for letting the free trade agreement come on board. We would have to run the traps.

Some loose ends still had to be tied down, but we were 99 percent of the way there. It was 7:00 p.m. on Monday, July 28. As the bipartisan negotiators walked from Lott's office, we told the waiting news reporters that we had reached "a tentative agreement."

TUESDAY, JULY 29, 1997

The budget agreement produced banner headlines. The press got it right. The agreement was a win for the country and the bipartisanship that had enabled the agreement. The fiscal integrity of the nation had been restored by responsible leaders.

Amazing amounts of activity were still going on on two fronts. One front involved taking credit for the win. The Republicans did their victory lap at the Capitol as Lott had long ago decided, while we invited every Democratic member of Congress to the White House for a celebration on the South Lawn. More than one hundred Democratic legislators gathered to hear speeches by the president, vice president, Daschle, Spratt, Lautenberg, and, in a bit of irony, House Democratic whip David Bonior, who would vote for the spending bill that balanced the budget. Notable for his absence was House minority leader Richard Gephardt, who voted against both the balanced budget bill and the tax bill.

The other level of exertion focused on wrapping up the loose ends. With the agreement announced and celebrated, there was no more leverage on either side. All we had was what we had had all along—a sense of purpose and goodwill that allowed us to seize a historic moment.

I STOPPED BY the Speaker's office to coordinate the remaining efforts. Gingrich walked in and announced he had a problem: it was about capital gains. There had been some misunderstanding about the holding periods and rates. I started to get that uneasy, sinking feeling. If there were one issue that could reopen or even kill the deal, it was capital gains.

Ken had reached the final agreement without Archer in the room, and they had gotten their signals crossed. Archer had thought that the rate for assets held between twelve and eighteen months would be the current 28 percent capital gains rate, not the top ordinary income tax rate of 39 percent. This was the first I had heard of the lower rate for these assets. I would have to get back to them.

AFTER THE WHITE House celebration, Erskine, Bob, and I went to Erskine's office. I told them of the problem as relayed by Gingrich and that I had completely missed the discussion on rates and holding periods if there was one. But Bob hadn't. He said he had explicitly clarified that the regular income tax rate would apply to assets held for less than eighteen months. It was hard to tell if Ken had made an error and gone beyond his guidance or if they were trying to come back for more. If we couldn't settle this one, we might be undone again.

ERSKINE, BOB, AND I reconvened with Gingrich and Lott at 7:00 p.m. in the Speaker's Dinosaur office. All sides had claimed victory, but we were still working the issues.

Almost unbelievably, we were still doing cleanup on penny-ante differences in allocations for the children's health program. More important, we also had to settle on the amounts and length of time that spending for kids' health would be incorporated into the budget baseline. If the funding was assumed to expire after five years, the budget rules would force us to pay for its extension beyond that.

In addition, the Hyde abortion language had not yet been settled. I took it down the hall from the Speaker's office to Lott's chief of staff, Dave Hoppe, the lead Republican negotiator on this issue. The galling part was that we had agreed not to use kids' health money for abortion services, but we needed language to ensure the prohibition would not reach into other areas. It was abortion politics, after all. We were hung up on one phrase until Representative Bliley's counsel came up with a new version. We ran it by our folks and it was good. That one was closed.

Back in the Dinosaur office, Erskine and Bob had given Gingrich what Archer wanted on the capital gains holding period. That concession cleared the way for us to secure our position on funding for the kids' health initiative for the next decade, as well as our Medicaid and business incentives for the District of Columbia.

We had been at it for three hours and we were done again except for the Caribbean Basin Initiative. Roth would not let us attach it to the reconciliation bill unless we helped muscle his Amtrak authorization on as well. I agreed to work on it but the odds were long. It was late and the bills were going to be filed the next morning.

IT WAS 11:00 p.m., and at the White House Dan Tate and Andy Blocker of my staff were working Amtrak. But it was rife with union and liability issues. To add to the difficulty, Gingrich would not agree to attach the Amtrak authorization without the assent of House Transportation Committee chairman Shuster. And Shuster was not a big fan of Amtrak. Dan and Andy would work it through the night, and we would try one last time in the morning.

WEDNESDAY, JULY 30, 1997

Bright and early and the Amtrak crowd was in full attendance in a Capitol meeting room: Roth, Moynihan, Joe Biden of Delaware, Shuster, Lott, and many others. Lott started the meeting by asking what we could offer. Did we have anything new to offer? He said that if we didn't, there was no point in proceeding. Having run the traps on the labor issues, we had come as far as we could. We had no more to give. I said that our offer was our offer. The meeting was over in three minutes. Neither the Amtrak authorization nor the Caribbean Basin Initiative would be part of the balanced budget agreement.

THROUGHOUT THE DAY, the White House and administration staff kept working with congressional leadership, committee, and legislative counsel staff to make sure the language was right. Everyone was exhausted, running on the knowledge and exhilaration that this was really it.

The afternoon was wearing on and the tax bill had not yet been filed—the one that had to be voted after the spending bill that balanced the budget. Then I got a call from Ken Kies. They had filed the tax bill. I looked at the clock. It was 4:00 p.m. on July 30, 1997. We were really, really done.

I could feel the pressure start to ebb. It had been just over six months of nonstop exertion since the first meeting with Pete Domenici and Bill Hoagland.

THE VOTES ON both bills that emerged from conference were bipartisan and overwhelming in both chambers of Congress. The House voted 346-85 for the spending bill on July 30 and 389-43 for the tax bill on July 31. The Senate took up both conference reports on July 31, voting 85-15 for the spending bill and 92-8 for the tax package. From the beginning, we had told Democrats that the White House would only negotiate an agreement that a majority of Democrats could endorse. In the end, three-quarters of the Democrats in the House voted for the spending bill, and 80 percent for the tax bill. Democratic support in the Senate was even better.[2] The two bills were signed in a White House ceremony on August 5, 1997, with Speaker Gingrich and thirty-seven other members of Congress attending.

It had taken the nation sixteen years to put the deficit genie back in its bottle. Two presidents—one Republican, one Democrat—did most of the lifting—George H. W. Bush and Bill Clinton. One was not rewarded for his fiscal virtue, while the other benefited greatly from the soaring 1990s which he did so much to create.

The foundation they had laid had made it possible for us to craft a budget in the middle that garnered the overwhelming support of all four party caucuses. The nation's leaders had reached across the aisle and pulled together, forging an agreement that served the national interest. For a brief shining moment, bipartisanship had fulfilled its promise in the triumph of responsibility.

The Limits and
Potential of
Bipartisanship

I have told the story of how responsible leaders rose to the challenge of legislation, reaching across party lines to balance the federal budget while enacting significant policies in the national interest. In this postscript I want to
address four questions. Why did bipartisanship succeed in 1997? Why isn't
bipartisanship more common? What is the potential for bipartisanship? What
are the lessons of 1997 for the future?

WHY DID BIPARTISANSHIP SUCCEED IN 1997?

Bipartisanship succeeded in 1997 because the American people were squarely
behind the goal of a balanced budget. Following the fiscal implosion of 1981,
budgetary responsibility became a driving domestic political force. In the
1980s, not a year went by without congressional leaders trying to repair the
damage. That momentum was amplified by the presidential campaigns of
Ross Perot, the bold fiscal actions of President George H. W. Bush, the 1992
campaign of President Bill Clinton (It's the economy, stupid!), the Democrats-
alone deficit reduction of 1993, and the Republican Contract with America.[1]

Second, each party had taken its turn at deficit reduction while also trying
to advance its political goals. But both the Democratic package of 1993 and
the Republican effort in 1995 were rewarded with political defeat. What both
parties learned the hard way was that behind the laudable goal of balancing
the budget were a bunch of tough policy choices guaranteed to make many
important constituencies unhappy. Both Democrats and Republicans realized that they had severely depleted their political capital trying to turn a dif-

ficult problem to partisan advantage. Bipartisanship, they decided, was a better way.

Third, by 1997 the deficit problem had become manageable. Thanks to the politically perilous efforts of Presidents Bush in 1990 and Clinton in 1993, as well as a robust economy that was filling the Treasury with revenues, it was clear that the budget could be balanced by curbing spending alone. There would have been no bipartisan agreement if tax increases had been part of the program; not only the Republicans, but also many Democrats would have opposed a deficit reduction package that raised taxes. With a manageable deficit hole to be filled, the challenge could be solved within the political box of reducing spending.

Fourth, the policies that were part of the bipartisan deficit reduction effort were fully understood in their political and substantive dimensions. The budget battles leading up to 1997 had largely delimited the universe of policies that could be considered and implemented. The negotiators were not starting from scratch; they thoroughly understood the political tolerances of each side, as well as the expected effects of the policy changes that were on the table. For example, the savings in Medicare and Medicaid had been fought over, scrubbed, and refined for years. Each side understood the policy levers that could be pulled and the political and policy implications of each choice. That knowledge allowed the participants to quickly assemble a budget package that could withstand a variety of opponents. Of course, part of that successful triage involved throwing overboard substantively compelling policies, such as the CPI adjustment, that simply caused too much political turbulence.

Fifth, the leaders on both sides were seasoned and responsible. Although they were tough partisans, each understood that an important national objective could be achieved by working together. None of the central players was so rigid that he could not negotiate in good faith and remain open to the viewpoint of the other side. These were also professionals who knew how to drive the legislative process. They understood the political and personal leanings of their colleagues and the policies they would and would not support. That knowledge and their leadership skills provided the foundation for an agreement that could command the overwhelming support of their caucuses.

WHY ISN'T BIPARTISANSHIP MORE COMMON?

What must be obvious to any citizen is that when it comes to the big issues, bipartisanship is the exception. Although every Congress sees the enactment of numerous bills by bipartisan majorities, these bills tend to fly below the radar screen; they are not the stuff of the nightly news nor the stuff of election campaigns. This should be no surprise. At the base of our democratic system of government is a competition for elective office; political competition among partisans is how we Americans pick winners and losers and empower the winners to make the big decisions. Winning elections is the essential precondition for exercising government's considerable powers.

Americans are bound together by innumerable ties that far outweigh our differences, but those differences are very real and very important. They are the propellant behind our political competition, the substance beneath the platforms on which the parties stand. In elections, the emphasis is on the differences among candidates and the parties, not on what they share in common. And although most candidates pay lip service to the idea of bipartisanship, campaigns are won or lost by drawing ideological, political, and policy differences.

Recall from the story of 1997 the first meeting between the president and the bipartisan congressional leadership. All those present knew that several issues were not even eligible for bipartisan consideration. These hot-button issues—abortion, labor issues, gay rights, and the like—were the grist for elections and the partisan legislative battles within the House and the Senate, issues on which deep substantive disagreement or political expediency ruled out a bipartisan approach.

Recall also that even within the bipartisan effort to balance the budget, many policies that were worthy on the merits were not part of the solution because the politics were too severe. These policies included the CPI adjustment, income-tested Medicare premiums, and an increase in EITC spending. Despite this, a bipartisan solution to the deficit problem was possible because the middle ground was large enough to allow leaders to balance the budget without exposure to severe political attack.

Bipartisanship is uncommon because partisan competition for office is at the core of our political system. The parties and participants stake their claims for office on issues that are raised, mediated, and fought through the news media, advertising, and an array of outreach efforts. Party cohesion and financial resources play a critical role in drawing the differences and getting the message out. The winners emerge committed to party platforms and policies that emphasize the differences with the other side rather than what they share in common. In such a setting, bipartisanship is not the first instinct; it is an option to be considered within the context of perceived electoral imperatives. Despite this, there are important opportunities for bipartisanship to play a constructive role in our political system.

WHAT IS THE POTENTIAL FOR BIPARTISANSHIP?

America's brand of representative democracy has proven amazingly resilient. Our vibrant, messy, contested, but fundamentally open and fair form of government has allowed the American people to steer their ship of state, deal with new challenges, and overcome many differences of belief and opinion. Over the long haul, our political system has proven remarkably good at inventing and enacting a positive and expansive American consensus. This consensus defines the political landscape on which bipartisanship can potentially flourish.

Here is a brief rendition of some key elements of the current American consensus. We should be free citizens who are secure in our fundamental rights; we should be secure as a nation and in our persons and possessions; we should have an open and competitive economy that rewards work and fair play; the doors of education should be open to everyone as the gateway to opportunity; we should live in a clean and safe environment; we should guarantee that our seniors, the disabled, and those who have sacrificed for their country have access to the basic essentials of life; and we should provide a safety net for the poor, as well as the tools they need to lift themselves out of poverty. This American consensus did not spring forth full grown; many of its elements emerged relatively recently, made possible by the serendipitous combination of economic growth, the goodness of a free people, and our competitive politics.

Political competition has been a prime catalyst propelling the values, ideas, and policies through which the American consensus has emerged. And that progression has often been contentious. To take a few examples, Social Security, civil rights, Medicare, and environmental measures were fought over, sometimes bitterly and for prolonged periods. Partisan competition has been at the center of our struggle to advance as a people and a nation. It has been our most important engine for adaptation and change—one that remains in full motion.

While competitive politics is the driving force behind the nation's evolution, bipartisanship has a significant role to play. Bipartisanship is important because it offers a constructive way to settle differences on a politically determined middle ground. Take the example of the children's health initiative in 1997. Both parties shared the goal of extending health care to more of America's children. But behind that shared goal there were strong and principled disagreements about the extent of the coverage and its cost, the role of states, the benefits to be covered, eligibility standards, and on and on. The bipartisan approach allowed the various interests and issues to be fully represented. Each side had to argue the merits of its positions in a bid for the other's support. The constructive tension between Democrats and Republicans forced policies to be thoroughly scrubbed and run to ground. Proposals on the extremes were eliminated, improving the final product. Often, however, the compromises in the middle resulted in greater complexity as both sides sought to incorporate elements of their favored policies.

The arenas where partisanship and bipartisanship dominate are not fixed but under dynamic stress, existing within a vibrant political system in which partisans fight for dominance. Take the example of Medicare. In 1995 the parties' disagreements about the scope, nature, and funding of Medicare forced the issue into the sphere of partisan competition. The outcome of those battles delimited the changes to the program that could be undertaken and opened enough of a middle ground for a bipartisan solution in 1997. One of the linchpins of the bipartisan agreement thus emerged from the ashes of partisan conflict.

LESSONS FOR THE FUTURE

Going forward, Americans will continue to decide their deep differences through open political competition. But we also need to draw on bipartisanship to strengthen our common ground. There are opportunities now for bipartisan engagement in the areas of Social Security, health care, tax reform, and national security, among others. To improve the odds that such engagement will occur, I want to offer ten generic lessons from the 1997 balanced budget agreement.

Get under the Umbrella

In 1997 the umbrella of fiscal responsibility established a balanced budget as the box within which many political and policy differences could be resolved. The commitment to an overarching goal is absolutely essential to bipartisan accomplishment—whether that goal is a balanced budget, the solvency of the Social Security system, health insurance coverage for all Americans, security for our nation and people, or any number of important objectives that fall under the American consensus. The commitment establishes the basis for partisans to engage, to enact solutions consistent with the principle, and to be held accountable for their performance. It is also the indispensable signal to partisans that they are to undertake a different type of political competition, one in which winning means not imposing losses on the other side but finding common ground. Once an overarching goal is endorsed by both sides, it allows hard partisans to shift gears and focus on accomplishment, not opposition.

Cement the Center with Trust

The balanced budget of agreement of 1997 would not have been possible without the extraordinary efforts of a small group of partisans. They understood that a successful engagement required an act of faith and trust that the other side was committed to the common enterprise. That opened the door for the participants to begin acting like teammates, working together to solve problems. Each act of trust and goodwill built upon others, ultimately creating a bond and commitment to see the effort to a successful conclusion. The bonds of trust are indispensable to allowing the center to hold against the assaults of partisans on the outside, to defeat the special interests, and to accommodate the parties' competing agendas.

Avoid the Politics of Confrontation

Early and quiet outreach prevented the normal partisanship from gaining the upper hand. At all times, the channels were fully open between the key participants. Misunderstandings were avoided by phone calls and back-channel meetings outside the glare of the press and hidden away from those who wanted us to fail. Much of the work was done outside the normal partisan settings. The participants usually succeeded in raising, resolving, or putting aside their differences quietly and privately. This reduced the chances that those opposed to parts or all of the agreement could leverage the media, caucuses, and interest groups against the agreement. Message wars and mobilizing the troops are the tools of partisanship and opposition, designed to defeat the other side rather than find the middle. Disagreements litigated in public bestow inordinate influence on fringe elements, particularly those with financial resources. Deficit reduction is about distributing pain—someone's ox is going to be gored. That necessary exercise is best decided in quiet and packaged in a way that can carry the entire measure.

Most important, the president and congressional leaders involved in the effort went out of their way to maintain a bipartisan tone. Not only were the core negotiators in constant touch with each other, sharing information and possible solutions, but the president was actively engaged with leaders of both parties. On the occasions when public displays of partisanship were unavoidable, advance notice was usually given along with assurances that the bipartisan process would continue.

Keep Your Counsel

Controlling the flow of information was one of our most potent weapons. The tough decisions were argued out in private among those committed to the overall enterprise. We simply locked out those whose goal was to subvert the agreement. Within the core group, there were no unplanned leaks; information was distributed only to advance the legislation. Interest groups and many in opposition only knew what we wanted them to.

We drew no public lines in the sand, were disciplined in our use of words, and kept our mouths shut even as we kept plowing ahead and working together. We kept our heads down together until we had created an agreement that could not be picked apart and undermined. Ultimately, we were able to put the opposition on the defensive, having to oppose a balanced budget that invested in America while cutting taxes.

Understand the Other Side

In 1997 each side fully appreciated the needs and constraints of the other. Success came from participants being open about their problems and respectful of those of the other side. In all negotiations the working presumption was that disagreements were rooted in principle and were worthy of respect and consideration. Previous engagements allowed both sides to understand the political hot buttons that could undo the effort. That history, along with an openness to accommodation, allowed the participants to understand and separate the needs of the other side from the posturing going on in public venues.

Know Your Facts and Policies

We were fortunate that both sides had policy experts who could strongly represent their views, poke holes in the arguments of others, and be open to the shortcomings of their own positions and the strengths of others. Expertise is essential among partisans, but it also needs to be reinforced by nonpartisan agencies such as the Congressional Budget Office whose analyses are accepted by both sides as fair and unbiased.

Know the Process and How to Use It

In 1997 the negotiators understood and used rules, procedures, and conventions to their advantage—whether it meant inventing a new baseline, adopting a novel scoring convention, overriding the work of the committees, or working together to find presentations satisfying the predilections of very different caucuses. Working together, negotiators on both sides were able to delete poison pills from legislation, add necessary provisions, and otherwise control the lawmaking process.

Take on the Opposition

Any major legislation will generate opposition. Whenever they could, partisans opposed to the 1997 agreement did their best to subvert it by arguing on the merits, disclosing sensitive information, misrepresenting the facts, organizing interest groups, and more. This is the expected rough and tumble of our partisan world, a reality to be recognized up front and be prepared for. In 1997 House Democratic leader Richard Gephardt opposed our effort from the beginning. While respecting Gephardt's position, we were resolved to prevail. That required arguing the merits in party caucuses, rallying the moderates, and reaching out to all those prepared to listen.

Expect Surprises

Surprises and bad news are the daily staples of legislation and politics. A key chairman or committee goes off on his or its own, a powerful member takes offense at a real or imagined slight, a policy or position is misunderstood or misrepresented, a vote count turns out to be wrong, a leadership mutiny threatens a key participant, or an error in crafting a policy ignites a firestorm. Sometimes even good news can be bad news, as when the CBO put $200 billion in additional revenue on the table, almost killing the agreement. Policymakers must expect surprises and then be ready to work together to overcome them.

Leaders Lead

At the end of the day, the balanced budget agreement became a reality because of the leadership of President Clinton, a group of talented congressional leaders, and professional staff on both ends of Pennsylvania Avenue. The congressional leaders involved in the bipartisan effort did a masterful job informing, guiding, cajoling, and winning the support of their troops. They were open about the lines they could not lead their colleagues across, whether on the CPI adjustment, the EITC, Medicare policies, or any number of other issues. In the Senate both Republican leader Trent Lott and Democratic leader Tom Daschle supported the effort, easing the way past many substantive and procedural hurdles. In the House the Republican leaders and important elements of the Democratic and Republican caucuses helped keep the agreement alive. They steered the caucuses through many tough stages and provided the political judgment, support, and vision to craft legislation that could ultimately command the overwhelming assent of all four caucuses.

As they did in 1997, today's leaders need to address critical national problems by reaching across the aisle to strengthen the American consensus. Those efforts will be difficult; success is not ensured. Partisanship is the propelling force behind our political system, and that partisanship has become professionalized and perfected. The hopes, fears, and anxieties of American voters are thoroughly plumbed and processed, then repackaged and amplified for partisan purposes. Our leaders are given very little leeway to find the middle. In such a world, it becomes much more difficult for the country to present a united front either at home or abroad.

In 1997 we reached across the aisle and trusted each other to do the right thing. Today, there is a crying need for bipartisanship on national security, taxes, health, retirement, the environment, and many other issues. After a decade of overblown opposition, it is time for the bond of bipartisanship to be renewed.

Primer on the
Budget Process

The budget process is the set of procedures by which the government decides its tax and spending policies for the upcoming year. It begins in early February when the president submits his budget proposal to Congress for the next fiscal year, which begins on October 1. Within each chamber, a budget committee is then charged with creating an initial blueprint to guide congressional action. Each of these two committees writes a budget resolution that sets the overall levels of federal revenues, spending, and the resulting surplus or deficit. Within the spending total, the budget resolution sets the total amount to be spent for government programs funded annually under the jurisdiction of the appropriations committees. The budget resolution may also trigger a reconciliation bill that is used to enact changes in government entitlement programs and tax policies in order to reduce the deficit. The reconciliation bill is considered under expedited procedures that limit hours of debate and cannot be filibustered.

The committee-reported budget resolution is considered, possibly amended, and passed by the full membership in each house. The differences in the Senate and House versions of the budget resolution are resolved in a conference among representatives of the two bodies. That nonamendable conference agreement is then adopted by both houses of Congress. Upon passage, the budget resolution becomes binding and is enforced by procedural points of order such as those that preclude, or create higher voting thresholds to retain, provisions that violate the budget resolution. The budget resolution is not presented to the president for signature but is intended to guide Congress's budget deliberations.

As mentioned, the budget resolution sets the amount that can be spent under the jurisdiction of the House and Senate Appropriations Committees. This spending is often referred to as *discretionary* to distinguish it from *entitlement* or *mandatory* spending, which is fixed in law and does not require annual appropriations. Deficit reduction in appropriated spending is achieved by restricting the total amount that can be spent to less than would be spent if the previous year's level of funding were increased at the rate of inflation.

Once the total pot of money that can be spent in the annual appropriations process is determined by the budget resolution, the Appropriations Committee in each house allocates that total among its thirteen subcommittees. After gathering input and testimony from interested parties, each subcommittee reports a bill funding programs under its jurisdiction. Each subcommittee-reported bill is considered, possibly amended, and reported by the full Appropriations Committee for consideration by the entire House or Senate. Upon consideration, possible amendment, and passage of each appropriations bill by each house, the differences between the bills are resolved in a conference. That nonamendable conference agreement is adopted by both houses of Congress and sent to the president for signature. If signed, the appropriations bill becomes a law. If vetoed, it is returned to Congress, where the veto is either overridden or sustained. If overridden, the bill becomes a law. If the veto is sustained, the bill dies, and another one must be considered with the goal of gaining passage in Congress as well as the president's signature. In the event that one or several appropriations bills are not enacted by the start of the fiscal year, the common practice is to pass a continuing resolution, which funds the activities of government until full-year funding can be enacted. The continuing resolution must be signed by the president to become a law.

The budget resolution may trigger a reconciliation bill to reduce the deficit either by reducing spending in entitlement or mandatory programs (such as Medicare, Medicaid, agriculture, and others), by increasing taxes, or by a combination of the two. On the spending side, budgetary savings are achieved by legislating programmatic changes to reduce spending below what would occur under laws currently in place. Programmatic changes might include changing benefit formulas, qualification standards, or federal payments to service providers, for example. Deficits can also be reduced by increasing taxes. Federal taxes largely fall under the jurisdiction of the Ways and Means Committee in the House and the Finance Committee in the Senate. The budget resolution establishes a numerical target for each committee charged with achieving deficit reduction in its jurisdiction. The budget resolution might suggest policies to achieve the required budget savings, but those suggestions are not binding on the committees. Each committee considers and reports policies in its jurisdiction to achieve the assigned numerical deficit reduction target. These committee-reported bills are packaged together and reported by the Budget Committee in each chamber in the form of a reconciliation bill. That privileged legislation—which cannot be filibustered—is considered, possibly amended, and passed in each body and the differences are resolved in conference. The nonamendable reconciliation conference report is adopted by both houses and presented to the president for signature. If signed, the reconciliation bill becomes a law. If vetoed, the bill is returned to Congress and the veto is either overridden or sustained. If overridden, the bill becomes a law. If sustained, the bill dies and a new one must be passed by Congress and signed by the president to become a law. (Readers seeking additional information on the budget and budget process should consult www.senate.gov/~budget.)

IMPORTANCE OF BUDGET PROJECTIONS

Budget projections play a crucial role in the budget process. There are two official arbiters of budgetary matters: Congress relies on the Congressional Budget Office (CBO), and the administration's budgetary agency is the Office of Management and Budget (OMB). As might be expected, these arbiters often disagree when projecting government spending, revenues, and deficits. These projections depend on three broad sets of factors: laws in effect, economic projections, and technical assumptions. Using unemployment insurance as an example, projected spending depends on the structure of the program as fixed in law, such as the requirements to qualify for benefits and the benefit formulas for recipients. But projections of future spending also depend on assumptions about how many people might become unemployed, which depends on projections of the future state of the economy. In addition, some percentage of qualified recipients might not take advantage of the program, and these technical factors must be accounted for as well.

Differences in budget projections have a major impact on the job facing congressional and White House budgeteers. Throughout the budget process, CBO and OMB independently estimate or score the budgetary implications of suggested policy changes. The higher their estimates of the budget and the lower their scoring of budgetary savings, the larger the budgetary and political challenge becomes. With each side defending the projections of its own budget arbiter and with the outcome so important on budgetary and political grounds, budgetary projections often become a point of contention.

For example, in 1997 there were significant differences in budget projections. After adjusting both OMB and CBO deficit projections for the fiscal dividend—the expected improvement in economic performance flowing from a balanced budget agreement—the cumulative deficits projected by CBO from FY 1998 to FY 2002 were $787.2 billion. Under OMB's projections the cumulative deficits were $596.4 billion, a difference of $190.8 billion. In FY 2002 alone, the difference in deficit projections was $65.9 billion.

IMPROVING THE BUDGET PROCESS

Even within our competitive political system, the opportunities for bipartisanship can be strengthened by paying attention to rules and institutions. Here I make three specific recommendations to improve the congressional budget process.

First, bipartisan cooperation is bolstered when there are strong nonpartisan referees trusted by both sides to separate fact from partisan positioning. The principal arbiters are the Congressional Budget Office; the congressional Joint Committee on Taxation (JCT), which analyzes and estimates the impacts of tax policies; and the Government Accountability Office (GAO), which is the nonpartisan investigative arm of Congress. These agencies evaluate, estimate, and investigate the expected and actual effects of congressional and executive branch activities. They are in a difficult position, being charged with nonpartisanship in a highly charged political atmosphere. A natural result is that attempts are made to influence their decisions. At the micro level, interested parties consult with these nonpartisan agencies. At another level, partisans have attempted to intervene in appointments of key officials, funding, and the reach of these agencies' jurisdiction. It is important to further isolate and empower these nonpartisan arbiters, particularly the JCT, which is closely aligned with the politically attuned tax-writing committees.

Second, when agreements are reached, adequate enforcement mechanisms are needed to ensure they are not easily bypassed or overturned. From 1991 until 2002, Congress operated under effective budget enforcement rules. The first held spending by the appropriations committees to the agreed-to amounts by legislating fixed dollar limits on the three major categories of appropriated spending—defense, international, and domestic spending. The second major enforcement mechanism was called PAYGO. It required that increases in entitlement spending or tax reductions greater than those set in the agreement be paid for with offsetting budgetary savings. Provisions or amendments that violated this requirement were subject to higher vote thresholds for adoption. The lapse of these enforcement mechanisms after fiscal 2002 helped open the door to large deficits. Both of these mechanisms have proven their effectiveness and should be reinstated in law.

Third, the legislative playing field needs to be tilted to encourage partisans to work together and to make it harder to simply run over the other side. For example, the reconciliation process needs to be returned to its original purpose. As enacted in the 1974 Budget Act, this privileged legislative vehicle, which effectively disarmed the filibuster in the Senate, was intended for deficit reduction. This narrow purpose has been completely subverted, and reconciliation has become the engine for every manner of legislation. Rather than a vehicle to enable fiscal prudence, it is used to make partisan blitzkriegs easier, reducing the need for bipartisan cooperation. Reconciliation needs to be returned to its original purpose or eliminated.

Key Budget Terms

APPROPRIATED SPENDING Federal spending determined annually through the enactment of appropriations bills. These amounts are also called discretionary spending in distinction to entitlement spending, which is determined by spending formulas set in law, such as Social Security and Medicare. Discretionary spending is frequently divided between defense spending ($271.7 billion in FY1997) and nondefense spending ($275.1 billion in FY1997). Nondefense discretionary spending can be divided into international discretionary spending ($19.0 billion in FY1997) and domestic discretionary spending ($256.6 billion in FY1997).

Appropriated spending is under the jurisdiction of the Appropriations Committee in each house. Each Appropriations Committee is divided into thirteen subcommittees, each of which is responsible for reporting a funding bill for government programs under its jurisdiction.

AUTHORIZING COMMITTEES Congressional committees that have jurisdiction over legislation that determines the programs and policies of the federal government. Legislation originating in authorizing committees can have a direct impact on spending or revenues through the passage of laws obligating the federal government to make payments under particular programs (such as Social Security, unemployment insurance, or Medicare) or to collect revenues from various sources (individuals, corporations, and the like).

BASELINE A projection of spending, revenue, and deficit amounts over time. The budgetary impact of policy changes is measured against the baseline amounts. For example, spending less than the baseline amount is scored as a budgetary saving— reducing the baseline spending and deficit projection.

There is no single convention for constructing a baseline. The baselines devised by both the Office of Management and Budget (OMB) and the Congressional Budget Office (CBO) reflect laws that are in effect. For amounts that are appropriated annually, the baseline is assumed to rise with the rate of inflation, based on the view that it is the real value of government services and benefits that is maintained over time. The baseline projections of OMB and CBO may vary significantly because of differences in underlying economic and technical assumptions. For example, differences in the projected unemployment rate generate different estimates of spending on safety net programs.

A "freeze" baseline assumes that spending is held constant over time at a fixed level without any adjustment to account for inflation.

BUDGET DEFICIT A unified federal budget deficit occurs when the government's total spending for a year exceeds the total revenues it takes in during that year. The budget deficit is financed by borrowing from the public. The accumulated borrowing of the federal government from the public is the national debt owed to the public.

BUDGET RESOLUTION The congressional budget blueprint that sets aggregate levels of spending, revenues, and deficits (generally over a five-year budget window). Within the spending total, the budget resolution sets the total amount to be spent for government programs funded annually under the jurisdiction of the appropriations committees. The budget resolution may also enable a reconciliation bill that is used to enact changes in government entitlement programs (Medicare, Medicaid, agriculture, and others), tax policies, or both, in order to reduce the deficit. The reconciliation bill is considered under expedited procedures that limit hours of debate and cannot be filibustered. The budget resolution is not a bill that is presented to the president for signature, but is Congress's own internal budget outline. The budget resolution is enforced through points of order that either preclude, or create higher voting thresholds to retain, provisions that violate the budget resolution.

BYRD RULE Named after its author, Senator Robert C. Byrd of West Virginia, the rule prohibits "extraneous" provisions as part of a reconciliation bill in the Senate. Of the several tests determining whether a provision is extraneous, three were particularly important in 1997: provisions would be removed if they had no budgetary impact and violated the intended use of the reconciliation vehicle; if they led to changes in revenues or outlays that were merely incidental to the intent of the provision; or if they caused an increase in the deficit beyond the five-year budget window. Provisions judged to be extraneous by the Senate parliamentarian faced a sixty-vote hurdle to waive the Byrd rule in the Senate and be retained in the bill.

CAPITAL GAINS TAX A preferential tax rate applied to the gains on assets held for a certain period of time. The reduction in the tax rate is achieved by excluding a proportion of eligible gains from taxation. In the final compromise in 1997, 50 percent of the gain was excluded from income, leading to a top capital gains rate of 20 percent.

CAUCUS A politically affiliated group within Congress. The major caucuses were the Republican and Democratic caucuses in the House and Senate. Caucus affiliation can include smaller groups such as the Black Caucus, Hispanic Caucus, and so on.

CHILD TAX CREDIT A credit on taxes of $500 per year for children under 17. In the final compromise, income limits for eligibility were set at $75,000 for single filers and at $110,000 for married filers.

CHILDREN'S HEALTH The final compromise provided $24 billion to expand health insurance to uninsured children, mainly those with family incomes up to 200 percent of the poverty level. Coverage could be provided through expansions of Medicaid coverage, state-sponsored health insurance, or a combination of the two. States could use up to 10 percent of the funding to provide direct health services to children.

CONFERENCE REPORT The final version of a bill in which differences between the House and Senate have been resolved. The agreed-upon bill must be passed in both the House and Senate before being sent to the president. The conference report cannot be amended, but on a reconciliation bill, provisions in the conference report were subject to the Byrd rule. The purpose of applying the Byrd rule to conference reports was to permit provisions to be struck from a conference report that could not be filibustered.

CONGRESSIONAL BUDGET OFFICE (CBO) A nonpartisan congressional organization created under the 1974 Budget Act. CBO undertakes a wide variety of analyses of the budgetary and other impacts of policy proposals and programs. It is the recognized estimator of the budgetary effects of congressional spending. The **Congressional Joint Committee on Taxation** is Congress's official estimator of the budgetary impact of tax policies. It is separate from CBO and is under the broad control of the tax-writing committees—the Finance Committee in the Senate and the Ways and Means Committee in the House.

CONSUMER PRICE INDEX (CPI) The government's official measure of the rate of inflation. It is used to determine inflation-based adjustments in government entitlement programs, such as Social Security, for which there are automatic cost-of-living adjustments (COLAs).

CONTINUING RESOLUTION A legislative vehicle under the jurisdiction of the appropriations committee. It provides temporary funding for government programs when regular appropriations bills have not been enacted into law by the end of the fiscal year on September 30.

CORPORATE ALTERNATIVE MINIMUM TAX (AMT) REPEAL The alternative minimum tax was adopted in 1969 to ensure that wealthy businesses and individuals could not avoid all income tax liability by claiming large numbers of deductions, credits, and exemptions. Because the AMT, unlike the rest of the tax system, was not adjusted for inflation, by 1997 the number of businesses and individuals subject to it had grown substantially. In the final compromise, businesses with less than $5 million of annual receipts were no longer subject to the AMT.

DISPROPORTIONATE SHARE HOSPITAL PAYMENTS Payments made under the Medicaid program to hospitals serving a high proportion of the needy. In 1997 the president proposed to reduce the total Medicaid payments while retargeting the remaining payments toward hospitals serving vulnerable populations.

DISTRICT OF COLUMBIA PROVISIONS The agreement raised the federal Medicaid matching rate from 50 percent to 70 percent; established an enterprise zone in several areas of the District, provided tax incentives for businesses to locate and hire workers there; and established a means-tested credit for homebuyers.

DOMESTIC DISCRETIONARY SPENDING Federal spending for domestic programs (not defense and international programs) determined annually through enactment of bills under the jurisdiction of the appropriations committees. In FY 1997 domestic discretionary spending was $256.6 billion. Funds provided within domestic discretionary spending cover a wide range of programs: education, health, science, transportation, commerce, banking, veterans services, labor, justice, environment, and more.

EMPOWERMENT ZONES AND ENTERPRISE COMMUNITIES A program enacted in 1993 to spur business investment, jobs, training, and community development in distressed areas using tax incentives, federal grants, and flexibility in the use of federal funds.

ENTITLEMENT SPENDING Government spending and payment amounts that are set in law. Legal criteria determine which individuals or organizations are eligible and the amounts they receive. The largest entitlement programs are Social Security, Medicare, and Medicaid.

EARNED INCOME TAX CREDIT (EITC) A program providing refundable tax credits for low-income working families. The EITC amount depends on income and the number of children. If the EITC amount is greater than the tax liability against which it can be counted, the difference is paid to the qualifying taxpayer. This payment is the refundable aspect and is counted as spending.

ESTATE TAX In the final compromise, the unified tax credit for estates and gifts was increased. This exemption from taxation was increased over time, set to reach $1 million in 2006.

FISCAL YEAR The year-long period for the federal budget, commencing on October 1 and ending on the following September 30. For example, fiscal year 1998 refers to the period beginning on October 1, 1997, and ending on September 30, 1998. Funding for the federal government's appropriated programs must be passed into law by October 1. If one or several appropriation bills have not been signed into law by that time, the normal practice is to pass a continuing resolution providing temporary funding.

FOOD STAMPS A federal program providing the means to purchase food and other essential items. In 1996 over 25 million people received food stamps with an average monthly value of $73.

GRAMM-RUDMAN-HOLLINGS (GRH) The 1985 revision to the budget process in which deficit goals were established in law, backed up by an enforcement mechanism—sequestration—that cut spending in order to meet the deficit targets.

GROUP OF EIGHT The shorthand name for the expanded group of White House budget principals. In alphabetical order they were Erskine Bowles, John Hilley, Jack Lew, Frank Raines, Bob Rubin, Gene Sperling, Larry Summers, and Janet Yellen.

GROUP OF FIVE The shorthand name for the core group of White House budget principals. In alphabetical order they were Erskine Bowles, John Hilley, Frank Raines, Bob Rubin, and Gene Sperling.

HOME HEALTH CARE BENEFIT A Medicare program providing home health visits for the sick elderly. Under the president's proposal, the first 100 home health visits following a three-day hospital stay would continue to be reimbursed under Part A of Medicare. All other visits, including those not following hospitalization, would be reimbursed under Part B of the Medicare program, which covers the costs of physician, nursing, and related health services. The transfer of these expenses was part of the final agreement.

HOPE SCHOLARSHIP A $1,500 per year refundable tax credit for the first two years of postsecondary education expenses. The president's original proposal for a lifetime learning tax deduction of $10,000 was dropped in favor of a lifetime tax credit of 20 percent of qualified education expenses, up to $5,000. In 2002 the expense limit would be raised to $10,000.

HYDE LANGUAGE Named after Representative Henry Hyde of Illinois, the Hyde language prohibited the use of federal funding for abortion-related health services as was applied to the new children's health initiative.

IMMIGRANT PROVISIONS COMPROMISE Under the final compromise, elderly or disabled legal immigrants in the United States as of August 22, 1996, were reinstated as eligible for SSI and Medicaid whether they were disabled on August 22, 1996, or became so afterwards. Before enactment of the 1996 welfare reform bill, legal immigrants had been eligible for these services.

INFLATION INDEXATION OF CAPITAL GAINS A proposal that was adopted in the Ways and Means Committee but was not part of the final compromise. Indexation of capital gains uses an inflation index to measure the amount of capital gains that are attributed to inflation. Only capital gains above inflation are subject to taxation.

INDIVIDUAL RETIREMENT ACCOUNTS (IRA) A tax-favored savings vehicle. The "front-loaded IRA" is funded with before-tax dollars, but the individual must pay taxes at the time of withdrawal. A "back-loaded IRA" is funded with after-tax dollars, but the accumulated earnings can be withdrawn tax-free. In the final compromise, the use of IRAs was restricted by income level.

MARKUP A term describing the actions of a congressional committee in creating legislation. The custom is for the chairman to offer a "mark," or draft, of the legislation. That mark can then be amended or replaced with a complete substitute under majority votes. Bills reported out of committee for consideration by the full body are placed on the calendar. It is normally the prerogative of the majority leader in the Senate and the Speaker in the House to determine which of the reported committee bills shall be considered by the full body.

MEDICAL SAVINGS ACCOUNT A program allowing the use of tax-exempt accounts for health care costs. Individuals would be required to carry a high-deductible insurance policy to guard against catastrophic health expenses. The final compromise called for a demonstration project limited to 390,000 participants.

MEDICAID The federal-state program that helps fund health care for people with incomes below certain levels.

MEDICARE The federal program funding health care for seniors sixty-five and older. It is not means-tested—beneficiaries do not lose or pay more proportionately for benefits as income rises. Part A of Medicare primarily pertains to hospital services, while Part B pertains to physician, nursing, and related services.

NONDEFENSE DISCRETIONARY SPENDING Spending on discretionary programs covering domestic and international areas. In FY1997, $275.1 billion was spent on programs under this broad category. Spending is determined annually through the enactment of appropriations bills.

OFFICE OF MANAGEMENT AND BUDGET (OMB) The executive branch agency charged with analyzing and estimating the budgetary and other impacts of proposals, policies, and programs. OMB is the administration's official budget estimator.

PAYGO An important budget enforcement mechanism requiring that spending or tax legislation be paid for in a deficit-neutral manner. Violations of the PAYGO, or "pay as you go," provisions were subject to sixty-vote budgetary points of order in the Senate.

PELL GRANTS Named after Senator Claiborne Pell of Rhode Island, the grants assist low-income students to cover the cost of attending college.

POINT OF ORDER When a point of order is raised in the Senate, the Senate parliamentarian determines whether it applies to the provision (or bill) in question. If judged so, the point of order may be waived, but only if there are the necessary votes to waive it. Since the reconciliation bill cannot be filibustered, the sixty-vote hurdles were important in helping to keep out provisions that did not conform to the intended purposes of the reconciliation bill.

PRIVATIZATION OF SOCIAL SECURITY A proposal to allow individuals to allocate a portion of Social Security taxes to private investment accounts. At the time of retirement, the individual investment account would provide financial support in addition to reduced Social Security benefits.

RECONCILIATION BILL A protected legislative vehicle established as part of the 1974 Congressional Budget Act. The reconciliation bill could not be filibustered and was considered under expedited procedures that limited the hours of debate. Protections such as the Byrd rule were adopted in an attempt to prevent misuse of the reconciliation vehicle and restrict it to budgetary purposes.

RULES COMMITTEE, HOUSE The House Rules Committee is the gatekeeper for bills to be considered by the entire House. Normally under the direction of the Speaker of the House, the Rules Committee determines which bills will be considered, which amendments (if any) will be allowed, and the time limits for debate. The "rule" passed by the Rules Committee that enables consideration of a particular bill must be adopted by a majority vote of the House of Representatives.

SECTION 127 The final compromise extended through 2000 the exemption from taxation of employer-provided education expenses for undergraduate studies.

SEQUESTER The cancellation of spending to achieve the Gramm-Rudman-Hollings deficit targets.

SPECTRUM FEES The amounts garnered by the federal government from auctioning parts of the electromagnetic spectrum.

SPENDING CAPS Limits enacted in law setting ceilings on the amounts that can be spent in the defense and nondefense discretionary accounts.

STACKING Term used to distinguish different proposals relating to the child credit and its interaction with the EITC. Regular stacking allowed income tax liability to be netted against the $500 per child credit before application of the EITC. Full stacking referred to allowing both income tax liability and the employee share of the FICA wage tax to be netted against the $500 per child credit before application of the EITC.

SUPPLEMENTAL APPROPRIATION A spending bill enacted outside the normal budget process.

SUPPLEMENTAL SECURITY INCOME (SSI) A federal program providing cash assistance to poor aged, blind, and disabled adults and children. In 1996 over 6 million individuals received SSI payments.

SUPPLEMENTAL SECURITY INCOME KIDS An administration proposal adopted in the agreement that extended Medicaid benefits to disabled children who would have come off the welfare rolls under the stricter tests of the 1996 welfare reform law.

STATE MAINTENANCE OF EFFORT The House proposed allowing states to cut or eliminate federal maintenance-of-effort requirements on state supplementation of SSI and Medicaid benefits.

WELFARE-TO-WORK The agreement provided a wage credit to employers hiring former welfare recipients and provided $3 billion of welfare-to-work grants to states and localities to assist in moving individuals off of welfare.

WORKFARE Government-sponsored programs in which participants are required to work a number of hours in order to qualify for certain of the government's means-tested safety net programs such as SSI and Medicaid.

Chronology of Important Dates

January 24, 1997: First outreach on the budget by the White House to Senate Republicans.

February 6, 1997: President submits fiscal year 1998 budget proposal to Congress.

March 12: House Republicans pass a nonbinding resolution calling on the president to resubmit his budget.

March 19: White House and congressional leaders agree to negotiations to achieve a balanced budget by 2002.

April 30: Bipartisan agreement reached on major spending and tax components of a balanced budget.

May 1: CBO surprise, in which CBO reveals a forthcoming upward revision in revenue projections of $45 billion a year.

May 2: Announcement of a bipartisan budget agreement that was reconfigured in fewer than twenty-four hours to incorporate the CBO surprise.

May 15: Details of bipartisan compromise are agreed to, including two letters outlining commitments on tax policies and consultation.

May 21: House defeats Shuster amendment on transportation spending and passes the budget resolution.

May 23: Senate defeats Hatch-Kennedy amendment on tobacco tax and passes the budget resolution.

June 5: Conference report on budget resolution is passed by the House and the Senate.

June 25: House and Senate pass the reconciliation spending bill.

June 26: House passes the tax bill.

June 27: Senate passes the tax bill.

July 30: House passes the conference report on the reconciliation spending bill (HR 2015).

July 31: Senate passes the conference report on the reconciliation spending bill (HR 2015).

July 31: House and Senate pass the conference report on the tax bill (HR 2014)

August 5: President signs the Balanced Budget Act of 1997 (PL 105-33) and Taxpayer Relief Act of 1997 (PL 105-34).

List of Key Participants

The Clinton Administration

White House

William Jefferson Clinton, president of the United States
Al Gore, vice president of the United States

Erskine Bowles, chief of staff to the president
Susan Brophy, principal deputy, Office of Legislative Affairs
Barbara Chow, Office of Legislative Affairs
Rahm Emanuel, senior adviser to the president
Martha Foley, Office of the Chief of Staff
John Hilley, senior adviser to the president and head of Legislative Affairs
Chris Jennings, senior White House health adviser
Ron Klain, chief of staff to the vice president
Mike McCurry, White House press secretary
Dick Morris, political adviser to the president
Janet Murguia, House deputy, Office of Legislative Affairs
Mark Penn, political adviser to the president
Bruce Reed, head of the Domestic Policy Council
Gene Sperling, head of the National Economic Council
Janet Yellen, chairperson, Council of Economic Advisers

United States Treasury

Bob Rubin, secretary
Larry Summers, deputy secretary
Linda Robertson, assistant secretary for legislation

Office of Management and Budget

Frank Raines, director
Jack Lew, deputy director
Nancy Ann Min, program associate director for health
Ken Apfel, program associate director for human resources

Department of Health and Human Services

Donna Shalala, secretary
Rich Tarplin, assistant secretary for legislation

Department of State

Madeleine Albright, secretary

UNITED STATES SENATE

Senator Trent Lott, Republican leader
Senator Don Nickles, Republican whip
Senator Tom Daschle, Democratic leader
Senator Wendell Ford, Democratic whip

Senator Robert C. Byrd, ranking member of the Senate Appropriations Committee
Senator Pete Domenici, chairman of the Senate Budget Committee
Senator Frank Lautenberg, ranking member of the Senate Budget Committee
Senator Daniel Patrick Moynihan, ranking member of the Senate Finance Committee
Senator Bill Roth, chairman of the Senate Finance Committee
Senator Ted Stevens, chairman of the Senate Appropriations Committee

Randy DeValk, senior adviser to Daschle
Jim English, staff director, Senate Appropriations Committee Minority
Bill Hoagland, staff director, Senate Budget Committee Majority
David Hoppe, chief of staff to Lott
Bruce King, staff director, Senate Budget Committee Minority
Sue Nelson, senior analyst, Senate Budget Committee
Mark Patterson, staff director, Senate Finance Committee Minority
Lindy Paull, staff director, Senate Finance Committee Majority
Pete Rouse, chief of staff to Daschle
Larry Stein, policy director to Daschle

United States House of Representatives

Representative Newt Gingrich, Speaker of the House
Representative Dick Armey, Republican majority leader
Representative Richard Gephardt, Democratic leader
Representative David Bonior, Democratic whip

Representative Bill Archer, chairman of the Ways and Means Committee
Representative Michael Bilirakis, chairman of the Subcommittee on Health
    and Environment, Commerce Committee
Representative Thomas Bliley, chairman of the Commerce Committee
Representative Sherrod Brown, ranking member on the Subcommittee on
    Health and Environment, Commerce Committee
Representative John Dingell, ranking member of the Commerce Committee
Representative Cal Dooley, prominent member of New Democrats
Representative John Kasich, chairman of the House Budget Committee
Representative Bob Livingston, chairman of the House Appropriations
    Committee
Representative Jim Moran, prominent member of New Democrats
Representative John Murtha, ranking member of the Subcommittee on
    Defense, Appropriations Committee
Representative David Obey, ranking member of the House Appropriations
    Committee
Representative Charlie Rangel, ranking member of the House Ways and
    Means Committee
Representative Tim Roemer, prominent member of New Democrats
Representative Clay Shaw, chairman of the Subcommittee on Human
    Resources, Ways and Means Committee

Representative John Spratt, ranking member of the House Budget Committee

Representative Charlie Stenholm, prominent member of House Democratic Blue Dogs

Representative Bill Thomas, chairman of the Subcommittee on Health, Ways and Means Committee

Representative Henry Waxman, ranking member, Subcommittee on Health and Environment, Commerce Committee

Arne Christenson, chief of staff, Speaker of the House

Tom Kahn, staff director, House Budget Committee Minority

Ken Kies, chief of staff, Joint Committee on Taxation

Rick May, staff director, House Budget Committee Majority

Notes

The events portrayed in this volume were taken largely from my own notes and materials collected during the period in which I was working on the balanced budget agreement. A main source for additional information was the series of *CQ Almanacs*, published annually by Congressional Quarterly in Washington.

CHAPTER 1

1. Joining the Congressional Budget Office in 1983, I moved to the Senate Budget Committee under Senator Lawton Chiles at the beginning of 1985. With Chiles's retirement in 1988, I became staff director of the Democratic staff of the Senate Budget Committee under Senator Jim Sasser, serving two years before accepting the chief of staff position for Senate Democratic leader George Mitchell in 1991. After Mitchell's retirement in 1994, I worked a year for Democratic leader Tom Daschle before going to the White House at the beginning of 1996.

2. Domenici lost the race for leader to Bob Dole in 1984, and in 1994 he was defeated by Don Nickles in the race to become chairman of the Republican Policy Committee.

3. In 1985 Domenici joined Bob Dole to rally the Republican caucus around a major deficit reduction package that included a freeze on cost-of-living adjustments (COLAs), including those for Social Security. But President Ronald Reagan undermined their effort by reaching a deal with House Speaker Tip O'Neill, a Massachusetts Democrat, to drop the COLA freeze in exchange for more spending on defense. They reached this compromise while strolling under an oak tree on the White House grounds—leading the agreement to become known as the "Oak Tree Framework." *1985 CQ Almanac*, p. 456.

4. The congressional budget resolution sets the overall levels of spending, revenues, and the resulting deficit (or surplus) for the federal government. As part of this effort, it establishes numerical targets for appropriations and other committees whose actions affect spending and taxes, seeking to ensure that their legislative activities conform to the overall budget targets. The congressional budget resolution is an internal blueprint adopted by Congress and does not require the president's signature.

5. In 1997 the twelve Republicans on the Senate Budget Committee were Domenici, Grassley, Nickles, Gramm, Bond, Gorton, Gregg, Snowe, Abraham, Frist, Grams, and Gordon Smith. The ten Democrats were Lautenberg, Hollings, Conrad, Sarbanes, Boxer, Murray, Wyden, Feingold, Tim Johnson, and Durbin. *1997 CQ Almanac*, B-29.

6. A resolution can be directly placed on the Senate calendar under Rule XIV of the Standing Rules of the Senate. See Committee on Rules and Administration, *Senate Manual* (Government Printing Office, 1993) pp. 12–13.

7. In 1996 the Senate Finance Committee created a commission to examine this question, under the leadership of Michael Boskin, who had headed the Council of Economic Advisors under President George H. W. Bush. The Boskin Commission concluded that the overstatement was quite large and that the consumer price index could be adjusted downward by slightly more than a full percentage point. By 1997 the Bureau of Labor Statistics (BLS), the official arbiter of the CPI, was in the process of revising its measure, creating the expectation that a downward adjustment would be forthcoming.

8. Legislative accomplishments in the months immediately preceding the 1996 elections are described in *1996 CQ Almanac*, pp. 1–9.

9. Poison pills are controversial legislative provisions that are usually attached to major bills. They are inserted either to disrupt prospects for passage or, in the alternative, to be swallowed as the price of gaining passage of the major bill.

10. For a discussion of the Speaker's ethics problems, see *1997 CQ Almanac*, pp. 1-11–1-15.

11. Until the 1996 Democratic convention, Dick Morris was the president's lead political adviser. Now the political meetings were conducted by Mark Penn, Bob Squier, Doug Schoen, and Bill Knapp, all veterans of the presidential campaign.

12. Spratt originally sought the chairmanship of the House Budget Committee in 1992 but was defeated for the post by Representative Martin Sabo of Minnesota. Spratt won election as ranking minority member in December 1996.

13. The Breaux-Chafee plan was offered as an amendment to the fiscal 1997 budget resolution on May 23, 1996. It was defeated by a vote of 46-53. This seven-year balanced budget plan contained $679 billion of budget savings and would have resulted in a balanced budget in 2003. It adjusted the CPI downward by a half a percentage point and made way for a $105 billion tax cut; see *1996 CQ Almanac*, p. 2-23.

14. The deficit reduction package enacted under President George H.W. Bush projected five-year deficit savings of $496.2 billion, of which $146.3 billion was in the form of increased revenues; see *1990 CQ Almanac*, p. 112.

15. In his acceptance speech at the 1988 Republican National Convention, Bush famously declared: "Read my lips: no new taxes."

16. The projected deficits faced by President Clinton in January 1993 are based on estimates found in Congressional Budget Office (CBO), *The Budget and Economic Outlook: Fiscal Years 1994 to 1998* (GPO, 1993), p. 28, table 2-1.

17. In comparison, the 1993 deficit reduction package had projected five-year savings of $496 billion, of which $240 billion was from increased revenues; see *1993 CQ Almanac*, p. 108.

18. *1995 CQ Almanac*, p.1-10.

19. The congressional budget resolution passed by the House in 1995 called for $895 billion in spending cuts; see *1995 CQ Almanac*, p. 2-20.

20. For details of the president's budget proposal, see Office of Management and Budget (OMB), *Budget of the United States Government: Fiscal Year 1998* (GPO, 1997).

21. Defense numbers are from CBO, *Budget and Economic Outlook: Fiscal Years 2007 to 2016* (GPO, 2006), table F-7.

22. In 1996 Social Security spent $347 billion, Medicare $191 billion, and Medicaid $92 billion. CBO, *The Budget and Economic Outlook: Fiscal Years 1998–2007* (GPO, 1997), table F-12.

23. Between 1982 and 1996, Medicare expenditures grew by $142 billion, while Medicaid

expenses grew by $75 billion. CBO, *The Budget and Economic Budget Outlook: Fiscal Years 1998–2007*, table F-12.

24. For the president's proposed entitlement spending, see OMB, *Fiscal Year 1998 Budget*, table S-6.

25. For a transcript of the State of Union address, see *1997 CQ Almanac*, pp. D-17–D-21.

26. The first two bills introduced by Republicans in 1997 (S1 and S2) reduced the capital gains rate and the estate tax and contained a $500-per-child tax credit. To these proposals were added Finance Committee chairman Bill Roth's proposals regarding individual retirement accounts (IRAs). Together, the proposed tax cuts totaled approximately $193 billion over five years, and $565 billion over ten years. *1997 CQ Almanac*, p. 2-20.

CHAPTER 2

1. The Medicare trust fund is an accounting convention tracking the receipts and expenditures for Part A of the Medicare program. Dedicated receipts come from a 2.9 percent payroll tax, split equally between employers and employees. Part A reimburses hospital, skilled nursing, home health, and hospice services for qualified beneficiaries.

2. The president's budget proposal would extend the life of the trust fund until 2007; see OMB, *Fiscal Year 1998 Budget*, p. 187.

3. The expenses proposed to be moved from Medicare Part A to Part B were the costs of home health care visits above 100 following a three-day hospital stay, as well as all home health visits not following hospitalization.

4. Triggered by President Richard Nixon's impoundment of congressionally mandated spending, Congress enacted the Congressional Budget and Impoundment Control Act of 1974, which established new budget structures. A budget committee in each chamber was responsible for reporting a congressional budget resolution that set the aggregate levels of federal spending, revenues, and the deficit. Once adopted by Congress, the resolution set the aggregate budget limits on appropriations, or spending, bills passed by Congress. To propel the budget process, a new legislative vehicle was created in the form of a reconciliation bill whose purpose was to reduce the deficit. It was endowed with procedural protections that effectively disarmed the filibuster in the Senate and increased the odds that budgetary gridlock could be avoided. For a brief history of the 1974 budget act, see David R. Tarr and Ann O'Connor, eds., *Congress A to Z*, 4th ed. (Washington: CQ Press, 2003), pp. 41–45.

5. In a surprise move in September 1985, three senators launched a major revision to the federal government's budget process. Known as Gramm-Rudman-Hollings (GRH) for its three original cosponsors, the legislation took the Senate and House by storm, and was enacted into law just two months later. The GRH revisions to the budget process centered around two key concepts. First, a sequence of declining deficit targets was established, mandating a balanced budget by 1991. Second, GRH contained an enforcement mechanism that would kick in if Congress and the president failed to hit the targets. That enforcement mechanism was sequestration—an across-the-board reduction in spending weighted heavily toward defense and domestic spending under the jurisdiction of the appropriations committees. The size of the sequestration would be the amount by which the budget deficit for the fiscal year just beginning was projected to exceed the GRH target for that year. For a discussion of the Gramm-Rudman-Hollings deficit reduction measure, see *1985 CQ Almanac*, pp. 459–64.

6. For a description of the president's fiscal 1998 enforcement mechanism, see *1997 CQ Almanac*, pp. 2–4. Also see OMB, *Fiscal Year 1998 Budget*, p. 16.

7. The 1996 welfare reform bill funded child care as well as a health safety net for the children of welfare recipients. It helped move people from welfare to work and had tough enforcement measures for child support payments. For provisions, see *1996 CQ Almanac*, p. 6-3.

8. The president proposed spending $14.6 billion to allow disabled legal immigrants to receive Medicaid and Supplemental Security Income, thereby reversing the loss of these services as enacted in the 1996 Welfare Reform Act. See *1997 CQ Almanac*, pp. 2-4–2-5.

9. Not only were Democrats more frequent users of the bank and its interest-free, penalty-free overdrafts, but the abuses largely implicated the majority Democratic Party as the administrators of the House. The House banking scandal was an important factor in weakening Democratic control leading up to the Republican takeover in 1994. See *1992 CQ Almanac*, p 23.

10. At the end of 1996 the White House and the Republican Congress had come to loggerheads on many of the appropriations bills; particularly troublesome were several "legislative riders" attached by House Republicans. These provisions had little relevance to the legislation and usually dealt with the environment, abortion, labor, and other points of contention. With the elections looming, Gingrich decided it was time to get out of Washington and let his Republican legislators hit the campaign trail. Walking into one of the last negotiations, he had said, "O.K., what's the price for leaving town?" In the end the price was $6.5 billon—funding for education, national service, Head Start, and more—even funding for the National Endowment for the Humanities, whose choices of projects to support many Republicans found culturally suspect. And all the legislative riders were quickly swept clean.

11. Under the Constitution, the vice president is the president of the Senate, a largely ceremonial position, but one that carries two important rights: the right to break tie votes, and the right to recognize a particular senator, thereby granting control of the Senate floor. Vice President Gore had cast the deciding vote on the Democrats-alone 1993 deficit reduction bill, which then passed 50 to 49. He had also used the right of recognition to help Democrats gain control of the Senate floor to offer and debate amendments.

12. The National Economic Council had the lead on domestic issues for which economic and budgetary issues were at the fore. It coordinated its work with OMB, and in many cases with the Domestic Policy Council, which had the lead on noneconomic domestic policy issues.

13. A capped entitlement is a hybrid form of funding. Like an entitlement, funds do not have to be appropriated annually, but the maximum level is set in the authorizing legislation that enacts the program. As well, the requirements to qualify for the benefit are set in law. But unlike entitlements such as Medicare, Social Security, and many others, the funding is limited to a fixed amount. If the estimated funding to serve the target population turns out to be inadequate, either the program must be adjusted to fit within the funding constraint or new legislation must be passed to increase the level of funding.

CHAPTER 3

1. The president's five-year budget proposed $98.4 billion in gross tax cuts. These cuts were offset by revenue increases of $76 billion, leaving a net tax cut proposal of $22.4 billion. See OMB, *Fiscal Year 1998 Budget*, table 8-1, p. 112.)

2. The Medicare Catastrophic Coverage Act was passed by overwhelming margins in both the House and Senate and signed into law on July 1, 1988. The program was to be largely self-financed. Although the poorest seniors were exempted from paying the new catastrophic premiums, 40 percent of the 33 million enrollees faced annual premiums of up to $800 in 1989, rising to $1,050 in 1993. The political firestorm unleashed by this financing mechanism led Congress to repeal the act the very next year, by votes of 360-66 in the House and 99-0 in the Senate. See *1989 CQ Almanac*, p. 149.

3. The privatization of Social Security refers to proposals to allow individuals to allocate a portion of their Social Security taxes to individual investment accounts. At the time of retirement, the individual investment account would provide financial support to supplement reduced Social Security payments. Proponents claim that these investments would generate a higher rate of return than that implicit in the payments currently coming from Social Secu-

rity. Opponents point to the increased risk of such investments, the possible high transaction costs that would reduce net payments to beneficiaries, and the potential for privatization to undermine political support by well-to-do seniors for the Social Security program.

4. For a description of the furor over the defeat of the constitutional amendment requiring a balanced budget, see Eric Pianin, "Clinton Budget Plan Panned, 'More Honest' Try Demanded by Republicans," *Washington Post*, March 6, 1997, p. A4.

5. Lautenberg had a letter from the CBO stating that thanks to the enforcement mechanism contained in the president's budget, that budget would get to balance in 2002, not just under OMB numbers but CBO's as well.

6. Over the weekend of March 8–9, 1997, the White House quietly proposed to Senator Lott a commission on Social Security in place of the failed CPI commission. The idea was to keep the CPI issue alive within the framework of a longer-term examination of the policies needed to maintain the solvency of the Social Security system. Lott immediately squashed the idea, fearing the political exposure of drawing a direct link between balancing the budget and Social Security. In addition, he emphatically felt that Congress and the White House needed to stay focused on the immediate budget problem.

CHAPTER 4

1. For a comparison of economic assumptions, see OMB, *Fiscal Year 1998 Budget*, p. 31, and CBO, *The Budget and Economic Outlook: Fiscal Years 1998–2007*, p. 2, table 1-1.

2. For example, the White House health policy effort was led by Chris Jennings, deputy assistant to the president and senior health advisor, and OMB's Nancy Ann Min. Their guidance was fully integrated into the ongoing White House deliberations of the group of eight in the chief of staff's office. Once a position was adopted, they had wide leeway to engage their congressional counterparts in seeking acceptable policy solutions. This method of including and deploying White House and cabinet agency policy experts extended to all major programmatic areas.

3. In 1996 the cost of the EITC program was $24.3 billion, counting revenue lost to reduced taxes and payments made to those receiving the refundable credit. The average EITC credit was $1,400 that year, and more than 20 million working families received the EITC. OMB, *Fiscal Year 1998 Budget*, p. 190.

4. The Blue Dog budget is described in a February 26, 1997, handout, "Coalition Budget, Summary of Major Provisions." The Social Security surplus in 2005 was $170 billion; see CBO, *The Budget and Economic Outlook, Fiscal Years 2007 to 2016*, table F-1.

5. In 1992 Conrad had refused to run for reelection, upset that Congress had done so little to turn the tide of red ink. But after Senator Quentin Burdick died in late 1992, North Dakota Democrats drafted Conrad to fill Burdick's seat. Conrad won that seat in a special election and thus never left the Senate despite relinquishing his former seat.

6. For a description of committee and floor action on the fiscal 1991 budget resolution, see *1990 CQ Almanac*, pp. 127–29.

7. The House passed the Democratic budget resolution on May 1, 1990. On May 2 the Senate Budget Committee passed its budget resolution. The key meeting with the president occurred on May 6.

8. Jackie Calmes, "Clinton Calls for Bipartisan Budget Talks: President Asks Negotiations Start Today in Bid to Fix Relations with Congress" *Wall Street Journal*, March 19, 1997, p. A-2; Eric Pianin and Clay Chandler, "Gingrich Backs Move to Put Off Tax Cuts; Speaker, House Leaders at Odds With Lott," *Washington Post*, March 18, 1997, p. A-1.

CHAPTER 5

1. The CBO reestimate of the president's Medicare proposal appears in "Preliminary Analysis of the President's Budgetary Proposals for Fiscal Year 1998," prepared by CBO at the request of the Senate Committee on Appropriations, March 3, 1997.

2. Richard W. Stevenson, "President Offers $18 Billion More in Medicare Cuts," *New York Times*, April 9, 1997, p. A-1.

3. Trends in domestic discretionary spending are shown in CBO, *The Economic and Budgetary Outlook: Fiscal Years 1998–2007*, table F-11. Nondefense discretionary spending includes domestic and international programs.

4. Budget baselines are projections of spending, revenue, and deficit amounts over time. The impact of policy changes on the budget is measured against the baseline amounts. For example, spending less than the baseline amount is scored as a budgetary saving, reducing the baseline deficit projection. There is no single convention for constructing a baseline. The baselines constructed by both OMB and CBO reflect laws that are in effect. For amounts that are appropriated annually, the baseline is assumed to rise with the rate of inflation, based on the view that it is the real value of government services and benefits that is maintained over time. CBO and OMB baseline projections may vary significantly because of differences in underlying economic and technical assumptions. For example, a difference in the projected unemployment rate generates different estimates of spending on safety net programs.

5. The president's tax proposals are summarized in OMB, *Fiscal Year 1998 Budget*, p. 112, table 8-1.

6. Roth briefly described his own recently released budget plan, which he said could pay for large tax cuts. He included the Boskin Commission recommendation for a 1.1 percentage point reduction in the CPI. And he had also taken the OMB economic and budget projections. Those two proposals would bring in a lot of money, balancing the budget and leaving plenty for a hefty tax cut.

7. A continuing resolution is a stopgap funding measure to keep the federal government operating. For government programs under the jurisdiction of the appropriations committees, funding expires on September 30. If funding amounts for the new fiscal year have not been enacted by October 1, a continuing resolution can be used to fund these programs. As with any law, it must be passed by Congress and signed by the president.

8. A supplemental appropriations bill is the legislative vehicle used for additional funding of programs outside the normal yearly appropriations process, necessitated by natural disasters, cost overruns, or a desire to win more funding for favored programs.

9. The president's Medicaid proposal is described in OMB, *Fiscal Year 1998 Budget*, p. 52.

10. One aspect of increased flexibility endorsed by both parties was abolition of the so-called Boren rule, which required states' Medicaid programs to pay standard rates to hospitals and nursing homes, limiting their freedom to bargain for a better deal. Named after its chief sponsor, former senator David Boren of Oklahoma, the amendment was repealed as part of the budget agreement.

11. Neither the concurrent resolution on the budget nor the reconciliation bill can be filibustered. Not having to meet the sixty-vote hurdle to end a filibuster, the fifty-five Republican senators could prevail on majority votes.

CHAPTER 6

1. For a discussion of the 1990 changes in the budget process, see *1990 CQ Almanac*, pp. 173–76. Dick Darman, director of OMB under President George H. W. Bush, was instrumental in enacting and implementing the new rules. On the congressional side, Jim English of the Senate Appropriations Committee, Bill Dauster and Sue Nelson of the Senate Budget Com-

mittee, and Richard Kogan of the House Budget Committee, as well as the congressional parliamentarians, also played important roles.

2. Only the child credit carried immediate budgetary costs, and those could be reduced by phasing in the increase in the tax credit. A capital gains tax cut would actually increase federal receipts in the short run as investors were induced by the lower rate to realize gains and pay taxes at the lower rate. As for their IRA proposals, the hit on the Treasury would come far in the future as retirees cashed in their nest eggs and paid no income taxes at the time of withdrawal.

3. The idea was to frontload five-year defense spending, thereby allowing greater savings by 2002 when the budget was to be balanced.

4. The leaders of the DLC, Al From and Will Marshall, had a great deal of influence with the president and members of Congress. They had pointed a lot of Democrats, including the president, in successful directions in the 1992 and 1996 election campaigns.

5. We had deployed Jennings to the Hill to start confidential discussions with the health committees. Representative Thomas, chairman of the Ways and Means Health Subcommittee, had rejected a compromise Blue Dog proposal subjecting home health care recipients with annual incomes greater than $30,000 to the 25 percent premium. That proposal would raise only $3 billion to $4 billion over five years, and Thomas had judged that amount too little.

6. By Sunday night Jennings had made the rounds of the key health committee leaders. The idea of phasing in the 25 percent premium on home health care looked like it might fly. But there was a problem on a possible income-related Medicare premium. Someone had to calculate the amount due and collect it. The IRS was the obvious choice. The agency had the right income and tax data and the infrastructure to administer it. But the Republicans refused, saying IRS involvement would make the premium look like a tax increase. The alternative was to have the Department of Health and Human Services take on the administrative chores. But that was beyond their technical capability. The revenue loss could reach $1 billion a year with HHS administering the program.

CHAPTER 7

1. Martha Foley knew more about appropriations than anyone else. She had been Leon Panetta's right-hand person on the budget when he served as White House chief of staff, and she had agreed to stay on with Erskine. Foley was indispensable on those thirteen appropriation bills, with all their complexity and poison pills sprinkled in strange places.

2. Pension reversion involves the alteration of a business entity's pension plans to make pension assets or income available for general business purposes.

3. Barbara Chow, like Martha Foley, was part of the White House team and an expert on the budget and its politics, having spent many years on the Hill before moving to the White house. Barbara knew the domestic side of the budget and was both analytic and convincing. Having served on committee and leadership staffs, she knew how to move bills toward agreement.

4. At a macro level, projections of revenue depend in part on estimates of national income and its division among its taxable components—corporate profits before tax, wages and salaries, other taxable income (rent, interest, dividend, and proprietor's components of personal income). Different assumptions about the size, distribution, and tax rates to be applied to these tax bases lead to different projections of federal revenues. In 1997 OMB was projecting larger taxable income than was CBO as well as a greater share of that income in the form of corporate profits—leading to projections of greater federal revenue. See OMB, *Fiscal Year 1998 Budget*, p. 31, table III-1, and CBO, *The Budget and Economic Outlook: Fiscal Years 1998–2007*, p. 15, table 1-5.

CHAPTER 8

1. As distinct from the appropriations committees, authorizing committees have jurisdiction over mandatory or entitlement programs whose spending flows automatically from the enacted policies, such as spending for Medicare, Medicaid, and farm price supports. By and large, these programs do not require annual appropriations. To meet its assigned deficit reduction target, an authorizing committee must enact policy changes in its jurisdiction that reduce spending, for example, by changing benefit formulas, requirements to qualify for programs, or rates at which service providers are reimbursed. These policy changes enacted by individual authorizing committees are packaged together by the budget committee in each chamber as a reconciliation bill, which is then considered by the whole body.

2. The Senate Finance Committee reported its tax bill on June 12, 1996, on a unanimous voice vote; see *1996 CQ Almanac*, p. 2-37.

3. The Goals 2000 program, initiated in 1994, was designed to help states raise educational achievement. It set national targets for education but allowed states wide leeway on the means to achieve them. Another component of Goals 2000 directly aided individual school efforts to improve education performance.

4. Named after its author, Senator Robert C. Byrd, the Byrd rule prohibits "extraneous" provisions as part of a reconciliation bill. Of the several tests determining whether a provision is extraneous, three were particularly important: if the provision had no budgetary impact and violated the intended use of the reconciliation vehicle; if the provision led to changes in revenues or outlays that were merely incidental to the intent of the provision; and if the provision caused an increase in the deficit beyond the five-year budget window. Sixty votes were needed to waive the Byrd rule for provisions judged to be extraneous by the Senate parliamentarian.

5. Recall that although the agreement called for a net tax cut of $85 billion over five years, the tax-writing committees could raise taxes to help pay for tax cuts in other areas. The numbers quoted by the president reflected our assessment of the overall size of the gross tax cut.

6. The America Reads program would bring government, business, and school resources together with the goal of ensuring that all children read well and independently by the end of the third grade. A central component would be individual tutors to provide after-school and summer help.

CHAPTER 9

1. The Shuster amendment is described in *1997 CQ Almanac*, p. 2-25.

2. E. J. Dionne, "Clinton Welcomes 'Big Fight' Over Taxes," *Washington Post*, May 17, 1997, p. A-25.

3. After passage by both chambers, the budget resolution goes to a conference where differences are worked out. That agreement, in the form of a conference report, is then voted on by both houses, at which point it becomes binding as the congressional budget blueprint. The resolution does not require the president's signature.

4. The Shuster amendment failed by a vote of 214-216. Forty-eight Democrats voted against it. For details, see *1997 CQ Almanac*, p. H-48.

5. For the House vote on passage of the budget resolution, see *1997 CQ Almanac*, p. 2-25.

6. A reserve fund confers procedural protections on a legislative vehicle and protects it from budget act points of order. The Kennedy-Hatch amendment paid for itself while reducing the deficit and therefore could not be attacked under the Byrd rule.

7. The Domenici motion to table the Hatch-Kennedy amendment carried by a vote of 55-45, effectively killing the amendment. Republicans supplied forty-seven votes to Democrats' eight. See *1997 CQ Almanac*, p. S-15.

8. Conference reports are not open to amendment on the floor. Nor can the budget resolution conference report be filibustered. On June 5, 1997, the conference report on the budget resolution passed the House by a vote of 327-97 and the Senate by a vote of 76-22. See *1997 CQ Almanac*, pp. 2–27.

CHAPTER 10

1. In most years, the reconciliation process produces a single bill, but for political reasons, we had agreed to a two-bill strategy to separate the spending reconciliation bill from the one that cut taxes. From the Republican viewpoint, this allowed the tax cuts to be separated from the spending cuts, particularly in Medicare. From the Democratic viewpoint, legislators were eager to vote for a balanced budget before agreeing to tax cuts.

2. In the ongoing White House budget meetings in Erskine Bowles's office, the policy experts working an issue would participate fully at the substantive and political levels. At any one time dozens of senior administration staff could be working with their Hill counterparts to resolve the long list of issues. Understanding the parameters and solutions that were needed, several policy experts were empowered to work out issues. There could not have been a bipartisan agreement without the likes of Chris Jennings, Nancy Ann Min, and Rich Tarplin on health care; Bruce Reed and Ken Apfel on welfare; and Martha Foley and Barbara Chow on almost every aspect of the budget; and the White House Legislative Affairs team on the front lines. And, of course, that went for all those capable Hill staff members who were part of the effort.

3. For an overview of the early history of the capital gains tax cut, as well as the failed 1989 attempt to reduce the rate, see *1989 CQ Almanac*, pp. 113–16. For an overview of the 1990 attempt to win a lower capital gains rate, see *1990 CQ Almanac*, p. 168.

4. Similar to the disagreement and debate about CBO versus OMB deficit projections, numbers were also central to the debate about tax policies. The evidence on equity had evolved into a consideration of distribution tables showing the impact of tax policy changes across income categories. As in the controversy over the deficit projections, there were two recognized, but often conflicting, arbiters of the numbers—the Treasury and the congressional Joint Committee on Taxation. To add to the confusion, each used a different methodology. On capital gains, the joint committee calculated the distributional impact based on taxes actually paid. The wealthy would receive the benefit of a lower tax rate, but they would also end up paying more taxes. From this perspective, the distributional impact of the capital gains tax cut did not appear so bad. But Treasury took a different approach, basing the distribution solely on the lower capital gains tax rate. Whenever the capital gains taxes were paid, they would be at a lower rate, substantially benefiting the asset holders. This method showed a much larger benefit to the wealthy.

5. We knew that the distribution of benefits in the final tax bill would be bad, and we had three bad choices for dealing with this predictable vulnerability. We could simply not perform the distributional analysis, but that was a nonstarter for institutional and political reasons. We could use the methodology used by the Joint Committee on Taxation, and the results would not look so bad, but that had the same institutional drawbacks. Finally, we could let the chips fall where they might, with our only degree of freedom the timing of the release of the size of the likely effects.

6. Whips are legislators who are part of the leadership organization. Each whip is assigned a specific number of colleagues and serves as a conduit between the leaders and his or her assignees. The whips count votes, attempt to steer their colleagues toward leadership positions, and convey information from members to the leaders.

7. Under a traditional IRA, contributions, including accumulated interest, were not taxed until they were withdrawn; since withdrawal usually occurred during retirement, the taxes

were lower because the individual taxpayer's income was usually lower. Contributions to back-loaded IRAs, however, had already been taxed, and any earnings accumulated were not taxed upon withdrawal. Depending on the amount that can be put into this tax-preferred savings vehicle and the income limits on those who can take advantage of them, the long-term losses to the Treasury can be substantial.

8. The unified credit is the amount of gifts and estates that are excluded from taxation.

9. The emergency supplemental was vetoed on June 9, 1997. A clean version that had been stripped of the automatic continuing resolution, as well as an extremely contentious provision concerning the use of statistical sampling on the national census, was sent to the president on June 12. It was quickly signed. The $8.9 billion emergency supplemental contained disaster aid for twenty-three states and funds for Pentagon peacekeeping operations. *1997 CQ Almanac*, pp. 9-84–9-85.

10. Under the proposals covering the District and Puerto Rico, the existing federal matching rate for Medicaid payments would be increased. See *1997 CQ Almanac*, p. 2-56.

11. The Rules Committee in the House is an instrument of the leadership. The leadership's alterations to the reconciliation bill could be packaged as an amendment, which the Rules Committee would make in order for consideration by the entire House.

12. Unlike in the House, the Rules Committee in the Senate does not have the ability to regulate the flow of legislation to the Senate floor; rather each senator has the right to offer amendments to bills. A leadership amendment is generally worked out behind the scenes in conjunction with key committees and senators, a process that normally ensures its passage.

13. The effective capital gains rate is lowered by excluding a percentage of qualified capital gains from taxation at the taxpayer's ordinary income tax rate. Under the Roth plan, the 50 percent exclusion implied an effective 20 percent rate on capital gains for those taxpayers in the top income tax bracket. For taxpayers in the 15 percent bracket, the effective rate was reduced to 10 percent.

14. On the spending reconciliation bill, the Senate version was better on immigrants but had not fully covered the disabled; like the House, the Senate had not provided the money for our Medicaid initiatives in the District and Puerto Rico and or to shelter low-income seniors from the Medicare beneficiary hits. The Senate version was better on the electromagnetic spectrum auction, but still short. But the structure of the welfare-to-work grants was much worse than the House measure.

15. The Chafee-Rockefeller child health amendment in the Finance Committee would have rationalized the Medicaid program to make children in the same family eligible for the same coverage. It would also have given states the flexibility "to choose Medicaid or a more flexible grant approach for uninsured middle-class children."

16. It would be easier to pry poison pills out of appropriations bills than out of the reconciliation bills that balanced the budget. The president could veto an appropriations bill, demanding that the offending provision be removed. If the standoff was not resolved, the portions of government funded by that bill would be provided for in a continuing resolution in which the normal custom is to throw all riders and poison pills overboard.

17. For details of the Finance Committee Medicare amendment, see *1997 CQ Almanac*, pp. 2-50–2-51.

18. The Finance Committee tobacco amendment raised the tobacco tax from 24 cents to 44 cents a pack. The additional revenue was to be used to bolster the kids' health initiative from $16 billion to $24 billion. A portion was also used to allow those receiving EITC to receive a portion of the benefit of the child credit. For details, see *1997 CQ Almanac*, p. 2-34.

CHAPTER 11

1. Congress enacted a major welfare reform bill in 1988, with Arkansas governor Bill Clinton playing a propelling role. For details, see *1988 CQ Almanac*, pp. 349–64.

2. The self-executing rule improved the bill by adding an additional $1 billion to offset the impact on the poor of the increased Medicare Part B premium arising from the home health transfer. It also increased the savings from the government's sale of portions of the electromagnetic spectrum by $10.6 billion. Finally, it extended the budget enforcement caps and PAYGO through 2002. Republicans favored the rule by a vote of 222-2 while Democrats opposed it by a vote of 197-6. For details, see *1997 CQ Almanac*, p. H-76.

3. The spending bill passed the House on June 25, 1997, by a vote of 270-162. For details on the vote, see *1997 CQ Almanac*, p. H-76.

CHAPTER 12

1. Although the conference report on a reconciliation bill cannot be amended or filibustered, provisions can be struck in the Senate under the Byrd rule. This important procedural protection discouraged conferees from attaching provisions unrelated to deficit reduction to this privileged legislative vehicle. In this case, because the labor provisions were extraneous to deficit reduction, sixty votes would be required to waive a point of order raised against them and keep them in the conference report. The key to flexing the Byrd rule was for the Senate parliamentarian to agree that the provision failed according to one of its several tests. On important provisions, it was common for the Senate parliamentarians to be lobbied by opponents and proponents, arguing the fine points of the legislation under the various Byrd rule tests. Legislative language would be written and rewritten in an attempt to fit within the rule, and it was often a very close call. Fortunately, under the guidance of Larry Stein and Bill Hoagland, we were able to present a united bipartisan front to the parliamentarians, enabling the Byrd rule to be used in our favor.

2. The House tax bill passed on June 26, 1997, by a vote of 253-179. All but one Republican supported the bill; Democrats voted against it, 177-27. For a breakdown of the vote, see *1997 CQ Almanac*, p. H-78.

3. For a breakdown of the vote, see *1997 CQ Almanac*, p. S-28.

4. For details of the Clinton tax proposal released on June 30, see *1997 CQ Almanac*, p. 2-37.

5. We preferred controversial legislative riders as part of appropriations bills. The prospect of a controversial provision being blamed for causing portions of the government to shut down gave the president great leverage in having them removed.

6. In the final compromise, businesses with less than $5 million in annual receipts were no longer subject to the AMT.

7. Both CBO and OMB score EITC amounts that exceed the income taxes owed as expenditures, not a tax reduction.

8. Even as we worked behind the scenes to fix the bills, it was critical to maintain our outreach to friend and foe. In the former category were the Blue Dogs, the New Democrats, and other moderate House Democrats whose resolve and support had been so crucial. Key influential moderates included Stenholm of Texas, Steny Hoyer of Maryland, Sabo of Minnesota, Fazio of California, and Murtha of Pennsylvania.

9. This White House proposal would continue Medicaid coverage for children of families who had lost their Supplemental Security Income benefits under the stricter eligibility standards of the 1996 welfare reform bill.

10. In the terminology of the day, the Republican approach "stacked" the child credit behind the EITC. The administration's original budget proposal to net the child credit against income tax before the EITC was applied was known as regular stacking.

11. Discussing the good news on deficit projections, the budget team had perhaps overabsorbed the lesson of the CBO surprise and was being extremely cautious. Gene Sperling wanted to leak the numbers showing the deficit rising over the next couple of years. Jack Lew wanted to put out the word that even with the economic and revenue adjustments, the budget would not balance in 2002 without the agreement. But we were already where we needed to be with the public and with Congress. Don't rock the boat.

12. Legislative assistants Elisa Millsap and Virginia Rustique played invaluable roles in scheduling, coordination, and every other aspect of running a very busy office.

13. Under this quiet scoring agreement, the EITC spending induced by the child credit provision would not be scored as part of the budget bill but would be counted in the new August spending baseline. The key participants agreeing to this finesse were senior congressional staffers Bill Hoagland and Larry Stein and White House aides Barbara Chow and Martha Foley.

14. On the attempted coup on July 16, see *Congressional Quarterly Monitor*, July 17, 1997, p. 1, and July 18, 1997, p. 1.

15. Following the meeting with Gingrich and Armey, but before the tax conference that night, Erskine and I met with Lott. Erskine went through our list for the umpteenth time. Lott responded that he needed a balanced budget, the $85 billion net tax cut, Medicare reform, a capital gains tax rate at "20-10," and estate tax relief. And he wanted the $500 child credit, and "something on IRAs." He was the one who would likely have to talk to Roth, and he needed something to offer.

CHAPTER 13

1. The note said, "Agree to stacking. Child credit + EITC cannot exceed income tax + FICA. 7/22/97."

2. On the very contentious labor provisions, the Republicans were floating a compromise. They would take out the offending language if the White House would agree to refrain from any new regulations in this area for nine months. Since the Labor Department had just issued the regulations we wanted, this sounded pretty good. The issue, however, was whether the Republican concept of a moratorium was retroactive.

3. On the income-related premium on Part B of Medicare, the Republicans refused to allow the Internal Revenue Service to administer the program, fearing it would appear to be a tax increase. The White House felt that the IRS was the only workable option. As well, the memory of the well-to-do seniors' opposition to the catastrophic health bill played a role in the White House decision to abandon the attempt to win passage of this provision.

4. Under legislation enacted in 1993, empowerment zones and enterprise communities develop plans to revitalize distressed urban areas. The federal government assists in these cooperative ventures through tax benefits, grants, and flexibility on the use of federal funds. Our proposal in 1997 was to increase the number and funding for these programs. For the president's proposal, see OMB, *Fiscal Year 1998 Budget*, p. 97.

5. Forget that these workers were already getting an EITC check—that was not the issue. The political focus was on allowing a broader concept of tax liability against which the child credit could be netted and the corresponding assurance that the government would not be writing more or larger checks to those who took advantage of the child credit. In pushing the envelope to expand the benefit of the child credit to the working poor, we had erected a political construction that was now biting us. When the Republicans had agreed to regular stacking—taking the child credit against income taxes before applying the EITC—the "welfare" issue had never come up. Everyone was used to using the EITC to offset income tax liability, with many workers getting a check for the difference whenever the EITC amount was larger than the taxpayer's income tax liability. Ken Kies and Bill Hoagland fully understood that this

policy would lead to more and larger EITC checks being written and had agreed to bury the increased outlays as an indirect effect in the new August baseline.

6. The concept had two sides. Holding other things the same, a worker with few children did not need as large a tax liability to get the sum of his family's credits. Also, a taxpayer with fewer children and standard deductions would have relatively more income tax due, making the inclusion of FICA again not as critical to take full advantage of the child credit. Under regular stacking, which permitted refundability, a worker with two children could potentially see his EITC check increase by a full $1,000 for two children. But under the full-stacking constraint, that EITC check could not rise as a result of the child credit.

CHAPTER 14

1. Those other education provisions included education savings accounts, penalty-free withdrawals from IRAs for education, tax deduction for interest paid on student loans, an exemption from taxation for education assistance provided by employers, and several provisions subsidizing the financing of education expenditures by government and private entities.

2. The medical savings account proposal would allow individuals to contribute to special tax-favored accounts that they could use to pay health care costs. Participants would be required to carry a high-deductible insurance policy to guard against catastrophic health expenses. In the final compromise, negotiators agreed to a demonstration project limited to 390,000 participants.

3. The HOPE scholarship was a credit of $1,500 per student for each of the first two years of postsecondary education. In place of the president's original proposal for a $10,000 higher education deduction, the negotiators agreed to substitute a 20 percent lifetime credit against education expenses, capped at $5,000 and increasing to $10,000 in 2002.

4. The quiet and off-line reply I was looking for was that he had accepted my latest proposal and buried the EITC outlays in the August baseline, as we had agreed to do earlier when both sides had accepted regular stacking.

CHAPTER 15

1. The language in question, involving worker displacement, sought to guard against employers using workfare workers to displace existing workers in similar lines of work or being used to undercut local wage rates. Displacement was a major concern of labor unions.

2. House Republicans supported the conference report on the spending bill, 193-32, while Democrats supported it, 153-52; see *1997 CQ Almanac*, p. H-104. Senate Republicans supported it, 43-12, while Democrats supported it, 42-3; see *1997 CQ Almanac*, p. S-36. House Republicans supported the conference report on the tax bill, 225-1, and Democrats supported it, 164-41; see *1997 CQ Almanac*, p. H-106. In the Senate, the tally was 55-0 among Republicans and 37-8 among Democrats; see *1997 CQ Almanac*, p. S-36.

POSTSCRIPT

1. Texas billionaire businessman Ross Perot ran as an independent for president in 1992 and again in 1996. Campaigning in 1992 on a platform of eliminating the federal deficit, enacting trade protection for American workers, and promoting generally conservative social policies, Perot won 19 percent of the popular vote but no electoral votes. In 1996 he received 8 percent of the popular vote and no electoral votes.

Index

Abortion issues, 169, 203, 204–05, 207, 223
Abraham, Katherine, 52, 92
Akaka, Dan, 136
Aliases, 178
Alternative Minimum Tax, 174, 181, 183, 184, 191–92, 196, 198, 203, 206, 207, 213
Alzheimer's respite care, 39, 73, 77
American Association of Retired Persons, 45, 52, 53–54
Amtrak, 120, 125, 223–24
Apfel, Ken, 80, 161
Appropriations process, 75–76
Archer, William, 73, 78, 117–19, 140–41, 144–45, 149, 162, 169–70; conference report negotiations, 174, 176, 180, 184–85, 186; leadership negotiations, 188, 196, 197, 198, 200, 208, 219, 222
Armey, Dick, 50, 67, 77, 118, 123–24, 173–74, 182, 188, 193; leadership negotiations, 200

Baer, Don, 63, 64
Balanced Budget Act (1997), writing and passage of: agreement on principle budget elements, 98–115; appropriations process, 137, 146–47, 154; Clinton Capitol Hill meeting after 1997 State of the Union, 30–34; conditions for success, xi–xii, 226–27; congressional budget resolution, 116–28, 129,

131–36; CPI commission proposal, 43, 44–45, 46, 47–50, 51, 53–54, 55–56; enforcement mechanism, 29, 62–63, 86, 166; final efforts, 215–25; first proposals for, 14–18; handoff to congressional budget committees, 41–42, 57–63, 64, 65–70; initial contact with Congress in preparation for, 1–8; lessons from, 230–34; political environment during, 1, 5–6, 7, 9, 47; public release, 19, 21–26; reconciliation process, 137–38, 147–48, 152–56, 157, 158–59, 161–67; significance of, xi, 222, 225; sources of savings in, 3, 13–14, 20–21; two-bill strategy, 42, 45, 46, 120, 124; vote, 224; White House team for, 37, 53
Baldacci, John, 100
Barton, Joe, 164, 166
Becerra, Xavier, 155, 158
Bentsen, Ken, 161
Berman, Mike, 186
Biden, Joe, 224
Bilirakis, Michael, 81–82
Bliley, Tom, 145–46, 148, 181
Blocker, Andy, 99, 223
Blue Dog Democrats, 8, 9, 25, 58, 64–65, 102, 131, 163, 164
Blum, Jim, 105
Bonior, David, 55, 222
Boskin, Michael, 92

Bosnia, 17

Bowles, Erskine, 1–2, 4, 7–8, 11, 21, 34, 37, 48, 50, 51, 67, 71, 74, 91, 95, 99, 106, 112–13, 113, 117, 122, 126–28, 143, 154, 164, 165, 173, 175, 182, 188, 191–92, 196, 203, 206, 207, 208, 210, 212, 213, 214, 222–23

Boxer, Barbara, 83, 103

Boyd, Allen, 100

Breaux, John, 38, 94, 135, 136, 153, 203. *See also* Breaux-Chafee group

Breaux-Chafee group, 9, 59–60, 63

Brophy, Susan, 166

Brown, Sherrod, 73, 82

Brownfields tax incentives, 113, 181, 198, 203, 206

Bryan, Richard, 153

Bureau of Labor Statistics, 46, 51, 52–53, 54, 92

Bush, George H. W., 4–5, 12, 13, 24, 65–66

Byrd, Robert, 76, 97

Byrd rule, 120, 123, 129–30

Capital gains tax: conference report negotiations, 171–72, 174, 180, 184; congressional committee negotiations, 78, 79, 139, 141–42, 146, 149; Democratic position, 78, 79, 141, 146; distribution, 139–40, 146, 191; final negotiations, 222; indexing, 141, 144, 149, 184, 191, 200; leadership negotiations, 203, 206, 207; Republican goals, 32, 77, 113; White House positions, 171, 191

Cardin, Ben, 159, 161, 163, 164

Caribbean Basin Initiative, 223, 224

Chafee-Rockefeller amendment, 153–54

Chapman, Max, 185–86

Chiles, Lawton, 220

Chow, Barbara, 110

Christensen, Arne, 48–49, 119, 152, 166, 200, 217

Christian Coalition, 43, 144, 200

Cleland, Max, 135

Clinton, William, 37, 185–86; budget knowledge, 22, 172; conference report preparation and, 172–73; Gingrich and, 35; in leadership negotiations, 207; Lott and, 5, 6–8, 114–15; tax bill negotiations with Democratic Party, 120–22

Clinton administration: bipartisanship of second term, 7, 38, 90; Breaux-Chafee group and, 59–60; Capitol Hill meeting after 1997 State of the Union, 30–34; Democratic Congress and, 24, 46–47, 77, 84; economic policy, 12; federal government shutdown (1995), 13, 21; first term, 12–13; goals for Balanced Budget Act, 3; handoff of budget plan to Congress, 57–70; Kennedy-Hatch bill and, 135–36; launch of balanced budget, 21–26; Medicaid reform negotiations, 81–82; Medicare reform negotiations, 73–74, 77; outreach in preparation for balanced budget proposal, 1–8, 10; preparations for leadership negotiations, 189–92; relations with Congress in second term, 1, 37–38; tax policy negotiations, 78–79, 150–52, 171, 202–3. *See also* Balanced Budget Act (1997)

Cohen, Bill, 6

Colton, Debra, 163

Condit, Gary, 102

Conference report: Daschle and, 171–72; Gephardt and, 169, 176; Gingrich and, 173, 174; House Democratic caucus and, 175; House tax bill, 169–70; Kasich and, 181–82; labor provisions, 173; Lott and, 170–71, 179; OMB deficit projections and, 177–78; president's role in negotiations, 172–73; Senate conferee appointments, 170; Senate Finance Committee and, 169; tax issues, 173–74, 176–77, 178–79, 180–86; White House tax goals, 171, 173–74, 183–84

Congressional Budget Office: budget projection revision, 104–07; corporate revenue projections, 111–12; deficit projections, 5, 20–21, 22, 62; estimates of Medicare reform savings, 58

Conrad, Kent, 54, 65, 94, 103

Constitutional amendment for balanced budget, 54–55

Consumer price index: Balanced Budget Act negotiations, 77, 89, 90–93; political sensitivity, 4, 51, 52, 53, 54, 77; proposal for commission, 43, 44–45, 46,

47–50, 51, 52, 53–54, 55–56; Republican Party policies, 90; significance of, in planning for Balanced Budget Act, 3, 51–52; White House goals for 1997 budget, 74

Contract with America, 5, 7, 12–13, 24, 27–28, 43

COPS program, 120

Corey, Marty, 53–54

Corporate tax, 58, 111–12, 144–45, 183, 191–92, 196, 198, 203, 207

Cost-of-living adjustments, 3, 54. *See also* Consumer price index

Coverdell, Paul, 216

Cuomo, Mario, 37

Currie, Betty, 109

Darman, Dick, 65

Daschle, Tom, 38, 208, 221; Balanced Budget Act negotiations, 19, 25–26, 47–48, 49, 68, 93, 103, 113, 131, 188, 201; conference report preparation, 171–72; CPI commission proposal and, 54, 55; influence of, 19, 23; partisan politics of, 33, 55

Davis, Jim, 161

Defense spending, 14, 17, 108, 110

Deficit projections: Balanced Budget Act negotiations, 17, 20–21, 58, 89; Balanced Budget Act projections, 5, 14, 177–78; Congressional Budget Office revisions, 104–7; corporate revenue projections, 111–12; Kasich's position, 5, 20, 34, 62; political sensitivity, 114; significance of, in budget negotiations, 62

DeLauro, Rosa, 100

Democratic Congress: budget factions, 9, 25, 64–65; Clinton administration and, 24, 46–47, 77, 84; House caucus meetings, 99–100, 142–43; as minority in House, 24; New Democrats, 25, 95, 100, 131, 163; outreach to, in planning for Balanced Budget Act, 4–5, 19, 23, 38; political goals for Balanced Budget Act, 7, 21–22; Shuster amendment debate, 131–33. *See also* Blue Dog Democrats; Partisan politics

Democratic Leadership Council, 95

Democratic Study Group, 9

DeValk, Randy, 59

Diabetes research, 208

Dingell, John, 145, 148

Dionne, E. J., 130

Discretionary spending, 75, 88–89, 96, 100, 102, 119–20

Disproportionate share hospital payments, 145, 148, 203, 209

District of Columbia, 31, 152, 206

Dodd, Chris, 19

Dole, Robert, 3

Domenici, Pete, 2, 8, 46, 55, 76, 77, 79, 85, 111, 119, 125; Breaux-Chafee group and, 59; consumer price index negotiations, 46, 77; domestic discretionary spending negotiations, 39, 75, 88–89, 96; enforcement process negotiations, 29, 62–63; entitlement spending negotiations, 27–28, 29, 39–40, 62, 72, 73, 88, 96–97, 106–07; handoff of budget plan to Congress, 68; initial planning for balanced budget proposal, 2–3, 6–7, 9–10, 11, 16–17, 18, 27; leadership negotiations, 192, 203; political relationships, 59–60; transfer of budget plan to Senate Budget Committee, 41–42, 59–60, 62–63, 67, 69

Domestic discretionary spending, 75, 88–89, 96, 100, 102

Dooley, Cal, 95, 100, 112

Earned income tax credit, 61–62, 113, 171, 173, 176–77, 179, 181, 189, 190–91, 192, 194, 209–14, 217, 218, 219, 220

Education spending: Balanced Budget Act negotiations, 15, 81, 126; conference report preparation, 177; congressional committee negotiations, 118, 119, 123, 146–47, 149; leadership negotiations, 206; tax policy negotiations, 140, 168, 201; White House tax goals, 78, 171

Electromagnetic spectrum auction, 14, 145–46, 148, 152

Emanuel, Rahm, 63–64, 105, 106, 196, 207, 213–14

Energy conservation programs, 120, 125

Enforcement of budget balancing requirements, 29, 62–63, 86, 166

Entitlement spending: Balanced Budget Act negotiations, 14, 26, 27, 28–29, 39, 81, 89, 100, 102–03; Contract with America policy, 13, 27–28; definition and scope, 17–18; initial planning for Balanced Budget Act, 3–4, 17, 18; political philosophies, 18. *See also* Medicaid; Medicare; Social Security

Environmental protections, xi, 125, 173–74. *See also* Brownfields tax incentives

Estate tax, 97, 113, 145, 174, 181, 191, 196, 197–98, 200, 202, 205–06, 207

Ethanol, 208, 219

Farm price supports, 18

Fazio, Vic, 38, 51, 95, 99, 112, 142, 164

Feinstein, Dianne, 103

FICA tax, 189, 192, 194, 195

Foley, Martha, 105, 110, 160–61

Foley, Tom, 24, 104

Food stamps, 18, 81, 152

Ford, Wendell, 94, 135

Frank, Barney, 99, 100

Gephardt, Richard, 19, 45, 67, 158, 222; capital gains tax policy, 139–40; in conference report preparation, 169, 176; consumer price index negotiations, 50, 77; partisan politics, 33, 46, 201; personal qualities and beliefs, 23–24; political influence, 24; proposal for CPI commission and, 50, 51, 52, 55–56; resistance to tax agreement, 121–22, 131; strategies for *1997* budget, 25, 33, 51, 79–80, 99, 142, 162; transfer of budget plan to congressional budget committees and, 63, 64

Gingrich, Newt, 36–37, 41, 55, 68, 91, 107, 109, 126; Clinton and, 35; conference report preparations and, 173, 174, 182; congressional committee negotiations, 118, 147, 155, 158, 160, 164, 165; consumer price index adjustment proposal, 43, 48–49, 91–92; delayed tax cut proposal, 66; entitlement program negotiations, 31–32; final negotiations, 216, 222–23; leadership negotiations, 188, 193, 194, 195, 197, 200, 203, 205,

206, 208, 209, 211, 213; nondefense discretionary spending negotiations, 119–20; political status, 5, 10–11, 30–31, 182, 192, 357; tax policies, 35–36, 112–13, 130, 182–83; two-bill strategy, 42, 124

Goals *2000*, 119–20, 125

Gordon, Bart, 145

Gore, Al, 32–33, 44–45, 63, 64, 77, 80, 114, 135, 147, 155, 209

Graham, Bob, 153

Gramm, Phil, 29

Grassley, Charles, 208

Greenspan, Alan, 48, 49

Harkin, Tom, 131

Hatch, Orrin, 133, 155

Head Start, 119–20

Health care issues: abortion issues, 169, 207, 223; final negotiations, 215–16, 218, 219–20, 223; Kennedy-Hatch bill, 74–75, 133–36, 140, 155, 158; leadership negotiations, 204–05, 206; significance of Balanced Budget Act (*1997*), xi; tobacco tax, 180–81; White House tax goals, 14, 15, 39, 171, 208. *See also* Medicaid; Medicare

Henreich, Nancy, 70

Hispanic Caucus, 9, 131, 155

Hoagland, Bill, 2–3, 9, 11, 16–17, 27–28, 29, 39, 59, 88, 96, 100, 101, 105, 108, 136, 139, 203, 221

Hobson, Dave, 160, 163

HOPE scholarships, xi, 58, 78, 97, 112, 118, 140, 144, 146, 168, 184, 189, 201, 202, 206

Hoppe, Dave, 143, 158, 223

House of Representatives: Appropriations Committee, 3, 20, 75–76, 76, 149; Budget Committee, 5, 8–9, 11, 57–58, 60–62, 67, 72, 128, 158–61; budget factions, 9, 25; in budgeting process, 10; leadership, 38–39; minority party status, 24; outreach to, in initial planning, 10; partisanship in reconciliation process, 157; passage of budget resolution, 129, 131–33; power relations in Congress, 27; Ways and Means Committee, 117–18, 141, 146, 148

Hoyer, Steny, 112
Hyde, Henry, 169, 204–05, 223

Immigrants, entitlement program eligibility, 30, 39, 58, 81, 89, 119, 148, 152, 154, 155, 156, 157–58, 169, 203–04
Inflation. *See* Cost-of-living adjustments
Inouye, Daniel, 136
Interest group politics, 44
IRA taxes, 144, 150, 151, 168, 174, 181, 184, 200, 202–03, 205, 218, 220–21

Jacoby, Peter, 99
Jennings, Chris, 74, 80, 96–97, 175, 216
Johnson, Broderick, 163
Joint Committee on Taxation, 174–75

Kasich, John, 8, 19, 55, 60, 67, 105, 106–07, 111, 117, 167; budget enforcement proposal, 86; budget resolution enactment, 119, 125, 127; conference report preparation, 181–82; consumer price index negotiations, 20–21, 62, 77, 90; domestic discretionary spending negotiations, 75, 88–89, 96, 119; on earned income tax credit, 61–62, 192; influence of, 5, 6–7, 11; initial budget goals, 5, 20, 34, 38, 72, 81; leadership negotiations, 192, 203; Medicare policies, 57–58, 61, 69–70, 88; personal qualities and beliefs, 5, 36; in reconciliation, 155, 158–61; Shuster amendment negotiations, 131–32
Kassebaum, Nancy, 6
Katfield, Mark, 6
Keating, Tim, 99
Kennedy, Ted, 133, 155
Kennedy-Hatch health bill, 74–75, 133–36, 140, 155, 158, 171
Kennelly, Barbara, 112
Kerrey, Bob, 94, 103
Kerry, John, 94, 103
Kies, Ken, 139, 141, 144, 171, 174, 176, 178, 181, 183, 184, 192–93, 194–95, 200, 205, 210, 214, 217, 222–23, 224
King, Bruce, 103
Klain, Ron, 105, 106, 135, 209
Kohl, Herb, 136

Labor unions: congressional committee negotiations and, 152–53, 154, 158–61, 163, 167; consumer price index adjustments and, 4, 52, 53–54; political status, 152
Lautenberg, Frank, 3, 7, 38, 54, 58–59, 69, 70, 79, 93, 96, 103, 110–11, 113, 134
Leadership negotiations: child tax credit agreement and, 192–96, 199–200, 201, 209–14; participants, 188, 196; shuttle diplomacy for, 196–97; spending issues, 203–5; White House strategy, 189–92
Lew, Jack, 53, 126–28, 158, 160, 161, 175
Lieberman, Joe, 136
Livingston, Robert, 76
Lott, Trent, 19, 42, 130–31, 143–44, 215–16; Clinton and, 5, 6–8, 114–15; conference report preparation, 170–71, 179; consumer price index negotiations, 51–52, 77; Domenici and, 3, 9, 85; final negotiations, 218, 224; handoff of budget plan to Congress, 68; House of Representatives and, 10–11, 38–39; initial budget goals, 26, 32, 43, 67, 68, 87; Kennedy-Hatch bill and, 134, 135–36, 158, 171, 179; leadership negotiations, 188, 193, 203, 205, 206, 208, 212–13; leadership style, 10; national service program negotiations, 124–25; political considerations in budget negotiations, 5–6, 82–83; tax issues, 103–04, 112–13, 114–15, 124, 149–50
Lowey, Nita, 50
Low-income housing tax credit, 113
Lunch Bunch, 9

Maldon, Al, 99
Marguia, Janet, 99, 161, 162, 166
May, Rick, 203
McCain, John, 80, 145
McCurry, Mike, 126
McDermott, Jim, 99
Medicaid, 97, 204; block grant proposal, 40, 82; congressional committee negotiations, 145, 148, 152, 153; Contract with America policy, 13; Democratic Party policy development, 89; disproportionate share hospital payments, 145, 148, 203, 209; legal immigrant

eligibility, 30, 39; per capita cap, 82, 108, 145; program history, 17–18; reform goals, 18, 40; state autonomy issues, 81–82. *See also* Entitlement spending

Medicare, 4; Alzheimer's respite care, 39, 73, 77; budget goals and negotiations, 3–4, 14, 18, 27, 28, 31–32, 57, 62, 73–74, 77, 88, 93, 94, 96–97, 98, 100, 102, 106–07, 108, 110, 119; conference report preparation, 175; congressional committee negotiations, 152, 154–55; Contract with America policy, 13, 27–28; Kasich's position, 57–58, 61, 69–70, 88; leadership negotiations, 194, 204; program history, 17–18; trust fund, 28, 29, 57–58, 88. *See also* Entitlement spending

"Meet the Press," 10

Miller, George, 51, 142

Min, Nancy Ann, 73, 86–87

Minge, David, 100, 161

Minimum wage, 61

Mitchell, George, 24

Moran, Jim, 95

Morris, Dick, 178

Moynihan, Daniel Patrick, 45, 49, 78, 146–47, 151–52, 168–69, 180, 201

Murray, Patty, 54, 84

Murtha, John, 108

Nadler, Jerry, 100

National Economic Council, 37

National service program, 120, 123, 124–25

Nelson, Sue, 58–59, 64, 139

New Democrats, 25, 95, 100, 131, 163

Nickles, Don, 180–81, 186

Nondefense spending, 14–15, 75, 98, 100–102, 119

No-shutdown provision, 80, 145

Obey, David, 50, 76, 100

Office of Management and Budget, 27; Balanced Budget Act projections, 177–78; budget agreement memorandum, 117; corporate revenue projections, 111–12; deficit projections, 5, 14,

20–21, 62, 89; estimates of Medicare reform savings, 58, 73

O'Neill, June, 105

Oxley, Michael, 181

Panetta, Leon, 66

Parker, Mike, 160

Partisan politics: bipartisan effort in Balanced Budget Act passage, 226–27; bipartisan goals of Clinton administration, 1, 7, 38, 90; in budgeting process, 4–5, 29; budget wins and losses, 83, 91; Bush administration *1990* budget negotiations, 65–66; Clinton Capitol Hill meeting after *1997* State of the Union, 32–34; Clinton first term, 12–13; of congressional Democratic leaders, 33, 46, 55, 77, 201; cost-of-living and CPI adjustments and, 4, 50, 55–56, 91–92; Democrat's rationale for *1997* bipartisan budget agreement, 47; earned income tax credit policies, 61–62; entitlement program policies, 18; federal government shutdown (*1995*), 5, 6, 13, 21; goals of bipartisan action, xi–xii; in House reconciliation process, 157; interest group politics and, 44; no-shutdown provision and, 80; opportunities for bipartisanship, 227–34; outreach in preparation for balanced budget proposal, 1–8; prior to Balanced Budget Act launch, 21–22; Senate Budget Committee, 83; in Senate vs. House, 2; at start of second Clinton term, 1, 6, 9, 19–20; strategies for passing Balanced Budget Act, 25–26; transfer of budget plan to congressional budget committees and, 63–65, 66, 67

Paull, Lindy, 144

Penn, Mark, 49, 63, 64, 82, 150

Pension reversions, 113

Public opinion: beginning of second Clinton administration, 7; bipartisan balanced budget agreement, 176; consumer price index commission, 49; federal government shutdown (*1995*), 13; political implications of budget proposals, 82; tax bill proposals and, 150–51

Raines, Frank, 8, 9, 17–18, 22, 27, 37, 39, 50–51, 75, 84, 93, 99, 100–01, 105, 110, 114, 136, 158, 160, 203, 206
Rangel, Charles, 73, 74, 78, 180, 201, 218
Reagan administration, 4–5, 11–12, 72
Reconciliation, 137–38, 147–48, 152–56, 157, 158–59, 161–67
Reed, Bruce, 37, 63, 64, 161, 218–19, 221
Refundability provision, 189–91, 192–94
Regular order, 10, 19, 33, 46, 83–84
Reid, Harry, 103
Republican Party: budget factions, 9; Clinton administration and, 24; Contract with America, 5, 7, 12–13; exit strategy for collapse of budget negotiations, 60, 63, 64, 66, 84; first proposals for Balanced Budget Act, 16–18; House–Senate relations, 10; motivation for balanced budget, 7; negotiating strategies for 1997 budget, 71–72; outreach to, in planning for Balanced Budget Act, 1–8, 10, 37–38; solidarity, 25, 26; tax proposals for 1997 budget, 25–26, 78, 172; White House budget goals and, 80–81. See also Partisan politics
Retirement account taxation, 78
Rivlin, Alice, 27
Robb, Chuck, 135
Robertson, Linda, 180
Rockefeller, Jay, 147
Roemer, Tim, 95, 99, 110, 143
Rostenkowski, Dan, 44
Roth, William, 73, 78, 81–82, 118–19, 144, 148–49, 150, 151, 168–69, 180, 181, 184, 185, 188, 196, 200, 218, 221
Rother, John, 53–54
Rothman, Steve, 100
Rouse, Peter, 49
Rubin, Robert, 11, 37, 44, 78, 79, 98, 104, 114, 117, 143, 151, 165, 168–69, 175, 176, 180, 184, 186, 188, 196, 197–98, 207, 213, 218, 222–23

Sabo, Marty, 50–51, 100, 165–66
Sarbanes, Paul, 84, 94, 131
Sasser, Jim, 65–66
Sawyer, Tom, 145
Shuster, Bud, 129, 223, 224

Shuster amendment, 131–33
Section 8 housing, 101
Senate: Appropriations Committee, 76, 149; bipartisan culture, 2; Budget Committee, 2–3, 41–42, 58–60, 62–63, 67, 72, 84, 86–87, 128; budget resolution passage, 129–30, 133–36; Finance Committee, 118, 144, 146–47, 149, 150, 153–54, 154–55, 158, 169; power relations in Congress, 27
Shalala, Donna, 82
Shaw, Clay, 148, 155, 163, 164, 203
Social Security, 4, 17–18; consumer price index and, 3, 45; Contract with America policy, 13; initial planning for balanced budget proposal, 3
Sperling, Gene, 37, 44, 50–51, 56, 63, 67, 80, 93, 100–01, 150, 175, 199, 200, 203, 213, 217
Spratt, John, 7, 8–9, 38, 50–51, 58, 68, 69, 89–90, 93, 96, 97, 103, 109–10, 110, 112, 113, 127, 131, 158–59, 163, 164, 165–66, 201
Stark, Pete, 73
State of the Union address (1997), 4, 7, 19
Stein, Larry, 59
Stenholm, Charlie, 50–51, 64–65, 100, 110, 112
Stevens, Ted, 76
Stupak, Bart, 145
Summers, Larry, 53, 97, 180
Superfund, 32–33, 206. See also Brownfields tax incentives
Supplemental Security Income, 18, 30, 39

Talent, Jim, 160, 163, 164
Tanner, John, 100, 110, 112
Tate, Dan, 99, 223
Tauscher, Ellen, 100
Tax policy: budget enforcement, 86; budget factions, 8, 9, 25; Bush (G. H. W.) administration, 12; capital gains, 171–72; child credit, 43, 78, 97, 144, 149, 151, 168, 171, 173, 176–77, 178–79, 184, 189, 192, 193–96, 199–200, 201, 202, 205, 209–14, 218, 219, 220; conference report, 176–77, 180–86; congressional committee

negotiations, 117–19, 123–24, 139, 140–41, 144–45, 148–52; Contract with America policy, 13, 27–28; corporate taxes, 58, 111–12, 144–45, 183, 191–92, 196, 198, 203, 207; Democratic Party disagreement, 121–22; earned income tax credit, 61–62, 171, 173, 176–77, 179, 181, 184, 189, 190–91, 192, 194, 209–14, 217, 218, 219, 220; estate taxes, 97, 113, 145, 174, 181, 191, 196, 197–98, 200, 202, 205–06, 207; FICA tax, 189, 192, 194, 195; first Clinton term, 12; IRA taxes, 144, 150, 151, 168, 174, 181, 184, 200, 202–03, 205, 218, 220–21; leadership negotiations, 188–201, 205–06, 209–14; negotiations, 14–15, 42, 43, 78–79, 81, 97, 98, 100, 103–04, 106–07, 108, 109, 110, 112–13, 139–40; Reagan administration, 11–12; reconciliation process, 137–38; sunset provisions, 42; ten-year revenue loss, 104, 109, 113–15, 184, 185; tobacco tax, 74–75, 133–36, 155, 158, 171, 174, 180–81, 182–83, 198, 219; two-bill strategy, 42, 45, 46, 120, 124; White House proposal, 171, 189–92, 202–03. *See also* Capital gains tax

Taylor, Gene, 100
Ten-year projections, 104, 109, 113–15, 184, 185
Thomas, William, 73, 88
Thornton, Tracy, 161
Thurmond, Strom, 33
Tobacco tax, 74–75, 133–36, 155, 158, 171, 174, 179, 182–83, 198, 219
Torricelli, Bob, 54
Transportation spending, 108, 120, 125, 129; Shuster amendment, 131–33
Two-bill strategy, 42, 45, 46, 120

Unemployment insurance, 18
United Nations, 123

Waters, Maxine, 99
Waxman, Henry, 82, 100
Welfare reform: Clinton administration policies, 30; immigrant eligibility, 58; leadership negotiations, 204; workfare program, 152–53, 159–61, 173–74, 203, 204, 218–19
Wellstone, Paul, 131
Wyden, Ron, 54
Wyman, Lucia, 99

Yellen, Janet, 52